MUSICAL BIOGRAPHY

VOLUME I

Da Capo Press Music Reprint Series
GENERAL EDITOR
FREDERICK FREEDMAN
VASSAR COLLEGE

MUSICAL BIOGRAPHY

*Memoirs of the Lives and Writings of the
Most Eminent Musical Composers and Writers
Who Have Flourished in the Different Countries
of Europe During the Last Three Centuries*

By William Bingley

VOLUME I

𝒮 DA CAPO PRESS · NEW YORK · 1971

A Da Capo Press Reprint Edition

This Da Capo Press edition of
Musical Biography is an unabridged
republication of the second edition
published in London in 1834.

Library of Congress Catalog Card Number 70-127286
SBN 306-70032-8

Published by Da Capo Press
A Division of Plenum Publishing Corporation
227 West 17th Street, New York; N.Y. 10011
All Rights Reserved

Manufactured in the United States of America

MUSICAL BIOGRAPHY

VOLUME I

MUSICAL BIOGRAPHY;

OR,

MEMOIRS

OF THE

LIVES AND WRITINGS

OF THE MOST EMINENT

MUSICAL COMPOSERS AND WRITERS,

WHO HAVE FLOURISHED

IN THE

DIFFERENT COUNTRIES OF EUROPE

DURING THE

LAST THREE CENTURIES.

BY

WILLIAM BINGLEY, A.B. F.L.S., &c.

Author of " ANIMAL BIOGRAPHY," &c. &c.

SECOND EDITION.

IN TWO VOLUMES.

VOL. I.

LONDON:

PUBLISHED FOR HENRY COLBURN

BY R. BENTLEY. SOLD BY ALL BOOKSELLERS.

1834.

PREFACE.

——

THE present work was orginally compiled, nearly twelve years ago, for the Editor's own information and amusement. From this period to the present he has not, from time to time, omitted to add to his former collections such further anecdotes and memoirs as he has been able to derive from every authentic source of information which has been accessible to him. In addition to his own investigations, he has, of course, been much indebted to the works of Sir John Hawkins and Dr. Burney, as well as the publications of numerous other English authors on the subject ; nor has he neglected an accurate inspection of such of the works of the continental writers as he has been able to procure. He has likewise been supplied, by his musical friends, with some original memoirs.

With respect to the arrangement of his work,
chronologically, into classes and countries, he trusts
that it will be found useful in affording a general
view of musical history, which a mere alphabe-
tical arrangement would not have done.   It is, he
acknowledges, liable to some objections (though,
upon the whole, they are not of great importance),
arising chiefly from the want of certainty, in
several instances, respecting the places in which
the persons spoken of were born, and from the
circumstance of many persons passing the greater
part of their lives in other countries than those
which gave them birth.

In this arrangement it has been found necessary
to place the Prussian and Danish musicians under
the general head of Germany, and the natives of
Ireland under that of Great Britain.

That there are numerous omissions in his work,
the Editor freely confesses, and has greatly to lament,
particularly where these omissions respect persons
of eminence in the profession ; but he ventures to
hope, that the indulgent reader will consider these
as in some measure necessarily attendant upon a
work, in which persons living as well as deceased
are spoken of.

Any additions, either of memoirs or anecdotes, addressed to the publisher, and properly authenticated, will be extremely acceptable; and if these be found of sufficient importance to be printed as a supplement to his work, the Editor will be most happy to have this done in such manner that they may be bound up with, or incorporated in, the copies of the present edition.

When he first resolved to submit his labours to the Public, he proposed to insert in the second volume a priced and arranged catalogue of such music of the respective composers therein mentioned as is now in print in this country; but to this some objections were stated, which induced the publisher rather to wish that such a catalogue might be printed separately. Considerable preparations have been made for it; and if at last such should be considered desirable, its separate publication will not long be delayed.

CONTENTS

OF THE

FIRST VOLUME.

———

INTRODUCTION.

ORIGINAL Introduction of Music into the Church.—
Ambrosian and Gregorian Chants.—Introduction of
the Organ.—Choral Music in England.—Music in
Consonance. — Improvements by Guido. — Musical
Stave and Cliffs. — Time. — Secular Music in the
Fourteenth and Fifteenth Centuries.—Musical Charac-
ters. — Descant.—Score.—Counterpoint. — Introduc-
tion of Discords.—Choral Service in the Fifteenth
Century.—Fugue.—Canon.—Concert Music.—Fan-
tazias.—Concertos.—Church Music after the Refor-

CHAP. I.

English Musical Composers and Writers,
who flourished from 1500 to 1600.

CHAP. II.

Italian Musical Composers and Writers,
who flourished from 1500 to 1600.

CHAP. III.

German Musical Composers and Writers,
who flourished from 1500 to 1600.

CHAP. IV.

English Musical Composers and Writers,
who flourished from 1600 to 1650.

CHAP. V.

Italian Musical Composers and Writers,

w hoflo ur ished from 1600 *to* 1650.

CHAP. VI.

English Musical Composers and Writers,

who flourished from 1650 *to* 1700.

CHAP. VII.

Italian Musical Composers and Writers,
who flourished from 1650 to 1700.

CHAP. VIII.

German Musical Composers and Writers,
who flourished from 1600 to 1700.

CHAP. IX.

French Musical Composers and Writers,
who flourished from 1500 to 1700.

CHAP. X.

English Musical Composers and Writers,
who flourished from 1700 *to* 1725.

CONTENTS

OF THE

SECOND VOLUME.

CHAP. XI.

Italian Musical Composers and Writers,
who flourished from 1700 to 1725.

CHAP. XII.

English Musical Composers and Writers,
who flourished from 1725 to 1750.

CHAP. XVII.

Spanish Musical Composers and Writers,
who flourished from about the year 1500 to 1750.

CHAP. XVIII.

British Musical Composers and Writers,
who flourished from about the year 1750 to 1812.

CHAP. XIX.

Italian Musical Composers and Writers,
from about the year 1750 to 1812.

CHAP. XX.

German Musical Composers and Writers,
from about the year 1750 *to* 1812.

Musical Biography.

INTRODUCTION.

——◆——

ORIGINAL INTRODUCTION OF MUSIC INTO THE CHURCH.—AMBROSIAN AND GREGORIAN CHANTS.—INTRODUCTION OF THE ORGAN.—CHORAL MUSIC IN ENGLAND.—MUSIC IN CONSONANCE. — IMPROVEMENTS BY GUIDO.—MUSICAL STAVE AND CLIFFS.—TIME.—SECULAR MUSIC IN THE FOURTEENTH AND FIFTEENTH CENTURIES.—MUSICAL CHARACTERS. — DESCANT. — SCORE. — COUNTERPOINT.—INTRODUCTION OF DISCORDS.—CHORAL SERVICE IN THE FIFTEENTH CENTURY.—FUGUE.—CANON.—CONCERT MUSIC.—FANTAZIAS.—CONCERTO.—CHURCH MUSIC AFTER THE REFORMATION.—PSALMODY.

IT appears that Music was first introduced into the service of the Christian Church at Antioch, so early as about the year of our Lord 350. The example of the metropolis of Syria was followed by other churches of the East; and, in the course of a few years, it received the sanction of public authority. By a Council of Laodicea, holden between the years 360 and 370, a canon was issued, directing that " none but the canons, which ascend " the *ambo,* or singing desk, and sing out of " the parchment, should presume to sing in the " church." Thus established in the East, it soon passed to Rome ; and from thence to all the western countries of the then civilized world.

St. Ambrose, who became one of the great patrons of church music, instituted in his church at Milan a peculiar method of singing, which has since received the name of *Cantus Ambrosianus,* the *Ambrosian Chant ;* and Pope Gregory the First, who lived about two hundred and thirty years afterwards, in order to introduce a greater variety into the service, is said to have somewhat enlarged the former plan, and to have begun a new method, called *Cantus Gregorianus, the Gregorian,* or, as it is frequently denominated, *the Ecclesiastical Chant.* What the difference was betwixt these, is at present entirely unknown. The Gregorian chant, however, is said yet to subsist in the churches of some parts of Italy.

The singing, in the primitive church, was sometimes by the whole assembly of choristers ; sometimes it was alternate, or, as it is called, antiphonal, the choristers being, for that purpose, divided into separate choirs ; and, lastly, it was sometimes by a single person, who, after singing the first part of a verse, was then joined by the rest in chorus. In the latter method we see clearly the origin of the office of *precentor,* whose duty it is, even at this day, to govern the choir, and to see that the choral service be properly performed.

It is supposed that some very considerable improvement must have taken place in church music, in consequence of the introduction of the *Organ,* which has usually been ascribed to Pope Vitalianus, somewhat after the year 663. When, however, we consider the intricate mechanism of this instrument, at the present day, and reflect upon the low state of the arts at that time, we cannot have any very exalted notion of the organ of the seventh century.

The missionaries who came over with Augustine, about the year 596, for the purpose of converting the inhabitants of this island to Christianity, adopted a musical service in their devotions. For some time the people were delighted with so pleasing a novelty ; but, after a while, it met with considerable opposition, and was at length entirely laid aside. During the papacy of Vitalianus, one of the principal singers was sent from Rome to instruct the Britons in the Roman method of singing; and the Cathedral Church of Canterbury claims the merit of having been the first in this country in which a regular *choral service* was performed. The true date of the introduction of music into our cathedrals is supposed to have been about the year 679.

Music in consonance seems to have been known in the eighth century. Bede speaks very particularly of a well-known species of it, called *Descant;* and an ancient manuscript, deposited among the Cottonian MSS. in the British Museum, describes the intervals, and the mode of singing, in so plain a manner, that it is impossible to be misunderstood. It is not, however, ascertained in what country it had its rise.

At the commencement of the tenth century, learning began to flourish throughout Europe. In France several of the abbeys became famous for learned men ; and that of Corbie in particular was so celebrated for a musical institution, that the younger monks were usually sent thither from England to be instructed in music, and in the true method of performing the choral service.

In the eleventh century an highly important reformation took place in the art, in consequence of the attention that had been paid to it by a Benedictine monk, GUIDO ARETINUS.

The difficulties that attended the instruction of youth in the church offices were at this time so great, that, in one part of his Works, he says, " Ten years were generally consumed in merely " acquiring a knowledge of the *canto fermo,* or " plain song." This consideration induced him

to study its amendment. It is stated, that, being
one day at vespers, and singing the hymn,

" Ut queant laxis, Resonare fibris
" Mira gestorum   Famuli tuorum
" Solve polluti   Labii reatum ;"

the idea occurred to his mind, that the syllables,
Ut, Re, Mi, Fa, Sol, La, of that hymn, being
easy of pronunciation, might be applied to an
equal number of sounds in regular succession, and,
by that means, remove the difficulties under which
the musical scale had hitherto laboured. The
scale, as it stood before the time of Guido, was not
adapted to the reception of the six syllables. This
therefore he changed, by converting the ancient
tetrachords into hexachords, and then applying
these syllables to it. He added a tone, to which
he prefixed the Greek letter Γ (whence the scale is
now called the *gammut*) below the lowest note of
the old scale, and, by so doing, the situation of
the semitone became clearly pointed out. To the
first note of the hexachord he applied the syllable
ut, and the rest of the syllables, in succession, to
the other notes. This is the origin of what is
usually denominated *solmization*.

His invention having thus far succeeded to his
utmost wishes, he next extended the scale, by the
addition of four other tones, from the lowest line,
G, in the bass, to the fourth space, E, in the treble;
which at the time was considered so high, that

from thence arose the proverbal expression, in use even at this day, to reprehend an hyperbolic speech, " *that is a note above* E LA." The notes in this improved scale were twenty-four in number.

The clergy were, of course, the first who favoured the improvements of Guido, since they (not only at that time, but for some centuries afterwards) were almost the exclusive cultivators of the science. Nearly a whole century was suffered to elapse before these improvements were adopted in England. As soon, however, as their utility was discovered, a considerable degree of emulation arose among the different fraternities, which should excel in the composition of their respective services.

Many of the musical writers have attributed also to Guido the invention of the *stave,* of parallel lines, such as is now used in the writing of music ; but this has been done erroneously, since it is known to have been in use long before his time. Guido indeed intimated that points might be placed as well in the spaces as on the lines ; and he reduced the old number of seven, eight, or ten lines, to five, or rather, for the purpose of ecclesiasticated notation, to four lines.

He was also the inventor of three characters, which he placed on the lower lines, at the head of his stave, called *cliffs.* These were Γ, C, and F ; the first of which indicated a progression of sounds from the lowest note in the scale upwards to E ;

the second, a series from C to A ; and the third, another series from F, through Bb to D. These cliffs were also termed *claves*, or *keys*.

Notwithstanding all the improvements that were made by Guido, and the perfection to which, from his industry and abilities, the scale had arrived, it no where appears from his writings, that any method was then known, by which the length or duration of sounds could be marked, except that very imperfect one, the cadence of the words to be sung. The invention of the method now in use for this purpose, called *time*, has been generally ascribed to Johannes de Muris, a Doctor of Sorbonne, about the year 1330 ; apparently, however, without sufficient foundation.

For several centuries the knowledge of music appears to have been chiefly confined to the clergy ; yet it must not be supposed that the laity were so entirely ignorant of it, as not to have had their songs of mirth, and ballads suited to their conceptions and character. Of these it is difficult to give any satisfactory account. The historians of the times seldom descended to what they considered such inferior particulars. Chaucer, however, who lived in the fourteenth century, informs us, that in his time the English people frequently had music at their weddings, banquets, and other solemnities ; and that even the lowest class were not without it in their humble amusements. The knowledge of the theory of music was still confined almost entirely to the clergy; and they were, for the most part, the composers of those songs and ballads which were the ordinary amusement of the common people.

These were various in their kinds: some were merely legends of saints; others were metrical romances; and others songs of piety and devotion. They had frequently, for their subject, the sufferings of the primitive Christians, or the virtues of some particular and favourite saint. Oftentimes they were exhortations from Christ himself, represented in all the agony of his sufferings, adjuring his hearers by the nails that fastened his hands and feet, by the crown of thorns on his head, by the wound in his side, and all the calamitory circumstances of his passion and death, to pity and love him.

The tunes of these ancient ballads are, at present, nearly all lost. One of the oldest now extant is that to the following words:

> " Sumer is i-cumen in,
> " Lhude sing cuccu,
> " Groweth seed,
> " And bloweth meed,*
> " And springth the wde † nu.
> " Aive‡ bleteth after lomb,
> " Lhouth‖ after calve, cu.§

---

* The flowers in the meadow.   † Wood.   ‡ Ewe.
‖ Loweth.   § Cow.

" Bulluc sterteth,*
" Bucke verteth,†
" Merrie sing cuccu,
" Wel sing thu cuccu
" Ne swik‡ thu naver nu.

This song is supposed to have been written about the middle of the fifteenth century ; and the music is calculated for six voices, and is of that species of composition called canon in unison. Sir John Hawkins has inserted a copy of it in his History of Music. In Dr. Burney's History there are the words and music of a song written on occasion of the victory gained by King Henry the Fifth at Agincourt, in 1415, and, as it is believed, very shortly after that event.

The oldest dance tune now extant is considered to be that called " Sellinger's Round." This may be traced back to the reign of King Henry the Eighth, when Bird made it into a virginal lesson for Lady Nevil.

It is not exactly known at what period the *musical characters* were invented. They have, indeed, been ascribed to Johannes de Muris (before mentioned as the supposed inventor of *time*), but they were certainly not in use till many years after his death. Thomas de Walsyngham, who

---

* Starteth.   † Goeth to vert, that is, to harbour amongst the fern.   ‡ Do not cease to sing.

flourished about the year 1400, speaks of them, and says that in his day the number chiefly in use was five, the *large*, the *long*, the *breve*, *semibreve*, and *minim ;* and he adds, that " of late " a new character has been introduced, called " a *crotchet*, which would be of no use, if musi- " cians would only remember, that beyond the " minim no subdivision ought to be made."

In music somewhat subsequent to the time of which Walsingham speaks, we find that the following characters were employed : 1. the *large ;* 2. the *long*, of the same shape, but in size considerably smaller, two of them being equal in duration to the large ; 3. the *breve*, which was half the long ; 4. the *semibreve ;* 5. the *minim*, which was half the semibreve ; 6. the *semiminim ;* 7. the *chroma*, which was half the semiminim ; and, 8. the *semichroma.** Any of these notes, written with *red ink*, were diminished a fourth part : thus, a red semibreve, instead of being equal to four of the present crotchets, would only have been equal to three.

Each of the several measures above enumerated had then, as now, their correspondent pauses or *rests*. These were originally contrived to give

---

* The marks by which these characters were represented are as follow : 1. ▭ 2. ▭ 3. ▭ 4. ◇ 5. ◆ 6. ◆

7. ◗ 8. ◖

time for the singers to take breath. There were likewise a variety of *neumas,* or *points,* introduced for the purpose of augmenting the notes.

Besides the characters invented to denote the measure of time, which were simple and distinct, there were certain combinations of them used by the ancient musicians, known by the name of *ligatures.* Of the invention of these, no satisfactory account is any where given.

In the *music in consonance,* or symphony, it appears, from several tracts written about this period, that the part most regarded was the *tenor.** This part contained the melody, and to it all the others were adapted.

Descant appears, in its original sense, to have meant only a kind of extemporaneous song; and before the time of Guido, no method of notation seems to have been thought of to fix it. The staves, of eight or more lines, were merely used for simple melody in one part. The stave of Guido, in which the spaces, as well as the lines, were rendered useful, and in which the parts could be separated and known by means of cliffs, rendered the practice of music in consonance infinitely less difficult than it had been before his time. Descant now denotes any kind of musical composition which is written in more parts than one.

---

* From the Latin word *teneo,* to hold, because it held or sustained the air.

Although the word *score* has only been used by modern writers of music, yet the practice of writing in score must have been known to the immediate followers of Guido; since, without this method, it is impossible to dispose the several parts of music regularly. In Guido's time there was no diversity in the length of notes; the consequence was, that those in each stave were placed in opposition to the others; and the *cantus*, or song, thus framed, was, with propriety, denominated *counterpoint*.

After the introduction of the mode of measuring music, other improvements took place; and amongst them, the *canto figurato, canon,* and other kinds of symphonical composition, came into use.

There is very satisfactory evidence that *discords,* with their preparation and resolution, were unknown in the beginning of the fourteenth century.

At the commencement of the fifteenth century, music had become so essential a part of the *choral service* in this country, that it was used in all cathedrals and collegiate churches; and the clergy were very zealous in its promotion. In the abbey and conventual churches the choral duty seems to have been performed by members of their own body, and by children educated among themselves; but in several of the cathedral churches there were large endowments for canons, minor canons, and choristers.

The era in which music became raised to such

estimation as to be ranked among those sciences that entitle the professors of them not merely to the character of learned men, but to high literary honours, will, by all such as are concerned for its reputation, be considered a very important one. In the year 1463, Henry Habington was admitted to the degree of Bachelor of Music in the University of Cambridge; and about the same year, Thomas Saintwix, a Doctor of Music, was made master of King's College in that university. It no where appears that it was the practice in other countries to reward students in music with academical degrees.

The commencement of the sixteenth century is memorable to the musical profession, from the invention of a species of symphonical composition, in which a certain air or subject is begun by one part, and followed by another, called *fugue*. This has been compared to an echo; and it is by no means improbable that the accidental reverberation of some passage of a tune, may have originally suggested the idea of composition in fugue. The merit of the invention cannot, however, at this distance of time, be ascribed to any particular person.

The first essays of this kind, it is natural to suppose, were fugues in two parts; and a fugue thus constructed was called "two parts in one," since the melody of each was to be found in the other. If the reply was in precisely the same notes with the subject, the composition had the name of *fugue in the unison;* and if in any other series of concordant intervals, it was denominated accordingly. If the reply was in longer notes than the subject, it was termed *a fugue by augmentation;* if in shorter, *a fugue by diminution.*

Fugues in the unison had also the name of *rounds,* from the necessarily circular progression of the melody; and this term suggested the idea of actually writing them in a circular form, which was sometimes done.

A fugue written in one line, whether in a circle or otherwise, with direction for the other parts to follow, is called a *canon.* No sooner was this term canon introduced, than it was applied to all perpetual fugues, even in score; and perpetual fugue and canon were considered to be convertible terms, than which nothing can well be more improper, for when a fugue is once written in score, it ceases to be a canon.

A *perpetual fugue* was that in which every note in the one part had its answer in the other.

In the course of a few years after the invention of the fugue, there were further additions made by the contrivance of fugues that were sung both backward and forward, or, as the musicians termed it, *recte et retro;* and of others that were sung *per arsin et thesin,* or in such manner that, as one part ascended, the other descended. Some of these canons were such as to allow of being written in he form of a triangle, others in the form of a cross ; and there is one extant, which, in its shape, represents a horizontal sun-dial.

The *catch* is a species of fugue in unison, in which, in order to humour some conceit in the words, the melody is broken and the sense interrupted in one part, and caught again or supplied by another.

There is very little reason to suppose that what is now denominated *concert music*, altogether instrumental, was known so early as the sixteenth century. The first attempts of this kind of music were called *fantazias ;* and in these, viols of different sizes seem only to have been used. They continued in practice even till the middle of the succeeding century, when they gave way to a species of composition much more elegant, called *sonata di chiesa* and *sonata di camera.* The former (adapted to the church service) was grave and solemn, consisting of slow movements intermixed with fugues ; the latter admitted of a variety of airs to regular measures, such as the Allemande, the Saraband, and others. These were succeeded by the *concerto*, a composition in four parts, with such a reduplication of them as to make seven in the whole.

In the age immediately preceding the Reformaation, it appears that church music had arrived at a very considerable degree of perfection. In the Romish Church the greater part of the service was adapted to music ; and the splendour and magnificence of the worship in the cathedral and conventual churches, particularly upon all the solemn festivals, were excessively great.

The leaders of the Reformation do not seem to have imbibed any of those aversions to music which might have been expected by the enemies of the Romish religion, when we consider how great a portion of their service was musical. Luther happened to be a passionate admirer of music, and was himself well skilled in the science. He was fully sensible of its importance, and, in conjunction with his friend Melancthon, framed a ritual little less solemn than that of the Church of Rome, retaining the choral service in as much splendour and magnificence as the circumstances of the times would allow. He was a strenuous defender of the use of music in religious worship; and he even composed several of the hymns that were adopted by his own sect.

Calvin (whose separation from the Romish Church was founded in opposition as well to its discipline as its tenets), in his establishment of a church at Geneva, laid the musical part of the service under great restraints. He retained none of the offices in the Romish service; but the whole of the music adopted by him consisted in that plain metrical psalmody which is now in general use among the reformed churches of the Continent, and in the parochial churches of this country.

This seems to have been the origin of the

practice of *psalmody*. A French version of the first
fifty psalms was made by a person whose name was
Marot : these he published by permission of the
Doctors of Sorbonne, who declared that they con-
tained nothing inimical to the Christian faith.
Marot soon afterwards died, and the version of the
remainder was supplied by his friend Theodore
Beza.

No sooner were these psalms completed, than
Calvin, who was then at the head of the church
at Geneva, determined to introduce the singing of
them among the people of his own sect. He employed a musician, Guillaume Franc, (who will be
hereafter more particularly mentioned) to set the
psalms to easy tunes of one part only ; and in this
work the composer succeeded so well, that the
people became almost infatuated with the love of
psalm-singing.

Even in the field of battle this has been made
an incentive to courage. In the frequent insur-
rections of the reformers against their persecutors,
a psalm, sung by four or five hundred of their
party, answered all the purpose, in this respect, of
warlike music.

Of the German psalmody very little is at this
time known. It is, however, imagined that the
High Dutch version was made shortly after
Luther's death by some of the ablest of the Dutch
clergy.

It now remains to speak of the part which the

Church of England acted at this period with respect to church music. As King Henry the Eighth and all his children were proficients in music, their influence must have tended very considerably towards its preservation. Numerous complaints were indeed made by the dignified clergy and others, of the great intricacy and difficulty of the church music of these times, and it was once proposed that organs and *curious singing** (as it was termed) should be entirely banished from the churches. Latimer, in his diocese of Worcester, went still further : it appears, by some injunctions which he gave to the prior and convent of St. Mary, that he forbade, in their service, singing of every kind.

By the laws established for the reformation of the church service in England, during the reign of King Edward the Sixth, music and singing were allowed to be retained, but with certain restrictions in respect to what was denominated *figurate and operose* singing, or such as was productive of confusion, and unintelligible to the congregation.

The rubric, as it stands in the first Common Prayer Books, published by command of King

---

* It is not meant, by this term, that the music of the church had (as some might be led to suppose) any affinity to our present theatrical music. Such was denominated *curious singing*, that was intricate and elaborate, abounding with fugues, responsive passages, and a mixture of various and intricate proportions.

Edward the Sixth, prescribes the saying or *singing* of matins and even-song ; and in the Communion, it is ordered that, for the *introite,* the clerks shall *sing,* in English, a psalm appointed for the day. It also directs that, on Wednesdays and Fridays, the English litany shall be said or *sung* in all places, in certain forms appointed by the king. From these and other directions it appears, that notwithstanding the objections which had been lately made in this country against choral music, and the practice of singing, in some of the re-formed churches, the compilers of our liturgy looked upon the solemn musical service as an aid to religion, and were therefore determined to re-tain it.

The abolition of the mass, and the adoption of a new liturgy in the church, to be either said or sung, rendered it necessary that a new musical service should also be composed. Many excellent musicians were now living, but few of them had hitherto embraced the protestant tenets, and the others could not be expected immediately to assist in it. In less however than two years after the compilation of King Edward's liturgy, a formu-lary was composed, so perfect in its kind, that, with some variation, it continues to be the rule for choral service, even at the present day.

The composer of this valuable work was John Marbeck, who will be hereafter particularly men-tioned. It was printed in the year 1550, with the

title of " *The Booke of Comon Praier noted ;*"
and it may be truly considered to contain the
foundation of the solemn musical service of the
Church of England which is now in use. It was
formed on the model of the Romish ritual ; and
to the different offices a very simple species of
melody is adapted. An uniform kind of intona-
tion runs through the greater part of this service,
having a slight inflection at the different clauses,
to assist in keeping the several parts distinct.

As, however, by this work, the whole was sung
in unison, and as the people had been previously
accustomed to more elaborate and ornamental
music, they, after a while, began to express their
dislike to it. A new musical service, the composition of several different persons, was consequently
published in the year 1560, entitled, " *Certaine*
" *Notes set forth in foure and three Parts, to be*
" *song at the Morning, Communion, and Evening*
" *Praier.*" The difference betwixt this and the
former was very little, except that the litany was
here set, and that the whole was in three and four
parts. This book also contains several prayers
and anthems, in some of which, it is to be remarked, that the bass parts are set for children.

About five years afterwards, another publication
of the same kind appeared. It is greatly to be
wished that the idea of printing these two works
in score had occurred to the publishers, as, in that
case, the world might have reaped some benefit

from their labours, even at the present day ; but, being published in separate parts, they could not, of course, be long kept together, and the books are now so dispersed, that it is a question whether a complete set of either of them is any where to be found.

With respect to the psalmody in this country, there was but a very short' interval betwixt the publication of the French version, and ours by Sternhold and Hopkins ; the former appearing in 1540, and the first fifty-one psalms of the latter in 1549. The first complete publication of our version, however, did not take place till the year 1562.

The *tunes* to which they were adapted were about forty in number, written in one part only, and in the tenor clef. Who the composers of these melodies were, we are unacquainted. Several of them were indisputably the work of foreigners. Those to the hundredth and to the eighty-first psalms are generally attributed to Luther, and many of the others are supposed to have been brought over from Germany. These were afterwards harmonized, and published in four parts by a person whose name was Damon.

With the view of promoting the practice of psalmody, some of the most eminent musicians of the reign of Queen Elizabeth undertook and completed a collection of church tunes, composed in four points, in counterpoint. In this work there appears no elaborate display of invention; the harmony is extremely plain and simple. It was published in 1594, and entitled, " The whole " Booke of Psalmes, with their wonted Tunes, as " they are sung in Churches, composed into foure " Parts, by ten sondry Authors." The principal of these were Dowland, Farmer, Allison, Johnson, and Farnaby.

About five years afterwards appeared another collection of psalms, in four parts, by Richard Allison. This seems to have been chiefly intended for private practice, and the four parts are so disposed on the page of the book (which is printed in folio), that four persons sitting round a table, were able to sing at the same time out of the same book : none of the melodies in this collection, however, are original.

Having thus, in a cursory manner, traced the progress of some of the principal musical inventions, from about the middle of the fourth until nearly the conclusion of the sixteenth century, we shall now commence our Memoirs with an account of such English musicians of eminence as flourished during the sixteenth century.

CHAP. I.

ENGLISH
MUSICAL COMPOSERS AND WRITERS,

WHO FLOURISHED

During the Sixteenth Century,

1500 TO 1600.

MARBECK. — TAVERNER. — DR. TYE. — WHITE. —
TALLIS. — FARRANT. — JOHNSON. — PARSONS. —
BIRD. — DR. BULL. — DOWLAND. — PHILLIPS. —
MORLEY. — JOHN AND WILLIAM MUNDY. —
WEELKES. — DAMON. — FARNABY. — MILTON.

JOHN MARBECK, who deservedly claims the first
place in the present sketches, was organist of the
Chapel of St. George at Windsor, and a person
to whom church music is under greater obligation than the world, in general, has been inclined
to allow. It is a common, but mistaken opinion,
that Tallis was the first composer of the cathedral
service of the Church of England; Marbeck
certainly preceded him in this labour; and the
original musical notes to the preces, the suffrages,

and responses, were undoubtedly of his composition. His "*Te Deum*" is inserted in the first volume of Smith's "Musica Antiqua," published about two years ago.

The history of Marbeck, which has entitled him to a place in the Martyrology of the zealous and laborious John Fox, is as follows :

About the year 1544, a number of persons living at Windsor, who favoured the Reformation, had formed themselves into a society. Among them were Anthony Person, a priest, Robert Testwood, a singing man in the choir of Windsor, John Marbeck, and Henry Filmer. On intimation being given that these persons held frequent and improper meetings, the Bishop of Winchester procured a commission from the king to search the suspected houses; and the above-mentioned four persons were apprehended, and their books and papers seized. Among other things there were found some papers of notes on the Bible, and an English Concordance, in the hand-writing of Marbeck. Upon his examination before the commissioners of the statute of the Six Articles, he gave the following account of himself. He said, respecting the notes, that as he was in the habit of reading much, in order to understand the Scriptures, it was his practice, whenever he met with any explanation of an abstruse or difficult passage, to extract it into his note-book, and there place it under the name of the author. As to the Concordance, he told them, that being a poor man, and not able to buy a copy of the English Bible, then lately published by Matthew, he had set about transcribing one, and had proceeded as far as the book of Joshua, when an acquaintance, of the name of Turner, knowing his industry, suggested to him also the plan of writing a Concordance; and for this purpose supplied him with a Latin Concordance and an English Bible. He said, in conclusion, that by the assistance of these, as his papers would shew, he had been able to proceed in his work as far as the letter L.

This story seemed altogether so strange, that the commissioners scarcely knew how to credit it. Marbeck, however, desired that they would so far indulge him as to take any words under the letter M, and give him his Concordance and Bible, and he would endeavour to convince them of its truth. In a single day he had filled three sheets of paper with the continuation of his work, and had got as far as the words given him would allow. His ingenuity and industry were much applauded even by his enemies, and Dr. Oking, one of the commissioners who examined him, said that he *seemed to have been much better employed than some of his accusers.*

Neither his ingenuity nor his industry, however, could prevent his being brought to trial for heresy along with his associates. Person and

Filmer were indicted for irreverent expressions concerning the mass ; and the charge brought against
Marbeck was for copying, with his own hand,
an epistle of Calvin against it. They were all
found guilty and condemned to be burnt ; and
the sentence was executed on all, except Marbeck,
the day after the trial. Three of the witnesses on
this trial were, however, afterwards accused and
convicted of perjury.

Marbeck, being a man of mild and harmless
disposition, was afterwards given up to the Bishop
of Winchester, who, from his persecutor, became
his patron.   The catholics held out to him many
temptations, but he steadily refused to betray any
of the persons with whom his party had been
concerned ; and at last, through the intercession
of Sir Humphrey Foster, one of the commissioners, he obtained the king's free pardon.*

Having thus escaped martyrdom, he applied
himself to the study of his profession ; and not
having been required to make any public recan-
tation of his opinions, he indulged them in secret till
the death of Henry the Eighth, when he found
himself at liberty to make an open profession of

---

* It is somewhat strange, that Fox, who was personally
acquainted with Marbeck, should, in the first edition of his
Acts and Monuments, assert that he had suffered in the
flames with the other three. He, however, corrected this
glaring error in the subsequent edition.

his faith; and accordingly he finished, and in 1500 published his Concordance. He wrote also, amongst other things, "The Lives of Holy Saints, " Prophets, Patriarchs, and others," published in 1574; " A Book of Notes and Common " Places, with their Expositions, collected and " gathered together out of the Workes of divers " singular Writers," in 1581; and "" The Rip-" ping up of the Pope's Fardels."

The musical service composed by Marbeck was formed on the model of the Romish ritual, and first published in quarto, in the year 1550, with this title, " *A Boke of Common Praier,* " *noted.*" The Lord's prayer, the creed, and such other parts as were most proper to be read, are written so as to be sung in a certain key or pitch, in a kind of recitative. To the other parts are given melodies of a grave and solemn con-struction, and nearly as restrained as those of the old *Gregorian Chant.* These have each an harmonical relation with the whole, the dominant of each being in unison with the key-note in which the whole is to be sung.

John Taverner was organist of Boston, in Lincolnshire, and likewise a member of Cardinal (now Christ-Church) College, Oxford. Being in his religion a Lutheran, and connected with John Frith the Martyr, and some others, he was with them accused of heresy. They were all seized and imprisoned in a deep cavern under the college, at that time used for the keeping of salt fish, the putrid stench arising from which actually suffocated one of them.   Frith was convicted and burnt at Smithfield in the year 1533; but Taverner had kept more within the bounds of moderation than the others, and was only accused of having concealed some heretical books under the boards of the school where he taught.   On this account, and from his great eminence as a musician, he was fortunate enough to escape condemnation.

It is necessary to remark, that there were two Taverners living about the same time, who had the same Christian name.   The one above-mentioned is known as Taverner the musician; the other was one of the Gresham professors, and the publisher of Matthew's Bible, in 1539.   This person, indeed, took a degree in music at Oxford, but he is not known to have at all excelled in the science.

CHRISTOPHER TYE, born in Westminster,* and educated in the Royal Chapel, was musical preceptor to Prince Edward, and the other children of King Henry the Eighth.   In the year 1545, he was admitted to the degree of Doctor of Music in

---

* Anthony Wood says he was a *western* man.

Cambridge; and in 1548, was incorporated a member of the University of Oxford. In the reign of Queen Elizabeth, he received the appointment of organist of the Royal Chapel. He was a man of considerable literary acquirements, and, for the age in which he lived, was truly excellent in his profession. Anthony Wood says of his compositions, that " there are some of " them among the ancient books in the Music " School at Oxford, but that they are antiquated, " and not at all valued :" there are, however, not many ancient compositions for the church, which can boast a degree of merit equal to that of his anthems. One of these for a full choir, " From " the depth I called on thee, O Lord," is to be found in Page's Harmonia Sacra; and the first part of another for four voices, beginning with the words, " I will exalt thee," in Dr. Crotch's Selections of the various Styles of Music, arranged for keyed Instruments. The latter appears to have been composed in 1545.

Dr. Tye began an arduous task in composing music to the whole *Acts of the Apostles*, which he had previously rendered into English verse; but he did not complete the undertaking. The first fourteen chapters were printed in the year 1553, with this singularly quaint title : " The " Actes of the Apostles, translated into Englyshe " metre, and dedicated to the kynge's most ex- " cellaunte maiestye, by Christofer Tye, doctor

" in musyke, and one of the gentylmen of hys
" grace's moste honourable chapell, wyth notes
" to eche chapter, to synge, and also to playe
" upon the lute, very necessary for studentes after
" their studye, to fyle theyr wyttes, and alsoe
" for all Christians that cannot synge, to reade
" the good and godlye storyes of the lives of
" Christ and his Apostles."

The following initial stanza of the fourteenth chapter is given as a specimen of the poetry. The New Testament translation runs thus : " It " came to pass, in Iconium, that they went both " together into the synagogue of the Jews, and " so spake, that a great multitude both of the " Jews, and also of the Greeks, believed."

> " It chaunced in Iconium,
>   " As they oft tymes dyd use,
> " Together they into dyd come
>   " The sinagoge of Jews;
> " Where they dyd preache and onlye seke
>   " God's grace then to atcheve,
> " That they so spake to Jue and Greke
>   " That manye dyd beleue."

This version of the Acts of the Apostles was occasionally sung in the chapel of King Edward the Sixth, and probably in other places where the choral service was performed. Its success however did not answer the author's ex-pectation ; and, instead of completing it, he applied himself to the composition of music to words selected from the Psalms of David, in four, five and more parts. To the latter species of harmony, for want of a better name, that of *anthem*, a corruption of antiphon, was given.

In the second volume of Dr. Boyce's Collection of Cathedral Music, there is an anthem of this great musician, " I will exalt thee, O God," which is a perfect model for composition in the church style, not only from its melody and harmony, but for the contrivance and general effect of the whole.

The following memorandum respecting Dr. Tye is transcribed from a note in the writing of Anthony Wood : " Dr. Tye was a pevish and humoursome " man, especially in his latter days ; and some- " times playing on the organ in the chapel of " Queen Elizabeth, which contained much music, " but little delight to the ear, she would send the " verger to tell him that he played out of tune, " whereupon he would send word that her Ma- " jesty's ears were out of tune " He adds, that Dr. Tye restored church music after it had been almost ruined by the dissolution of monasteries.*

The manuscript from which this anecdote was taken, contains " Brief Notes and Memoirs of famous Musicians, by " Anthony Wood." It is to be found in the Ashmolean Museum, f. 189

ROBERT WHITE, who preceded Bird and Tallis,
and who died before their fame was well established, was an excellent composer of church
services in the style of Palestrina ; this, however,
he could not have imitated, since he was a great
master of harmony before the productions of this
chief of the Roman school were published, or at
least circulated in other parts of Europe. There is
reason to suppose that he died before the year 1581.

His works seem never to have been printed ; but,
in the library of Christ-Church, Oxford, a sufficient
number of them in manuscript has been preserved
to excite not only wonder, but indignation, at the
little notice that has been taken of him by musical
writers.   Morley, indeed, has given him a place
in the list of composers at the end of his " Intro-
" duction to Practical Music," and ranks him
with Orlando di Lasso and other excellent men ;
he likewise places him with Fairfax, Taverner,
Shepherd, Mundy, Parsons, and Bird, " famous
" Englishmen who have been nothing inferior to
" the best composers on the Continent."   And no
musician had then appeared who better deserved to
be celebrated for knowledge of harmony and
clearness of style than Robert White.

Dr. Burney says he is in possession of a small
manuscript, which, by the writing and ortho-
grapy, seems of the sixteenth century, entitled,
" Mr. Robert White, his Bitts, of three parte
" Songs, in partition ; with Ditties, 11, without

Ditties, 16." These are short fugues or intonations in most of the eight ecclesiastical modes. Their harmony is extremely pure, and the answer to each fugue is brought in with great science and regularity.

THOMAS TALLIS, one of the greatest musicians that this or any other country ever produced, flourished about the middle of the sixteenth century. It has been generally said that he was organist of the Royal Chapel in the reigns of Henry the Eighth, Edward the Sixth, Mary, and Elizabeth ; but this is by no means certain. It is known, however, that he was a gentleman of the Chapel in the reigns of Edward the Sixth and Queen Mary ; and that he received for this service $7\frac{1}{2}d.$ per day. Under Queen Elizabeth he and **Bird** were gentlemen of the Chapel and organists.

The studies of Tallis seem to have been wholly devoted to the church, for his name is not to be found to any of the lighter kinds of music. He and Bird were favoured by letters patent, granted in the year 1575. which not only enabled them, for the term of twenty-one years, to print, exclusively, their own music ; but which forbade that any persons, except themselves or their assigns, should vend any ruled paper for writing music on, or any printed music whatever, either English or foreign, under the penalty of 40*s*. for every book, paper, or song, that should be sold. Under the protec-

tion of this patent they published, in conjunction,
one of the noblest collections of church music
that has ever appeared in any age or country :
namely, " *Cantiones, quæ ab Argumento Sacræ*
" *vocantur, quinque et sex Partium, Autoribus*
" *Thoma Tallisio et Gulielmo Birdo, Serenissimæ*
" *Reginæ Majestati à priuato Sacello Generosis*
" *et Organistis.*"

Some of the compositions inserted in this collection have been spoken of, by succeeding musicians, in terms of the highest praise ; and many of
them have been adapted to English words by Dr.
Aldrich and others, for the use of our cathedrals.
The canons, inversions, augmentations, diminutions, and other learned and fashionable contrivances of the times, which were very difficult of
accomplishment, are carried on in these compositions with wonderful ingenuity.

The most curious and extraordinary of all
Tallis's labours was his SONG OF FORTY PARTS,
which is still extant. This astonishing effort of
harmonical abilities is not divided into *choirs* of
four parts, like the compositions *a molti cori* of
Benvoli and others, but consists of eight trebles
placed under each other, eight mezzi soprani or
mean parts, eight counter-tenors, eight tenors,
and eight basses, with one line allotted to the
organ. All these several parts are not, as might
be imagined, in simple counterpoint, or filled up
in mere harmony, without meaning or design, but
have each a share in the short subjects of fugue

and imitation, which are introduced upon every change of words. The first subject is begun in G by the first mezzo soprano or medius, and answered in D, the fifth above, by the first soprano; the second medius, in like manner beginning in G, is answered in the octave below by the first tenor; and that by the first counter-tenor in D, the fifth above; then the first bass has the subject in D, the eighth below the counter-tenor: and thus all the forty *real* parts are severally introduced in the course of thirty-nine bars, then the whole vocal phalanx is employed at once during six bars more;* after which a new subject is led off by the lowest bass, and pursued by other parts severally for about twenty-four bars, when there is another general chorus of all the parts; and thus this stupendous, though perhaps Gothic, specimen of human labour and intellect, is carried on in an alternate flight, pursuit, attack, and choral union to the end, when the polyphonic phenomenon is terminated by twelve bars of universal chorus in quadragintesimal harmony.

It is somewhat difficult to account for the publication of the *Cantiones Sacræ* by Tallis and Bird, with Latin words, at a time when it is well known that our liturgy was completely settled,

---

* The entire composition consists of one hundred and thirty-eight bars in *alla breve* time.

and the whole of the church service was by law required to be performed in the English language. It is true that the first act of uniformity of King Edward the Sixth allowed much latitude in singing, and left in a great measure to the clergy the choice of adopting either the metrical psalmody of the Calvinists, or of persevering in the use of the solemn choral service. In consequence of this they were both in practice; but there is no authority for supposing that the singing of anthems or hymns in the Latin tongue was ever afterwards permitted. The composition of music to the Latin service by Tallis and Bird cannot be accounted for, but upon the supposition that they were of the Romish persuasion, and that the *Cantiones Sacræ* were written for the use of Queen Mary's chapel.

But notwithstanding the supposed attachment of Tallis to the Romish communion, it seems that he accommodated himself and his studies to those alterations in the form of public worship which succeeded the accession of Queen Elizabeth. With this view he set to music those several parts of the English liturgy which at that time was deemed most proper to be sung.

He composed also many *anthems* in four and five parts, which were published in a collection printed in 1648, and entitled, " The First Book of " selected Church Music, collected out of divers

" approved authors, by John Barnard, one of the
" Minor Canons of the Cathedral Church of St.
" Paul."

This deservedly eminent composer died on the
23d of November, 1585, and was buried in the
chancel of the parish church of Greenwich, in
Kent, with the following inscription on his tomb:*

" Enterred here doth ly a worthy wyght,
   " Who for long tyme in musick bore the bell:
" His name to shew, was Thomas Tallys hyght,
   " In honest vertuous life he dyd excell.

" He seru'd long tyme in chappel with grete prayse,
   " Fower souereygnes reygnes (a thing not often seene),
" I mean Kyng Henry and Prynce Edward's dayes,
   " Quene Mary, and Elizabeth our Quene.

" He maryed was, though children he had none,
   " And lyu'd in loue full thre and thirty yeres
" Wyth loyal spowse, whos name yclept was Jone,
   " Who here entomb'd, him company now bears.

" As he dyd liue, so also did he dy,
   " In myld and quyet sort, O happy man!
" To God ful oft for mercy did he cry,
   " Wherefore he liues, let deth do what he can.

RICHARD FARRANT, a fine old composer of
church music, was a gentleman of the Chapel

---

* Dr. Aldrich caused the stone on which this was engraved
to be repaired; but, on taking down the old church soon
after the year 1720, it was, with many others, entirely destroyed.

Royal in the year 1564, and afterwards master of the children of St. George's Chapel at Windsor. He was also a clerk and one of the organists: on his appointment to the latter office, however, he resigned his place in the Chapel; but being called to it again, he held it till 1580. He is supposed to have died in the year 1585.

His compositions are in a style remarkably devout and solemn; many of them are printed in Barnard's Collection of Church Music, and a few in Dr. Boyce's Cathedral Music. The full anthem, "Lord, for thy tender mercies' sake," is at this day in frequent use; and Dr. Crotch, who has inserted it in his work, has justly observed, that it is " remarkable for its serene effect, and for " being as beautiful as the nature of plain coun- " terpoint will admit."

ROBERT JOHNSON, an ecclesiastic and a learned musician, was one of the first of our church composers who disposed their parts with intelligence and design. In writing upon a plain song, moving in slow notes of equal length, which was so much practised in these times, he discovers considerable art and ingenuity in the manner of treating subjects of fugue and imitation.

ROBERT PARSONS, or, as his name has been spelt, *Persons,* was organist of Westminster Abbey. He was a gentleman of the Chapel Royal in the reign of Queen Elizabeth; and was drowned at Newark-upon-Trent in the month of January, 1569.

Many of his compositions are extant in manuscript, and some of them have been spoken of in terms of high commendation.

The following whimsical epitaph on Parsons is preserved in Camden's Remains :

" Death, passing by, and hearing Parsons play,
  " Stood much amazed at his depth of skill;
" And said, ' This artist must with me away,'
  " For death bereaves us of the better still.
" But let the choir, while he leaves time, sing on,
  " For Parsons rests, his service being done.

WILLIAM BIRD was the son of Thomas Bird, one of the gentlemen of the Chapel Royal in the reign of King Edward the Sixth. According to the assertion of Wood, he received the principal part of his musical education under Tallis. He was elected organist of the Cathedral Church of Lincoln in the year 1563; and, six years afterwards, on the death of Parsons, was appointed a gentleman of the Chapel.

It appears that, in 1575, Tallis and Bird were both organists of the Royal Chapel; but the time of their appointment to this office cannot now be ascertained.

Bird died in the year 1623, leaving a son named Thomas, whom he educated in his own profession.

His compositions are various: those of his younger years were mostly for the service of the church; and they favour strongly the supposition already mentioned in the account of Tallis, that at that time he adhered to the Romish communion. There are three *masses* of his composition in print.

The " *Cantiones Sacræ*," before mentioned as the joint production of Tallis and Bird, seem to have been the earliest of his publications.   He composed also, alone, a somewhat similar work, entitled, "*Sacrarum Cantionum, quinque Vocum*," printed in the year 1589.   Besides these he was the author of " *Gradualia, ac Cantiones Sacræ*" (of which there are two editions, the latter published in 1610), and of "*Gradualia, seu Cantionum* " *Sacrarum : quarum aliæ ad quatuor, aliæ vero* " *ad quinque et sex Voces editæ sunt.*"

Although, from these productions, it appears that Bird was, in the strictest sense of the word, a church musician, yet he occasionally gave to the world compositions of a lighter kind, and he seems to have been the first among the English who attempted that elegant species of vocal harmony called the *madrigal*.   The *La Verginella* of Ariosto, which he set for five voices, is the most ancient composition of that kind to be met with in the works of English authors.

His other compositions were, " *Songs of sundry* " *natures, some of Grauitie, and others of Myrth,* "*fit for all Companies and Voyces,*" printed in 1589;—"*Psalmes, Sonets, and Songs of Sadness* "*and Pietie, made into Musicke of five Parts;*"—and "*Psalmes, Songs, and Sonets: some solemne,* "*others joyful, framed to the Life of the Words,* "*fit for Voyces or Viols of three, four, five, and* "*six Parts;*" published in 1611.

Besides the above, he was the author of many compositions printed in the collections of other persons, but particularly in one entitled, "*Parthe-* "*nia, or the Maidenhead of the first Musick that* "*ever was printed for the Virginals, composed by* "*the three famous Masters, William Byrd, Dr.* "*John Bull, and Orlando Gibbons, Gentlemen of* "*her Majestie's Chappell.*" In the collections of services and anthems published by Day and Barnard, there are many of his compositions, and several others continue still in manuscript in the King's Chapel, and in the cathedral and collegiate churches of this kingdom.

That Bird was an excellent organist there cannot be the least doubt; we need but turn to his compositions to form an opinion of his style and manner of playing. To judge from these, his voluntaries must have been enriched with varied modulation, lofty fugues, artful syncopations, original and unexpected cadences, and, in short, with all those ornaments that constitute a style at once solemn, majestic, and devout.

He is considered to have been the finest player
on the virginal of his time ; and his music for that
instrument, or, as we should now term them, his
lessons for the pianoforte, are all so excellently
adapted to it, as to afford ground for supposing
that, if he had lived in a later age, his genius would
have expanded itself in works of invention, taste,
and elegance.   Several of these lessons are printed
in the collection entitled " Parthenia."   In a
magnificent folio manuscript, curiously bound in
red morocco, which is generally known by the
name of QUEEN ELIZABETH'S VIRGINAL BOOK,
there are also nearly seventy of his compositions.

The first piece by Bird in this book is a *fantasia,* which generally implies a *fugue,* in which
the subject is as frequently changed as in the ancient choral music, where new words require new
accents and intervals ; for as yet it was not the
custom, in composing fugues, to confine a whole
movement to one theme ; and here Bird introduces
five or six, wholly different and unconnected with
each other.

The subject of the second composition by Bird
in the Royal Virginal Book is the tune of an old
ballad, " *Jhon, come kiss me now ;*" of which,
with great labour and ingenuity, he has varied the
accompaniments sixteen different ways.   No. 52
is another *fancie ;* and 56, a pavan by Bird.   No.
58 is entitled *The Carman's Whistle.*   From

No. 58 to 69, the compositions are all by him; consisting chiefly of old tunes with variations.

It has been imagined, observes Dr. Burney, that the rage for variations was the contagion of the present century; but it appears, from the above manuscript, that this species of *influenza*, or *corruption of air*, was more excessive in the sixteenth century than at any other period of musical history.

The compositions of Bird were very numerous, and in great variety. The most permanent memorials of his excellence are, however, unquestionably, to be sought for in his motets and anthems. These were formerly considered to possess a degree of merit so eminent, that in the Cheque-Book of the Chapel Royal their author is styled " the " father of music ;" and they will continue to be admired so long as there is any genuine taste for sacred music left in the world. His canon of " *Non Nobis, Domine,*" is known to every one.

JOHN BULL was born in Somersetshire, about the year 1563, and, as it is said, was a descendant from the Somerset family. He was educated in music under Biltheman, who was organist of the Chapel Royal in the reign of Queen Elizabeth. At the age of twenty-three he was admitted to the degree of Bachelor of Music in the University of Oxford; and six years afterwards to that of Doctor. On the death of Biltheman, in 1591, he received the appoint-

ment of organist of the Chapel; and Anthony
Wood has said of him, that he had *" a most pro-*
" digious hand on the organ."

Dr. Bull was nominated the first professor of
music in Gresham College, London, and that at
the express recommendation of the queen.

In the year 1601, he went abroad for the recovery
of his health, which, for some time, had been greatly
impaired. He travelled *incognito* into France and
Germany, and Anthony Wood relates the following
whimsical anecdote respecting him whilst in France.
" Dr. Bull, hearing of a famous musician belong-
" ing to a certain cathedral at St. Omers, he applied
" himself as a novice to him to learn something of
" his faculty, and to see and admire his works. This
" musician, after some discourse had passed between
" them, conducted Bull to a vestry or music school
" adjoining to the cathedral, and showed him a
" lesson or song of forty parts, and then made a
" vaunting challenge to any person in the world to
" add one more part to them, supposing it to be so
" complete and full, that it was impossible for any
" man to correct or add to it. Bull, desiring the use
" of pen, ink, and ruled paper, prayed the musician
" to lock him up in the said school for two or three
" hours; which being done, not without great dis-
" dain by the musician, Bull in that time, or less,
" added *forty more parts* to the said lesson or
" song. The musician thereupon being called in,
" he viewed it, tried it, and retried it; at length

" he burst into a great ecstacy, and declared that
" he who had added those forty parts must either
" be the Devil or Dr. Bull.* Whereupon Bull
" making himself known, the musician fell down
" and adored him. Afterwards continuing in
" those parts for a time, Bull became so much
" admired, that he was courted to accept of any
" place or preferment suitable to his profession,
" either within the dominions of the Emperor, the
" King of France or of Spain ; but the tidings of
" these transactions coming to the English court,
" Queen Elizabeth commanded him home."†

Dr. Ward, who has given some account of
Dr. Bull, in the Lives of the Gresham Professors,
says, that he had the honour of entertaining King
James the First and Prince Henry with his performance on the organ at Merchant-Taylors' Hall,
on the 16th of July, 1607, the election-day of the
master and wardens. He relates also, that six
years afterwards, Dr. Bull quitted England, and
went to reside in the Netherlands, where he was
admitted into the service of the Archduke of
Austria.‡ Wood asserts that he died at Hamburgh, but others say at Lubeck.

---

* An exclamation perhaps suggested by the recollection of
the very celebrated one of Sir Thomas More, " *Aut tu es Eras-*
" *mus aut Diabolus.*"

† Fasti, Anno 1586.

‡ The following is a copy of an entry in the Cheque-Book

There is a picture of him yet remaining in the music school at Oxford. It is painted on board, and represents him in his habit of Bachelor of Music.

The only works of Dr. Bull in print are, *Lessons for the Virginal*, in the collection entitled " Parthenia ;" and an anthem, " Deliver me, O God," inserted in Barnard's " Cathedral Music."

From the long list given by Dr. Ward of Dr. Bull's compositions in manuscript, in the collection of the late Dr. Pepusch, it should seem that he was equally skilled in vocal and instrumental harmony. By some of the lessons in " Parthenia," it appears that he possessed powers of execution on the harpsichord far beyond what is generally conceived of the masters of that time. These lessons, in the estimation of Dr. Pepusch, were so excellent, not only for harmony and contrivance, but also for air and modulation, that he has not scrupled to prefer them to most of those of the com-

---

of the Chapel Royal : " 1613, John Bull, Doctor of Music, " went beyond the seas without license, and was admitted " into the Archduke's service, and entred into paie there " about Mich. ; and Peter Hopkins, a base from Paul's, was " sworn into his place the 27th of December following : his " wages from Mich. unto the daye of swearing of the said " Peter Hopkins, was disposed of by the Deane of his Ma- " jesty's Chapel." From this entry it should seem that Dr. Bull was not only one of the organists, but likewise a gentleman of the Chapel.

posers who flourished about his own time.   Dr.
Burney, however, considers them as by no means
deserving of so much credit ; and the assertion
of Pepusch, he says, rather proves that his own
taste was *bad*, than that Bull's music was *good*.
" Though," he continues, " I should greatly ad-
" mire the hand as well as the patience of any
" one capable of playing his compositions, yet,
" *as music*, they would afford me no kind of plea-
" sure—*ces sont des notes, et rien que des notes ;*
" there is nothing in them which excites rapture.
" They may be heard, by a lover of music, with as
" little emotion as the clapper of a mill, or the
" rumbling of a post-chaise.

 " In all Dr. Bull's vocal music there seems to be
" much more labour and study than genius.   Tallis
" and Bird had long accustomed themselves to
" write for voices, and the parts, in their compo-
" sitions, are much more natural than those of
" Bull."

JOHN DOWLAND, a celebrated performer on the
lute, was born in the year 1562, and, at the age of
twenty-six, was admitted to the degree of Bachelor
of Music in Oxford.*   He seems to have been a

---

* Wood says, that he was one of the gentlemen of the
Chapel Royal, but the truth of this assertion is very doubtful ;
for he does not assume that title in any of his publications;
on the contrary, he complains, in the preface to his Pilgrim's
Solace, that he never could obtain any public situation
whatever.

great favourite with the public. Anthony Wood says of him, that " he was the rarest musician " that the age did behold ;" and Shakspeare has thus immortalized him in one of his sonnets :

" If Music and sweet Poetry agree,
 " As they needs must (the sister and the brother),
" Then must the love be great 'twixt thee and me,
 " Because thou lov'st the one, and I the other.
" Dowland to thee is dear, whose heavenly touch
 " Upon the lute doth ravish human sense ;
" Spenser to me, whose deep conceit is such,
 " As passing all conceit, needs no defence ;
" Thou lov'st to hear the sweet melodious sound
 " That Phœbus' lute (the Queen of Music) makes,
" And I in deep delight am chiefly drown'd,
 " When as himself to singing he betakes ;
 " One god is god to both, as poets feign,
 ". One knight loves both, and both in thee remain."

In the year 1584, Dowland travelled through the principal parts of France. From thence he passed into Germany, where he was received in the most flattering manner by the Duke of Brunswick and the learned Prince Maurice, the landgrave of Hesse-Cassel. After a residence of some months in Germany, he crossed the Alps into Italy, and successively visited Venice, Padua, Genoa, Ferrara, and Florence.

He published, in 1595, " *The First Booke of* " *Songes or Ayres of foure Parts, with Tabla-* " *ture for the Lute* ;" and in the Second Book, printed in 1600, he styles himself lutenist to the king of Denmark. A Third Book of the same work was afterwards given to the public. Some time after this he printed his " *Lachrimæ, or Seaven* " *Teares figured in Seaven passionate Pauans,* " *with divers other Pauans,** *Galiards, and Al-* " *mands, set forth for the Lute, Viols, or Violins,* " *in five Parts.*" This work seems to have attained considerable celebrity. It is alluded to in a comedy of Thomas Middleton, entitled " No wit " like a Woman's," in which the servant tells his master bad news, and is thus answered,

" No, thou plaiest Dowland's Lachrimæ to thy master."

Dowland translated and published, in 1609, the " *Micrologus*" of Ornithoparcus, containing the substance of a course of lectures on music, delivered by that author, about the year 1535, in the universities of Tubingen, Heidelburg, and Mentz ; and in 1612 he published, " *A Pil-* " *grim's Solace, wherein is contained musical* " *Harmony of three, four, and five Parts, to be* " *sung and plaid with Lute and Viols.*" In the preface to this work he styles himself lutenist to Lord Walden. One of Dowland's madrigals for four voices, " Go, crystal tears," is inserted in Smith's Musica Antiqua; and another, "Awake, " sweet Love," which is full of elegance, taste, and feeling, in Dr. Crotch's Selections.

---

* The pavan was a peculiar species of Spanish dance.

He died in Denmark, as it is supposed, in the year 1615.

PETER PHILLIPS, an Englishman by birth, but better known by the Italianized name of *Pietro Phillipi*, was a composer of vocal music both sacred and profane. He styles himself *Canonicus Sogniensis*, or Canon of Soigny, a city in Hainault; and he was likewise organist to the Archduke and Duchess of Austria.

His principal works were published in the following order: " *Melodia Olympica ;*"—" *Madrigali à* 8 *Voci,*" in 1599 ;—" *Cantiones Sacræ,* 5 *Vocum,*" in 1612 ;—" *GemmulæSacræ,* 2 *et* 3 *Vocum,*" in 1613 ;—" *Litaniæ B. V. M. in Ecclesia Loretana cani solitæ,* 4, 5, 9, *Vocum,*" in 1623.

The situations which Phillips held, and the nature of his compositions, all denote him to have been of the Romish communion. The *Cantiones Sacræ* are dedicated to the Virgin Mary.

THOMAS MORLEY, one of the gentlemen of Queen Elizabeth's Chapel, the author of a well-known treatise on Practical Music, was, in his younger days, a pupil of Bird. He obtained his Bachelor's degree in 1588 ; and, about four years afterwards, was sworn into Bird's place in the Chapel Royal.

His " *Playne and Easie Introduction to Prac-*

" tical Musicke" was published, in a thin folio
volume, in the year 1597. It is written in dialogue betwixt a master and his pupil. This
valuable work is divided into three parts : the first
teaching to sing ; the second treating of descant,
and the method of singing upon a plain song ;
and the third of composition in three and more
parts. In the course of the conversation so many
interesting particulars occur, relating to the manners of the times, as tend to render the book entertaining even to those who are unacquainted
with the subject of it.

In the first book, which professes to teach the
pupil the rudiments of song, the precepts are
illustrated by notes, to some of which are joined,
for the greater facility of utterance, the letters of
the alphabet, introduced by a distich, and concluded by a direction. The following (transposed
from the original clef, and written in more modern notes) is here inserted as a curious specimen
of this mode of instruction :—

Christes cross * be my speede in all uertue to pro-

ceede.   A b c   d e f g   h i k l m n o p

q r s   & t   double w   v   x with y   ezod & per se

con per se tittle   tittle est amen.   When you have done begin

again   begin   again.   Christes crosse be my speede in   all

uertue to proceede.   a b c   d e f g   h ,†

The second book of this work contains the rules
for extemporary descant; and the third treats of
the mode of composing songs.

In the course of his directions, Morley censures

---

* The alphabet is frequently termed *Criss Cross,* or *Christ's
Cross Row,* on account of a cross constantly placed before the
letter A, which was anciently a direction for the child to cross
itself before it began its lesson, as it is now in the Mass-Book
for the same action in different parts of the service.

† The practice of annexing frivolous words to notes, by the
way of better imprinting them on the memories of the learners,
was originally begun by the monks long before the time of
Morley.

the practice of several musicians in using perfect chords of the same kind in succession. He says of Fairfax, Taverner, Bird, and some others, that they would scarcely have thought it a greater sacrilege to spurn at the image of a saint, than to take two perfect chords of one kind together.

At the end of the dialogue, the author has inserted what he calls the *Peroratio*, in which he exhibits much learning in his profession. In this he states as his opinion, that if it had not been for the industry and writings of Boëtius, the knowledge of music would not even yet have reached the western countries of the world.

Next follow some of the author's compositions for three, four, and five voices, to Latin, Italian, and English words, all of which have great merit.

The annotations at the end of the work are replete with curious learning. In these the author has been very severe on some pretenders to the science. Among the rest he speaks of an anonymous work, printed in 1596, entitled, " The Guide " of the Pathway to Music;" and says that, with some exceptions, " you shall not finde one side in all the booke without some grosse errour or other."

From his own works, and from the few scattered notes concerning him to be found in the Athenæ Oxonienses, Morley appears to have been a sensible, learned, and pious man, somewhat

soured in his temper by bodily infirmities, and by
the envy of some of his rivals in the science: of
these he complains, in feeling terms, in the prefaces to nearly all his publications.

He died in the year 1604, having survived the
publication of his Introduction not* more than
nine years.

His other works are, " *Canzonets or little*
" *short Songs to three Voices,*" printed in London in 1593 ;—" *The first Book of Madrigals*
" *to four Voices,*" in the following year ;—
" *Canzonets or short Airs to five or six Voices,*"
in 1595 ;—" *Madrigals to five Voices,*" in the
same year ;—" *The first Book of Aires or lit-*
" *tle short Songes to sing and play to the Lute*
" *with the Base Viol,*" in 1600 ;—and the first
book of " *Canzonets for two Voices,*" printed in
1595 and 1619. He composed also several divine
services and *anthems.* A funeral service of his
composition, the first of the kind to the words of
our liturgy, is printed in the first volume of Dr.
Boyce's "Cathedral Music." Morley also collected and published, in 1601, madrigals by different
authors, for five and six voices, under the title of
" The Triumphs of Oriana," and a set or two of
Italian madrigals adapted to English words.

The *Triumphs of Oriana* is a work which
seems to have arisen from the joint efforts of all
the musicians of Queen Elizabeth's time that
were capable of composing. The occasion of

its collection is said to have been this. The Earl
of Nottingham, who was the only person that
could prevail on Queen Elizabeth, in her last
illness, to remain in her bed, gave, with a view
to alleviate her concern for the execution of the
Earl of Essex, a prize subject to all the poets
and musicians in the kingdom. This was the
beauty and accomplishments of his royal mistress ;
and a liberal reward excited them severally to the
compostion of this work. There is, however,
some piece of secret history yet to be learned,
that must enable us to account for their having
given to the queen the romantic appellation of
Oriana.

As a practical composer, Morley has doubtless
shewn great ability ; he was an excellent harmonist, but did not possess any great powers of invention. His compositions seem the effect of
close study and intense labour, but they have
little of that sweetness of melody which is found
in those of some of his contemporaries. His burial service continued in use at the interment of
persons of rank till that of Purcel and Croft was
introduced, which can scarcely be excelled.

After the expiration of the patent for the exclusive printing of music, granted to Tallis and
Bird, it seems that Morley had interest enough
to obtain from Queen Elizabeth a new one of the
same kind, but with more extensive powers. It
was granted in 1598 ; and under the protection of

it, William Barley printed most of the music books which were published during the time it continued in force.

JOHN MUNDY was organist first of Eton College, and afterwards of the free chapel of Windsor, in the reign of Queen Elizabeth. In the year 1586, at the same time with Bull, he was admitted to the degree of Bachelor of Music at Oxford ; and, about forty years afterwards, to that of Doctor. He died in 1630, and was interred in the cloister adjoining to the Chapel of St. George at Windsor.

Mundy was an able performer on the organ and virginal, as is manifested by several of his compositions for those instruments, preserved in Queen Elizabeth's Virginal Book ; and among the rest, by a *fantasia*, in which he endeavours to convey an idea of *fair wether, lightning, thunder, calme wether*, and *a faire day*. In this attempt, if he has failed, it was not for want of hand, as the passages are such as seem to imply great command of the instrument.

He composed several *madrigals* for five voices, which were printed in the " Triumphs of " Oriana." He was likewise the author of a work, published in 1594, entitled, " *Songs and* " *Psalmes, composed into three, four, and* " *five Parts, for the Use of and Delight of all* " *such as either loue or learne Musicke.*" Some of these, says Dr. Burney, are considerably " above mediocrity in harmony and design. Indeed, I think I can discover more air in some of his movements, than is to be found in those of any of his contemporary musicians of the *second* class."

WILLIAM MUNDY was a composer of several church *services* and *anthems,* the words of which are to be seen in " Clifford's Collection of divine " Services and Anthems, usually sung in Cathe- " drals."* He was the son of John Mundy, though a composer so early as the year 1591. According to Wood, he was not a graduate of either of the universities.

His name appears to several of the anthems in Barnard's Collection ; but it has been placed by mistake to one (as Dr. Aldrich has taken the pains to detect), " O God, the Maker of all " things," which is, in fact, the composition of King Henry the Eighth.

---

* This book is frequently referred to by Wood. It is a collection of the words only of the services and anthems then in use, printed in 12mo. in 1664. The compiler was a native of Oxford, and a chorister of Magdalen College there. He afterwards became a minor canon of St. Paul's, and was a reader in some church near Carter Lane, and also chaplain to the Society of Serjeant's Inn, in Fleet Street.

THOMAS WEELKES, organist of Winchester, and afterwards of Chichester, was the author of a set of *madrigals* for three, four, five, and six voices, printed in 1597. He published also, in the year following, " *Ballets and Madrigals to* " *five Voices, with one to six Voices ;*" and in 1600, " *A Set of Madrigals in six Parts.*" He likewise composed many *services* and *anthems*, which are well known and much esteemed. There is a madrigal of his composition, printed in the " Triumphs of Oriana," and an anthem in Barnard's Collection. He was the author also of a work entitled, " *Ayeres or Phantasticke Spirites* " *for three Voices,*" printed in London in 1608.

By the Fasti Oxonienses it appears, that, in 1602, William Weelkes of New College was admitted to the degree of Bachelor of Music ; but Wood makes it a question, whether the registrar of the university might not mistake the name of William for that of Thomas Weelkes? and on considering the relation between New College and Winchester College, it appears more than probable that he did.

WILLIAM DAMON is chiefly known on account of the harmonies which he published to a collection of psalm tunes. He was organist of the Chapel Royal during the reign of Queen Elizabeth, and was a man of considerable eminence in his profession. His harmonies were intended for

the private use of a friend for whom he had composed them ; but this person, in the year 1579,
without the knowledge of the author, thought
proper to give them to the public in a volume
entitled, " *The Psalmes of David in English Me-*
" *ter, with Notes of foure Parts set unto them,*
" *by Gulielmo Daman, for John Bull,** to the Use*
" *of Christians for recreating themselves, instede*
" *of fond and unseemly Ballades.*"

Neither the reputation of the author, nor the
novelty of the work, could get it into circulation.
In consequence of this he undertook its entire re-
composition, and succeeded so well that all the
disgrace which had been brought upon him by the
former publication was done away.† It is by no
means improbable that Damon or his friends may
have bought up and destroyed as many copies of the

---

* This John Bull is stated in the preface to have been a
citizen and goldsmith of London.

† The title of the new one was, " *The former Booke of the*
" *Music of Mr. William Damon, late one of her Majesty's*
" *Musicians ; conteyning all the Tunes of David's Psalms as*
" *they are ordinarily soung in the Church, most excellently by*
" *him composed into 4 Parts ; in which Sett the Tenor singeth*
" *the Church Tune. Published for the recreation of such as*
" *delight in Music, by W. Swayne, Gent.*" 1591.

At the same time was published, " *The second Book of the*
" *Musicke of Mr. William Damon, containing all the Tunes of*
" *David's Psalmes, differing from the former in respect that*
" *the highest Part singeth the Church Tune.*"

former impression as possible, for at this day there is not one to be had.

The tunes adapted by Damon were forty in number. They are the same that are printed with the earliest impressions of the psalms ; but, by the repetitions of the words and notes, he has contrived to make each of them nearly as long again as it stands in the original. By adopting this plan he seems to have rather intended them for private practice than for the service of the church ; and this probably is the reason why none of them are to be found in any of those collections of psalms in parts, composed by different musical authors, which were written and printed about or somewhat sub-sequent to this period.

GILES FARNABY, of Truro, in Cornwall, was entered at Christ-Church College, Oxford, and in 1592 obtained the degree of Bachelor of Music.

There are extant of his composition, " Canzonets " to four Voices, with a Song of eight Parts," printed in London, in quarto, in the year 1598, and a few of the psalm tunes inserted in Ravens-croft's Collection.

JOHN MILTON, the father of our justly celebra-ted epic poet, was a native of Milton, near Halton and Thame, in Oxfordshire. He was educated to the law, and practised as a scrivener in Bread Street, London ; but he acquired a considerable celebrity as a musical composer.

Among the *psalm tunes* published by Ravenscroft, in 1633, there are many with the name John Milton to them. One of these, called the York tune, is well known at this day in almost every parish church in the kingdom. In the " Triumphs of Oriana" there is a *madrigal* of his composition for five voices ; and in the collection entitled, "The Teares or Lamentations of a sorrow-" ful Soule," composed by various authors, and published by Sir William Leighton, Knt. one of the gentlemen-pensioners, in 1614, there are several of his *songs* for five voices.

It is said, in Phillips's Life of his son, that Milton composed an *In Nomine* * of no fewer than forty parts, for which he was rewarded by a Polish prince, to whom he presented it, with a gold medal and chain.†

---

* The term *In Nomine* is very obscure as applied in musical composition, but it may signify a fugue in which the subject and the reply differ in the order of their notes. A fugue of this description is called a *Fugue in Nomine*, as not being a fugue in strictness.

† A golden medal and chain were the usual gratuity of princes to men of eminence in any of the professions.

CHAP. II.

===

ITALIAN
MUSICAL COMPOSERS AND WRITERS,

WHO FLOURISHED

During the Sixteenth Century,

1500 TO 1600.

===

FESTA. — ARKADELT. — BERCHEM. — CORTECCIA. — CROCE. — PORTA. — ANIMUCCIA. — PALESTRINA. — G. M. NANINO.—BERNARDO NANINO.—ANERIO.— GIOVANELLI.—VECCI.—MARENZIO.—GASTOLDI.— GESUALDO, PRINCE OF VENOSA.—BONA.

VINCENTINO. — ZARLINO. — ARTUSI. — TIGRINI. — TRACCONI.

THE Romans appear to have received their ideas of music, both vocal and instrumental, from the Greeks; and they used it in their triumphs, sacrifices, and other religious rites; on occasions of festivity, and on the stage. Towards the latter end of the Republic, the art had risen into great esteem; and in the voluptuous times of the Emperors, the stage flourished, the temples were crowded, the festivals frequent, and the banquets splendid. Musical and poetical contests were instituted in the public games ; and even the Emperor Nero himself mounted the stage at Naples, as a public singer. This same Emperor, after entering the lists with common musicians at the Olympic games, and bearing off the prize of music by corrupting the judges or bribing his competitors, travelled through Greece, with the low ambition of displaying his skill in singing and playing upon the cithara. He every where challenged the best performers, and, as may be imagined, was invariably declared the victor.

The study of music continued to receive great encouragement throughout the Roman states for many years after the death of Nero; yet the science appears to have advanced but little towards perfection. The works of the Latin writers consist chiefly of abridgments from those of the ancient Greek theorists ; and the occasional additions and alterations to be found in them are, in general, of trifling or of very inferior importance. The treatise " *De Musica*" of Boëtius, written about the year 510, was indeed an intrinsically valuable work, and continued, for many centuries after his death, to be held in the highest estimation. It is entirely theoretical, and contains no allusions either to the state of music of his time, or, in any manner, to the practice of the art. All the writings of Boëtius were collected with great care, and published at Venice in 1499, in one folio volume. Glareanus of Basil collated this volume with several manuscripts, and republished it in the year 1570. The treatise " *De Musica*" was formerly so much in use in England, that an admission to the first degree of music in both our universities could not be obtained without a previous examination in or exercise from it.

We have already given some account of the important reformation that was made in the musical scale by Guido Aretinus, a native of the city of Arezzo, in Florence. This person and Franchinus Gaffurius, who flourished in the fifteenth century, may (with respect to the theory) be considered as the fathers of modern music.

The latter was a native of Lodi, a town in the Milanese, and born about the year 1451. His youth was spent in a close application to learning, but particularly to the study of music. He was elected professor of music at Verona; and he afterwards resided successively at Genoa, Naples, Monticello, Bergamo, and Milan. In the latter place he was appointed conductor of the choir of the cathedral, and received many distinguishing marks of honour. He was living in 1520, so that he must have been at least seventy years of age when he died.

His first work, " *Theoreticum Opus Armonicæ* " *Disciplinæ*," was printed at Naples in the year 1480, and was little more than an abridgment of

Boëtius, with some additions from Guido. In 1496, he published at Milan his "*Practica Musica* " *utriusque Cantûs*," which treats chiefly of the elements of music, and the practice of singing according to the method of Guido. This is written in so clear and perspicuous a manner, as to show plainly that Franchinus was perfectly master of his subject.

Another work by this writer was entitled, "*An-* " *gelicum ac divinum Opus Musicæ*." It was printed at Milan in 1508, and, from its style and manner, seems to have contained the substance of the lectures which he had read at Cremona, Lodi, and other places. It however contains little more than what may be found in the writings of Boëtius and other preceding harmonicians. His treatise, " *De Harmonia Musicorum Instrumentorum*," printed at Milan in 1518, contains the doctrines of such of the Greek musical writers as had come to the hands of the author.

The writings of Franchinus, in the course of a very few years, became so famous, that they were spread almost over all Europe ; and the precepts contained in them were inculcated in most of the schools, universities, and other public seminaries of Italy, France, Germany, and England. The benefits arising from his labours were manifested, not only by an immense number of treatises on music that appeared in the world in the succeeding age, but also by the musical compositions of the sixteenth century, formed after the precepts of Franchinus, which became the models of musical perfection.

For some time previously to the commencement of the sixteenth century, it appears that the chief teachers of music in Italy, and some of the adjacent countries, were the monks and the provençal muzars, violars, &c. The former, as well as they were able, instructed youth in the general principles of harmony, and the method of singing the divine offices : the latter taught the use of musical instruments.

We shall now speak of some of the earliest of the modern Italian composers of music. With respect, however, to the first of these,

CONSTANTIUS FESTA, we are ignorant of the place both of his birth and residence. His compositions are generally considered to be excellent. One of his *motets* is to be found in the fourth book of *Motetti della Corona,* printed so early as the year 1519.

In the third book of Arkadelt's Madrigals, published at Venice in 1541, there are seven of Festa's compositions. In these, says Dr. Burney, " more rhythm, grace, and facility appear, than in any production of his cotemporaries that

I have seen. Indeed he seems to have been the most able contrapuntist of Italy during this early period; and if Palestrina and Constantius Porta be excepted, of any period anterior to the time of Carissimi. I could not resist the pleasure of scoring his whole first book of three-part *madrigals*, from the second edition printed at Venice in 1559; for I was astonished as well as delighted to find the compositions so much more clear, regular, phrased, and unembarrassed, than I expected."

JACQUES ARKADELT, supposed by some writers to have been an Italian, and by others a Frenchman by birth, was a pupil of Jusquin de Prez, a celebrated French composer, hereafter mentioned. It should seem that he chiefly resided in Italy, since the first editions of his principal works were printed at Venice between the years 1539 and 1575. At different periods of his life he composed a great number of *motets* and *madrigals*. The latter were received with so much avidity on the Continent, that four books of them were published at Venice in one year, 1541. He was an excellent composer; and, for the period at which he lived, his melodies have much smoothness and grace.

JACKET BERCHEM, or, as he is called by the Italians, GIACHETTO, composed many of the *madrigals* and *motets* which are to be found in the

collections published at Venice about the middle
of the sixteenth century. Those of his compositions which are preserved in the British Museum
have a clearness, simplicity, and purity of harmony and design, that have been seldom exceeded
by the early composers. He was living in the
year 1580.

FRANCESCO CORTECCIA, a celebrated Italian organist and composer, was thirty years chapel-master
to the Grand Duke Cosimo the Second. In his youth
he published at Venice a set of *Madrigals* for four
voices, afterwards a set of *Motets*, and lastly,
" *Responsaria et Lectiones Hebdomadæ Sanctæ.*"
Dr. Burney says that he scored one of his motets,
but found it dry and uninteresting both in fancy
and contrivance.

He died in the year 1581, and was succeeded at
the court of Florence by

ALESSANDRIO STRIGGIO, a lutenist and voluminous
composer, whom Morley and others have frequently mentioned. His *Madrigals*, in six parts,
were published at Venice in 1566. A copy of
them is preserved in the collection at Christ-
Church, Oxford; but they do not contain any
thing remarkable either for genius or science.

GIOVANNI CROCE was chapel-master at St.
Mark's Church in Venice, in which office it is

supposed he was the immediate successor to
Zarlino.

His compositions were all of a devout and serious
kind ; and of these his penitential *psalms,* which
have been printed with English words, are the
best. Peacham says of his compositions, that
" for a full, lofty, and sprightly vein, Croce was
second to none."

Costanzo Porta, a Franciscan friar, and a
native of Cremona, is highly celebrated among
the musicians of the sixteenth century. He was a
pupil of Willaert, and fellow-student with Zarlino.
In the early part of his life he was maestro di
capella at Padua; afterwards of the Cathedral
Church of Osimo, a small city on the river Musone,
near Ancona ; then at Ravenna, and lastly at
Loretto, where he died in the year 1691.

He has left behind him *Motets* for five voices,
printed at Venice in 1546, and other works of
the same kind, printed also there in 1566 and
1580. These are all excellent and elaborate compositions.

Giovanni Animuccia, a native of Florence, was
no less admired on account of his musical abilities
than respected for his morals. He is celebrated
as one of the companions of San Filippo Neri, who
first applied music to the purpose of attracting
company to the Chiesa Nuova, or New Church, at

Rome, on Sunday evenings; whence sacred dramas, or mysteries, or moralities in music, were afterwards called *oratorios*. Animuccia composed the first *laudi* or hymns in parts which were performed on these occasions.

He published at Venice, in 1548, *Madrigals* and *Motets* in four and five parts, and at Rome, in 1567, a set of *Masses*, dedicated to the canons of the Vatican.

GIOVANNI PIERLUIGI DA PALESTRINA was, as his name imports, a native of Palestrina, or, as it is usually called, Palestina, a city of Italy situate about twenty-five miles east of Rome; and was born about the year 1529.

Tradition states him to have been a disciple of Rinaldo del Mell, a well-known composer, and a native, as it is generally supposed, of some town in Flanders. At the age of thirty-three Palestrina was made chapel-master of the Church of St. Maria Maggiore, and, nine years afterwards, was appointed to the same office in the Church of St. Peter at Rome, which he held during the remainder of his life. In this situation he was honoured with the personal favour and protection of Pope Sextus the Fifth.

In conjunction with Giovanni Maria Nanin, an intimate friend, and formerly the companion of his studies, he established at Rome a music school; in which, notwithstanding the confinement necessary to his studies and to the various duties of his situation, he occasionally assisted the students in their exercises, and heard and decided the disputes between the masters who frequented it.

Palestrina died in the year 1594 ; and so greatly had he been admired and respected during his life, that his funeral was attended not only by all the musicians of Rome, but by immense crowds of people from that city and neighbourhood.   It was celebrated by three choirs, who sang a " *Libera* " *me, Domine,*" of his own composition. His body was interred, inclosed in a sheet of lead, in the Church of St. Peter, before the altar of St. Simon and St. Jude, a privilege due to the merits of so great a man.

In the course of his studies, Palestrina discovered the errors of the musicians of Germany and some other countries, who had greatly corrupted the practice of music by the introduction of intricate proportions. He began, in consequence, to form a style of church music, which was grave, decent, and plain, and without the unnatural commixtures of dissimilar times, that were become a disgrace to the science. Influenced by that love of simplicity which is discoverable in all his works, he, in conjunction with Francesco Soriano, reduced the ecclesiastical measures of time to three, namely, the *long,* the *breve,* and the *semibreve.*

Of the many works which Palestrina composed,

one of the most celebrated is that published at
Rome in 1572, containing his *masses*. These
are five in number ; four of them for four, and
one for five voices. Many parts of each are composed in *canon*, and carry the strongest evidence of
the learning and ingenuity of their author.

There is also extant, of his composition, *Motets*
and *Hymns* for four, five, and six voices, printed
in folio in 1589. It is in the motets of Palestrina
that we discover that grandeur and dignity of
style, that artful modulation and pleasing inter-
change of new and original harmonies, for which
he is so justly celebrated. To two of these Dr.
Aldrich adapted English words, and, thus arranged,
they have been frequently sung in our cathedrals.
One of them in the key of C major, " O Lord God
" of our Salvation," is inserted in Page's Harmonia
Sacra; and the other, " We have heard with
" our Ears," together with part of a *magnificat*,
in Dr. Crotch's Musical Selections.

Many of the *masses* of Palestrina are strict
canon, a species of composition which he tho-
roughly understood ; but his motets are, for the
most part, fugues, in which it is hard to say whether the grandeur and sublimity of the subject, or
the close contexture of the harmony, is most to be
admired. The subjects of his fugues, in general,
consist of but few bars, or even sometimes only
of a single bar ; and yet these have on many occasions been assumed as themes or subjects for

other compositions by masters of the first eminence.

The superior excellence of his compositions excited in contemporary musicians both admiration and envy ; and some infamous attempts were made to destroy his reputation and character, all of which, however, succeeded as they deserved.

Notwithstanding the assiduous attention that Palestrina paid to the duties of his station, and his industry in improving the church music, which was the chief object of his studies, he found time to compose a few *madrigals*, that have been preserved and published. A collection of these appeared in the year 1594, under the title of " *Madrigali Spirituali à cinque Voci.*" They are thirty in number, to Italian words, and in their style are remarkably chaste and pathetic.

The following catalogue of the works of Palestrina is inserted for the use of such persons as may be desirous of collecting them :

" *Joannis Petri Loysii Prænestini in Basilica*
" *S. Petri de Urbe Capellæ Magistri Mescorum,*
" *liber primus.*" Ed. in Roma, 1572.

" *Madrigali spirituali à cinque Voci.*" 1594.

" *Dodici Libri di Messe à* 4, 5, 6, 8 *Voci,*" published in Rome and Venice in 1554, 1567, 1570, 1572, 1582, 1585, 1590, 1591, 1594, 1599, 1600, 1601.

" *Due Libri d' Offertorii à* 5." Venice, 1594.

" *Due Libri di Motetti à* 4." Venice, 1571, 1606.

" *Quattro Libri di Motetti à* 5, 6, 7, 8 *Voci.*" Venice, 1575, 1580, 1584, 1586.

" *Magnificat* 8 *Tonum.*" Rome, 1591.

" *Hymni totius anni* 4 *Voc.*" Rome⁛and Venice, 1589.

" *Due Libri di Madrig. à* 4 *Voci.*" Venice, 1586, 1605.

" *Due Libri di Madrig. à* 5 *Voci.*" Venice, 1594.

" *Litanie à* 4." Venice, 1600.

Giovanni Maria Nanino, a fellow-student, under Rinaldo del Mell, with Palestrina, was a native of Valerano, and, in 1577, was appointed a tenor-singer in the Pontifical Chapel, where many of his compositions are yet preserved. He afterwards became chapel-master of the Church of St. Maria Maggiore, in which office he probably succeeded Palestrina.

There are extant some fine *madrigals* of his composition, and two manuscript treatises of music ; the one entitled, " *Centocinquanta Sette Contra-*
" *punti e Canoni à* 2, 3, 4, 5, 6, 7, 8, 11 *Voci*
" *sopra del canto fermo, intitolato la Base di*
" *Costanzo Festa;*" and the other, " *Trattato di*
" *Contrapunto con la Regola per far Contra-*
" *punto.*"

BERNARDO NANINO, a younger brother of the above writer, was distinguished as a surprising genius, and as having improved the practice of music by the introduction of a new and original style. There is, however, nothing extant of his composition, except a work printed at Rome in 1620, entitled, " *Salmi à* 4 *Voci per le Dome-* " *niche, Solennita della Madonna et Apostoli con* " *doi Magnificat, uno à* 4 *e l' altro à* 8 *Voci.*"

FELICE ANERIO was a pupil of the elder Nanino, and the immediate successor of Palestrina in the station of composer to the Pontifical Chapel. These two circumstances imply no common degree of merit.

According to Adami, many admirable compositions of this author were preserved in the library of the Chapel. There is extant a valuable collection of *madrigals* by him, which were printed at Antwerp in 1610.

RUGGIERO GIOVANELLI, of Velletri, was master of the Chapels of St. Louis and St. Apollinare, and the successor to Palestrina in the Church of St. Peter at Rome. He was also a singer in the Pontifical Chapel.

There is extant a collection of *madrigals* by Giovanelli, that were printed at Venice. He composed many *masses,* some of which have been much celebrated. In the year 1581 he published a work on music, which however contains very little that is deserving of attention.

HORATIO VECCI, a native of Milan, was, for many years, chapel-master at Padua. His vocal compositions have obtained considerable celebrity.

He composed *masses, hymns,* and one book of *madrigals;* but his principal compositions are *canzonets,** of which he was the author of no fewer than seven sets. Milton, who was a great lover of music, and very well understood the science, esteemed Vecci as one of the most accomplished masters of his time. There are two madrigals from the first edition of his first book, which was printed at Venice in 1589, inserted in Smith's "Musica Antiqua."

LUCCA MARENZIO, a native of Coccalia, in the diocese of Brescia, and an excellent composer of *motets* and *madrigals,* flourished about this time. His parents being poor, he was maintained and instructed by Andrea Masetto, the arch-priest of the place. Having a melodious voice, and discovering a strong propensity to music, he was

---

* The word *canzonet* is derived from *canzone,* which signifies in general a song, but, more particularly, a song in parts, containing passages in fugue. The *canzonet* is a composition of this kind, but shorter and less artificial in its contexture. Its invention has been ascribed to Alessandro Romano, a singer in the Pontifical Chapel in the year 1560.

placed under the tuition of Giovanni Contini, and became exceedingly famous. It is said that after he had been some time in Rome, he entertained a criminal passion for a lady, a relation of the Pope, whose fine voice and exquisite performance on the lute had captivated his heart. He soon afterwards retired to Poland, where he was well received, and had an appointment with a salary of a thousand scudi per annum. Here he remained for several years, till the queen, happening to express a desire to see the lady who had been the occasion of his retreat, he resolved to convey her into Poland; but when he arrived at Rome, he found the resentment of the Pope so strong against him, that he was not able to effect his purpose, and he died there of chagrin and disappointment about the year 1599.

Of one set of the madrigals of Marenzio, our countryman Peacham says, that "they are songs which the muses themselves might not have been ashamed to have composed." The subjects of fugue, imitation, and attack, are traits of elegance and pleasing melody, which, though they seem selected with the utmost care, for the sake of the words they are to express, yet so artful are the texture and disposition of the parts, that the general harmony and effect of the whole are as complete and unembarrassed as if the author had been writing in plain counterpoint without poetry or contrivance. One of these, "Disse

à l'amata mia," may be seen in Smith's " Musica
" Antiqua," and is an interesting specimen of
his composition.

The first set of his madrigals for five voices
seems the most elaborate ; the fugues and imitations here are more ingenious and frequent than
in his other works. He has, indeed, in those of
later date, more melody ; but as yet there was too
little to compensate for the want of contrivance.
Whoever takes the trouble to score and examine
this set, will discover marks of real genius with
respect to harmony and modulation, with many
attempts at melody of a more graceful kind than
is to be found in the works of his contemporaries.

The words of his ninth book of five-part madrigals are all from the *Canzoniere* of Petrarca ;
and of these the composition seems the most free
and fanciful of all his works. In Page's " Harmo-
" nia Sacra," there is a full anthem, " Save, Lord,
" hear us when we call," adapted from one of the
motets of Marenzio by the late Dr. Bever, fellow
of All-Souls College, Oxford.

GASTOLDI, sometimes called CASTALDI, born
at Caravaggio, was the author of thirty musical
works, the titles and dates of which may be
seen in Walther's " Musicalisches Lexicon."—
His ballads, printed at Antwerp in 1596, under
the title of " *Balletti à* 5 *co i Versi per cantare,*

" *sonare, e ballare; con una mascherata di Cac-*
" *ciatori à* 6, *e un Concerto de' Pastori è* 8,"
put the derivation of our word *ballad* out of all
doubt, which originally meant a song which was
sung and danced to at the same time. " The
tunes of Gostoldi," observes Dr. Burney, " are
all very lively, and more graceful than any I
have seen before the culivation of melody for
the stage."

CARLO GESUALDO, *Prince of Venosa,* (a principality of the kingdom of Naples) flourished
about the latter end of the sixteenth century. He
was the nephew of Cardinal Alfonso Gesualdo,
Archbishop of Naples, and received his instructions in music from Pomponio Nenna. The writers of all countries give to this prince the character of being an extremely learned, ingenious, and
artificial composer of *madrigals.*

He is generally believed to have imitated and
improved that plaintive kind of air which distinguishes the Scots melodies, and which had
been brought to considerable perfection in the
preceding century. Dr. Burney, however, says,
that in a very attentive perusal of the whole six
books of the Prince of Venosa's Madrigals, he
was utterly unable to discover the least simili-
tude to, or imitation of, the Caledonian airs; and,
instead of giving to his compositions the unlimited

praise that has been so liberally bestowed by others, he says that, " so far from Scots melodies, they seem to contain no melodies at all; nor when scored, can we discover the least regularity of design, phraseology, rhythm, or indeed any thing remarkable, except unprincipled modulation, and the perpetual embarrassments and inexperience of an amateur in the arrangement and filling up of the parts."

Notwithstanding this opinion of Dr. Burney, which indeed few persons would venture to question, it is well known that Geminiani has often declared that he " laid the foundation of his studies on the works of the Principe di Venosa."

The first five books of his Madrigals were published in parts, in 1585, by Simon Molinaro, a musician and chapel-master of Genoa. In the year 1563, the Madrigals of the Prince of Venosa (six books) were published together by the same person. The pieces contained in this edition were upwards of a hundred in number. Two other collections were afterwards printed, but it is probable that the edition of 1613 contains the whole of his works.

VALERIO BONA, an ecclesiastic and musical composer, printed, in 1595, a work on counterpoint and composition, of little use in the present day.

He also published several *motets, masses, the Lamentations of Jeremiah, madrigals,* and *canzonets.*

ITALIAN MUSICAL WRITERS,

Who flourished during the Sixteenth Century.

NICOLO VINCENTINO.—With respect to this writer there are few modern books on music in which some mention is not made. He published, at Rome, in 1555, a work entitled, " *L'Antica Musica ridotta alla Moderna Prattica,*" containing chiefly a series of dissertations on the music of the ancients, in comparison with that of the moderns. The author's principal design in publishing it seems to have been to revive the practice of the ancient music ; and, for this purpose, he invented an instrument of the harpsichord kind, so constructed and tuned as (he hath told us) to answer the division of the ancient tetrachord in each of the three genera. Such a multiplicity and confusion of chords as attended this invention introduced a great variety of intervals, to which the ordinary division of the scale, by tones and semi-tones, was by no means commensurate. He was therefore reduced to the necessity of giving to his instrument no fewer than six rows of keys, the powers of which he has attempted to explain, but in very obscure terms.

The success which he fancied he had attained by his instrument induced, after his death, many persons to attempt the recovery of the ancient musical genera ; and several alterations of different kinds were made in it by a reduction of the keys and other methods. All these were, however, to no purpose. The arrangements of the tones and semi-tones in the musical instruments, continue at this day precisely the same as they did when·Vincentino's ideas on the subject first occurred to his mind.

His work has been variously spoken of by musicians. Some have condemned it as containing the most absurd doctrines ; others have stood forward in its defence. Among the latter is to be numbered the late Dr. Pepusch. On the whole, however, it appears that Vincentino derived all his knowledge of the ancient writers from the works of Boëtius and his contemporaries ; and that, beyond some whimsical notions of his own, there is little contained in his publication which is not also to be found in them.

GIOSEFFO ZARLINO, of Chioggia, an episcopal city in one of the islands of the Gulf of Venice, a celebrated theorist and practical musician, was born in the year 1540. He was a man of very extensive learning ; and there is reason to suppose that he was not originally intended for the profession of music. From the recommendation, however, of Adrian Willaert, a well-known French composer of his time, he was induced to apply himself to this study.

He was made chapel-master of the Church of St. Mark, at Venice ; and he composed the music for the rejoicings at that place on the defeat of the Turks at Lepanto, which was much applauded. Notwithstanding this he is usually considered rather as a theorist than a practical composer ; and he was indisputably one of the best of the modern writers on the science of music. He died at Venice in the year 1589.

The best edition of his works was published at Venice about the time of his death, in four volumes in folio. The first volume contains his " *Institu-* " *tioni Harmoniche ;*" the second, " *Dimostra-* " *tioni Harmoniche ;*" the third, " *Sopplimenti* " *Musicali ;*" and the fourth, a collection of tracts on different subjects, which have no relation to music.

In the three first volumes Zarlino has entered into a long discourse on the theory and practice of music. He has considered the subject in all the various forms in which it appears in the writings of the ancient Greek harmonicians, and in those of later times. As he seems to have been well acquainted with the Greek language, there is little doubt but that he derived his intelligence from the genuine source ; and as to Boëtius and the other

Latin and Italian authors, he appears to have been possessed of all the knowledge which their writings were capable of communicating.

In the *Institutioni* the author sets forth the excellence of music, as applicable both to civil and religious purposes. Amongst numerous other subjects, he speaks of musical proportion, and of the ancient genera and their species, declaring at the same time his opinion of their futility. The third part of the *Institutioni* contains the elements of counterpoint, and precepts for the composition of fugue. The last part treats of the modes or tones, not only of the ancients, but also of those instituted by St. Ambrose and Pope Gregory, and adapted to the service of the church. He gives some rules for the accommodating of melody to words; but these are at present of little use.

The " *Dimostrationi Harmoniche*" are a series of discourses in dialogue. The author begins with the subject of proportion and the measure of intervals; and the whole of the first discourse is little more than a commentary on Boëtius; the second and third discourses consist, for the most part, of demonstrations of the ratios of the consonances and the lesser intervals; the fourth directs the division of the monochord, and treats, in general terms, of the ancient system; and the last contains the author's sentiments on the modes of the ancients; in which little is advanced that is not to be found elsewhere.

The " *Sopplimenti Musicali*" is styled, " A
" Declaration of the principal Things contained
" in the two former Volumes, and a formal De-
" fence of the Author against the Calumnies of
" his Enemies." The disputes from which these
calumnies arose were founded on Zarlino's opinions respecting the several species of the diatonic genus. His chief opponent was Vin-
centio Galilei. This part of the work contains
also a defence of some other opinions entertained
by the author, and has also in it many diagrams
and mathematical problems to illustrate his doctrines.

These volumes contain a great fund of musical
erudition, and have at all times been held in estimation by men of science.

Giovanni Maria Artusi, an ecclesiastic of
Bologna, was the author of a treatise on music,
entitled, "*L' Arte del Contraponto ridotta in Ta-
" vole,*" published at Venice in the year 1586.
This work contains a great variety of excellent
rules, selected with much judgment, from the
works of various modern writers. These are disposed in analytical order, and so well compres-
sed, that, small as the book is, it must have
been one of the most useful treatises that
had at that time been published. In the year
1589, Artusi printed a second part of his work,
in which he has explained the nature and uses of

the dissonances.   This is a curious and valuable supplement to the former.

In 1600, he published a discourse, in dialogue, entitled, " *L'Artusi, ouero delle Imperfettioni* " *delle moderna Musica, Ragionamenti dui,*" containing an interesting and curious account of the state of instrumental music in his time, with rules for the conducting of a musical performance, either vocal or instrumental.   Three years afterwards there appeared a supplement to this work, containing, amongst other things, an inquiry into the principles of some of the modern innovations in music.

In the following year Artusi printed, at Bologna, a small tract, in quarto, entitled, " *Im-* " *pressa del molto R. M. Giaseffo Zarlino da* " *Chioggia,*" which contains a kind of device, exhibiting the diagrams invented by him for the demonstration of consonances, with a commentary on them.

Orazio Tigrini, canon of Arezzo, published at Venice, in 1588, a musical work entitled, " *Com-* " *pendium della Musica,*" which he dedicated to Zarlino.   This compendium is both well digested and well printed.   Tigrini is the first that we have met with, who has censured the impropriety and absurdity of composing music for the church upon the subject of old and vulgar ballad tunes.   The cadences which he has given in three,

four, five, and six parts, and which are good examples of ecclesiastical counterpoint, have been all
used by Morley, without his once acknowledging
the obligation. It appears, from the Compendium
of Tigrini, that extempore descant upon a plain
song was still practised in the churches of Italy;
and instructions are here given for this species of
musical divination.

LODOVICO ZACCONI, an Augustine monk of Pe-
saro, and afterwards a musician in the service of
the Duke of Bavaria, was the author of an excellent work, printed at Venice, first in 1591, and
afterwards in 1596, under the title of " *Pratica*
" *di Musica.*" This is justly esteemed one of
the most valuable treatises on the subject of practical music that is extant; and although it seems
chiefly intended for the use of experienced musicians, it abounds with precepts which are applicable to practice, and suited even to ordinary
capacities.

In the year 1622, he published a second part
of this work, in which he treats of the elements
of music, and the principles of composition. The
rules for the composition of counterpoint, fugue,
and canon, are taken from the writings of Zarlino,
Artusi, and other Italians.

CHAP. III.

GERMAN
MUSICAL COMPOSERS AND WRITERS,

WHO FLOURISHED
During the Sixteenth Century,
1500 TO 1600.

JUSQUIN DE PREZ.—OKENHEIM.—BRUMEL.—DE LA
RUE.— HOBRECHTH. — DE MONTE.— DE KERL.—
ORLANDO DE LASSO. — GOMBERT. — LE COICK.—
CANIS.— MANCHICOURT. — BASTON.—CREQUILON.
CLEMENS NON PAPA.—KRUMBHORN.—REINCKE.
PRINCE MAURICE.—AGRICOLA.—KEPLER.

In Germany and the Low Countries we find that
music had arrived at considerable perfection as
early as the middle of the sixteenth century. In
the composition of church music the Italian masters were certainly superior to the Germans;
but the latter were by much the most skilful in
their knowledge and use of the organ. They
had discovered the power and excellence of this
noble instrument; and, from the duration of its
sounds, how particularly adapted it was to the

performance of music in consonance : that all the graces of modern music, such as fugues, imitative and responsive passages, and various kinds of motion, were no less capable of being expressed on the organ than by a number of voices in concert. To such perfection had the Germans carried their performance on the organ, that, even so early as the year 1480, one of their countrymen, whose name was Bernhard, invented the pedal, and thereby increased the harmony of the instrument, by the addition of a fundamental part.

It is generally understood that *vocal concerts* had their first rise in Flanders about the middle of the sixteenth century. Charles the Fifth, King of Spain and Emperor of Germany, for some time made Brussels the place of residence for himself and his court, and great numbers of eminent musicians were drawn thither from all parts of Europe. These were not only patronized and favoured by the prince, but likewise received the greatest encouragement from the opulence and generosity of the merchants of the place and neighbourhood.

It is true that concerts of merely instrumental music were then scarcely known ; but vocal music, in parts, was not only the entertainment of persons of rank at public solemnities, but began to be so much the common amusement at social meetings and in private families, that every well

educated person was supposed to be capable of
joining in it.

The kind of convivial harmony here alluded to
was a species of composition of three or more
parts for different voices, adapted to the words
of some short poem, and known by the name of
madrigal. It cannot be supposed that these
first essays had much to recommend them to notice besides the correctness of their harmony; and
although they were greatly admired at the time,
they fell far short, in point of excellence, of those
of the succeeding age.

JUSQUIN DE PREZ, or JODOCUS PRATENSIS, was
a native of some place in the Netherlands, and a
pupil of Okenheim. In the early parts of his life
he went to Paris, and was appointed chapel-master
to Lewis the Twelfth, who reigned from 1498 to
1515. When he was first admitted to this office,
the king promised him also a *benefice,* but by
some means or other it was forgotten. Jusquin
experienced some inconveniences, and at length
ventured upon an expedient to bring the circumstance to the king's recollection, without giving
offence. He had been ordered to compose a motet
for the royal chapel ; and he chose that part of
the 119th Psalm which begins, *Memor esto
verbi tui servo tuo,* " O think upon thy ser-
" vant as concerning thy word." This he set in
so supplicating and exquisite a manner that it

was universally admired. The king was delighted with it : he took the hint, and conferred on Jusquin the promised preferment. The grateful musician afterwards composed an anthem from another part of the same Psalm : *Bonitatem fecisti cum servo tuo, Domine,* " O Lord, thou hast dealt " graciously with thy servant."

In consequence of the neglect that had taken place respecting the benefice, Jusquin applied to a nobleman, in high favour at court, to exert his influence with the king. This person encouraged his hopes with ardent protestations of zeal for his welfare, and constantly ended by saying, " I " shall take care of this business, let me alone." " *Laisse faire moi, (laissez moi faire.)* At length, however, Jusquin's patience was exhausted by this vain and fruitless assurance ; and out of revenge he turned it into *solemnization,* and composed an entire mass on these syllables of the hexachord, *La, sol, fa, re, mi.* This mass is among the productions of our author deposited in the British Museum, and is an admirable composition.

The following circumstance likewise took place during Jusquin's residence at the court of France. The king, though extremely fond of music, had so weak and inflexible a voice that he had never been able to sing a tune ; and he defied his chapel-master to compose any piece of music in which it was possible for him to bear a part. The musician made the attempt. He wrote a canon for two voices, to which he added two other parts. The person who sang one of these two parts had nothing more to do than either to sustain a single sound, or alternately to sing the key-note and its fifth. Jusquin gave to his Majesty the choice of the two. He preferred that which consisted only of the long note; and after some time the royal scholar was enabled to continue this, as a drone to the canon, in despite of nature, which had never intended him for a singer.

Jusquin, among musicians, was the giant of his time; and he seems to have arrived at an universal monarchy and dominion over the affections and passions of the musical part of mankind. His compositions appear to have been as well known, and as much practised throughout Europe, at the beginning of the sixteenth century, as Handel's were in England about fifty years ago.

In the music book of Prince Henry, afterwards King Henry the Eighth, preserved in the Pepys Collection at Cambridge, there are several of his compositions; and we are told that Anne of Boleyn, during her residence in France, had collected and practised a great number of them. In a very beautiful manuscript deposited in the British Museum,* consisting of French songs of the fifteenth cen-

---

* Bib. Reg. 20. A. 16.

tury, in three and four parts, there are several
written by Jusquin. But probably the most capital collection of his works, and of those of contemporary contrapuntists, now extant, is a printed
one in the British Museum, containing masses in
four parts, the first that issued from the press
after the invention of printing. They consist of
the first and third set of the mass, which Jusquin composed for the Pope's chapel during the
pontificate of Sextus the Fourth, who reigned from
1471 to 1484 ; of the masses of Pierre de la Rue ;
of a set of masses by Anthony de Feven, or Feum,
Robert de Feven, and Pierzon; and of the
masses of John Mouton, and of other different
composers, *(missæ diversorum auctorum)*, namely, Obrecht, Bassiron, Brumel, Gaspar, and De
la Rue.

Whoever examines the compositions of Jusquin
in score, will find that no notes have had admission by chance, or for the sake of *remplissage*, as
the French term it, but that every thing not only
contributes to the principal design and harmony
of the whole, but each part has a specific character and meaning in itself.

His masses, though more frequently cited and
celebrated by musical writers than those of any
other author, and indeed than any others of his
own works, seem inferior in every respect to his
motets. The latter are not only all composed
upon subjects of his own invention, or upon frag-

ments of the most beautiful and solemn chants of the church, but are in a style considerably more clear and pleasing than those.

With respect to some of Jusquin's contrivances, such as augmentations, diminutions, and inversions of the melody, expressed by the barbarous Latin verb, *cancrizare*, from the retrograde motion of the *crab*, they were certainly pursued to an excess ; but to subdue difficulties has ever been esteemed a merit of a certain kind in all the arts, and consequently treated with respect by artists.

Canons difficult of solution were to musicians a species of problem, and served more to exercise the mind than to please the sense ; and however contemptuously these harmonical contrivances may be treated by the lovers of more airy and simple compositions, the study of them is still of such use to musical students, in their private exercises, that a profound and good contrapuntist has, perhaps, never yet been made by other means.

As Euclid ranks first among ancient geometricians, so Jusquin, for the number, difficulty, and excellence of his musical canons, seems entitled to the first place among those old composers who have been most assiduous and successful in the cultivation of this difficult species of musical calculation.

But although the style of Jusquin, even in his secular compositions, is grave, and chiefly in fugue, imitation, and other contrivances, with little air or melody ; yet this defect is amply supplied to contrapuntists and lovers of choral music by purity of harmony and ingenuity of design. " Indeed," says Dr. Burney, " I have never seen, among all his productions that I have scored, a single movement which is not stamped with some mark of the great master ; and though fugue and canon were so universally cultivated in his time, when there were many men of abilities in this elaborate and complicated kind of writing, yet there is such a manifest superiority in his powers, such a simple majesty in his ideas, and such a dignity of design, as wholly to justify the homage he received from the world."

Notwithstanding the favour in which he stood with the French king, Jusquin experienced, in his latter days, a sorrowful reverse of fortune, and, during the time he was in Italy, he seems to have complained to his friend Serasino Acquillano, the poet, of the splendour in which some fashionable buffoons lived, whilst he was left in want and obscurity. A sonnet which was produced on this occasion is preserved by Zarlino. We shall present it to the reader in an English dress.

> " Ne'er say, O Jusquin, Fate's to thee unjust,
>   " Blest with a genius so divine ;
> " Nor let the dress of vile buffoons disgust,
>   " Who but in borrow'd plumage shine.

" Nor gold nor silver want to be adorn'd,
 " Their price from worth intrinsic springs ;
" While structures formed of meaner wood are scorn'd
 " Till cover'd with more precious things.

" Of these buffoons how soon the favour fades,
 " Who ev'ry hour their trappings change;
" But short neglect true virtue ne'er degrades,
 " She safely through the world may range !

" Buoy'd up like one whom friendly cork surrounds,
 " Though plung'd in Ocean fathoms deep,
" Elastic still, with native force she bounds,
 " And still above the wave will keep."

According to Walther, Jusquin de Prez was
buried in the Church of St. Gudule at Brussels,
where his figure and epitaph are still to be seen.
His death must have happened early in the sixteenth
century, but the exact time of it we have not been
able to discover.

John Ockegem, or Okenheim, as he is called
by some writers, was a native of the Low Countries, and the master of Jusquin de Prez.

Glareanus speaks of a composition by Ockegem
for six voices, which, he asserts, was much admired for its contrivance : he does not, however,
state in what the parts consisted nor how they were
disposed.   It was in the composition of *fugue* that
this writer is said to have chiefly excelled.   A
canon, four in two, by him, beginning, " Sanctus

" Dominus Deus Sabaoth," is inserted in Smith's
" Musica Antiqua:"

ANTHONY BRUMEL was contemporary with Jusquin de Prez, and also a pupil of Okenheim. He
does not appear to have had much invention;
his harmony, however, is in general pure; and
his melody and notation are more clear and simple
than was common at the period when he flourished.
Glareanus seems to characterise him justly, when
he says, that he was a very able contrapuntist, but
that he possessed more learning than genius.—
" There is," says Dr. Burney, " more plain and
simple counterpoint in a mass of his, which I
have scored, and less fugue, canon, or imitation, than I have ever seen in a composition of
the same length and period."

PIERRE DE LA RUE.—One of the most voluminous composers of the sixteenth century was Pierre
de la Rue, or, as he is otherwise called, *Petrus Pla-
tensis*. He resided chiefly in Germany, and was
in great favour with Prince Albert and the Princess Isabella of the Low Countries. He published
at Antwerp, " *El Parnasso Espagnol de Madri-*
" *gales y Villancios, à quatro, cinco, y seis*
" *Voces;*" besides several *masses* and *motets* to
Latin words.

Many of his compositions are still extant in the
Collection of Masses and Motets preserved in the

British Museum, some of which were published early in the sixteenth century, immediately after the invention of musical types. He was a very learned and excellent contrapuntist.

JAMES HOBRECHTH or OBRETH, a Fleming, the preceptor in music to Erasmus, has the credit of having been an excellent musician; he is said to have had so great a celerity of invention that he composed in one night a whole *mass*, to the admiration and astonishment of all who knew him. Glareanus asserts that the compositions of Hobrechth contain much grandeur and majesty.

PHILIP DE MONTE, a native of Mons, in Hainault, born in the year 1521, was master of the chapel to the Emperor Maximilian the Second : he was also a canon and treasurer of the Cathedral Church of Cambray.

Besides several *masses* this writer composed *Four Books of Madrigals.*

JACOB DE KERL, canon of the Cathedral Church of Cambray, was born at Ipres, in Flanders.

His compositions, which are chiefly for the church, were published in different parts of Europe from 1562 to 1573. His *masses* were printed at Venice in 1562. Their style is dry and uninteresting ; the harmony, however, is good, and his answers to the fugues are warrantable.

ORLANDO DE LASSO, or, as he is sometimes called, *Orlandus Lassus,* was a native of the city of Mons. He was born in the year 1520, and was a contemporary and an intimate friend of De Monte. For the unrivalled sweetness of his voice while a child, and afterwards, in his riper years, for the excellence of his compositions, he is said to have been the admiration of all Germany. During his childhood he was, for some time, retained in Sicily and Italy by Ferdinand Gonzaga; and when grown up he resided and gave instructions in music two years at Rome. After this he travelled through other parts of Italy and into France, but at length returned to his native country, and lived many years at Antwerp; from whence he was called away by an invitation from Albert Duke of Bavaria, in whose court he married and settled. He was invited to reside in France by Charles the Ninth; but that king dying whilst De Lasso was on his journey, he returned into Bavaria, and died there in the year 1595, at the age of seventy-five.

He left two sons, who were also musicians, the one named FERDINAND, chapel-master to Maximilian Duke of Bavaria; the other RUDULPH, organist to the same prince. They published, in the year 1604, a collection of their father's compositions.

De Lasso was the first great improver of figurate music; for, instead of adhering to the stiff and formal rule of counterpoint, from which some of his predecessors seemed afraid to deviate, he gave way to the introduction of elegant points and finely wrought responsive passages. He was the author of upwards of seventy different works. In the " Musica Antiqua" Mr. Smith has introduced one of his madrigals, beginning " Susanna, " un jour."

NICHOLAS GOMBERT, a native either of France or of the Netherlands, was chapel-master to the Emperor Charles the Fifth. He was a pupil of Jusquin, and was well skilled in the science of harmony.

He furnished a very considerable portion of almost all the *songs* and *motets* that were printed in Antwerp and Louvain during the middle of the sixteenth century, besides a set of *masses* published at Venice in the year 1541, and two sets of *motets* in 1550 and 1564, all in four parts.

GIAN LE COICK, or LE COQ, was the author of several *songs* published in the collections of his time, particularly one in five parts, printed at Antwerp in 1545, in the sixth book of " *Chan-* " *sons à 5 et à 6 Parties.*" In this song the two upper parts are in canon, in which the second part inverts the melody of the first, while the other three move in free fugue. This kind of composition is curious; but it is valuable only from the difficulty of its construction.

CORNELIUS CANIS, whose name frequently occurs in the Antwerp and Louvain collections of songs, was the author of several *canons*. He died some time before the year 1556.

PIERRE MANCHICOURT, a native of Bethune, and director of the music in the Cathedral Church of Dornick, was a composer of *songs* and *motets*. From his compositions that are yet extant, he seems to have been not only a dry, but a clumsy contrapuntist.

JOSQUIN BASTON, who was living in 1556, wrote, says Dr. Burney, " in a clear and clean manner." One of his *songs* was printed in the Louvain Collection of 1559, in the music of which there are more facility, rhythm, and melody, than were common in his time: the key too is well defined. But all the compositions of this period, in the fifth or sixth ecclesiastical mode, or, as we should write, in F or G major, are the more pleasing to modern ears, on account of the key being ascertained.

THOMAS CREQUILON, a Fleming, was chapelmaster to the Emperor Charles the Fifth about the year 1536. He composed *hymns* for many voices, and some *French songs* in four, five, and six parts.

CLEMENS, otherwise called JACOB CLEMENS NON PAPA, was by birth a Fleming, and one of the musicians in the service of the Emperor Charles the Fifth. He was the author of several *masses* and other sacred offices.* Dr. Burney says, he has found no better music of the kind than that of this composer. His style is clear, his harmony pure, and every subject of fugue or imitation simple and natural.

In Smith's "Musica Antiqua" there is a beautiful chanson of Clemens, for four voices, adapted to the English words, "Ye nightingales "in green woods chanting," by the late T. Warren Horne, Esq.

CASPAR KRUMBHORN was a native of Lignitz, in Silesia, and born in the year 1542. In the third year of his age he lost his sight by the small-pox, and became totally blind. He was placed by his brother, who was many years older than himself, under the care of a famous musician of the name of Knobeln, by whom he was taught first to play on the flute, then on the vio-

---

*The Emperor was remarkably fond of music; and Roger Ascham has related, that one day being at his table, "his "chapel sang wonderful cunningly all the dinner while."

lin, and lastly on the harpsichord. On each of these instruments he became so excellent, that he excited the admiration of all who heard him. His fame procured him from Augustus the Elector of Saxony an invitation to Dresden. This prince was greatly astonished that a young man, deprived of the faculty of sight, should not only be an excellent performer on various instruments, but likewise be deeply skilled in the art of practical composition. He endeavoured, in vain, to retain Krumbhorn in his service; for, preferring his own country to all others, he returned to Lignitz, and was appointed organist of the Church of St. Peter and St. Paul there. This station he occupied for fifty-six years, during which time he had frequently the direction of the musical college. He died in 1621, and was interred in the church which he so long had served.

Although Krumbhorn is said to have been the author of many musical compositions, it does not appear that any of them were ever printed.

REINCKE was a celebrated German composer of this period, who lived to within a few months of the age of a hundred years. In his younger days, having been elected successor to the famous Scheidemann, organist of St. Catharine's Church in Hamburgh, it is related that a musician of Amsterdam declared that he must be so presumptuous a man to take Scheidemann's place, that he should

like to see him.   This observation having been repeated to Reincke, he sent him one of his compositions, thus superscribed :   " This is the portrait of the audacious youth whom you wished to
see."   The Dutchman found in the composition
so much genius and learning, that he immediately
went to Hamburgh for the purpose of hearing
him play on the organ.   After this he said he
could have kissed his feet, in testimony of the ve-
neration with which his talents had impressed him.

MAURICE, *Landgrave of Hesse-Cassel,* is said
to have composed eight or ten sets of *motets,*
and other pieces of solemn music, for the use of
his own chapel, of which, on the great festivals,
he frequently played the organ.   He completed
and published a work begun by Valentine Guc-
kius, entitled, " *Opera metrici sacri Sanctorum,*
" *Dominicalium et Ferarium.*"

GERMAN MUSICAL WRITERS,

Who flourished during the Sixteenth Century.

MARTINUS AGRICOLA, a chorister in the Cathedral Church of Magdeburgh, was the author of
several musical tracts.   The two first were published in the years 1528 and 1529, and were entitled " *Teutsche Music,*" and "*Musica instru-*

" *mentalis.*" The latter was republished in 1545
with considerable alterations; for the author acknowledges that the first edition was so difficult
to be understood, that few persons were able to
read it to any advantage. In this second edition,
after explaining the principles of music, he enters
largely into a description of the musical instruments in use at that time. Both the above-mentioned tracts are written in German verse.

The most celebrated work of Agricola is entitled, " *Melodiæ scholasticæ sub Horarum inter-*
" *vallis decantandæ,*" and was printed at Magdeburgh in the year 1612. There are also extant
of his writing, *A Tract on Figurate Music;*
another on *the Rudiments of Music;* another
" *De Proportionalibus;*" and a treatise entitled,
" *Scholia in Musicam planam Weneslai Philo-*
" *matis de nova Domo, ex variis Musicorum*
" *Scriptis collecta.*"

Agricola died on the 10th of June, 1556; and
in 1561, the heirs of George Rhaw, the printer
of Wittenberg, published his " *Duo Libri Mu-*
" *sices, continentes Compendium Artis et illus-*
" *tria Exempla.*"

The works of this writer seem principally intended for the instruction of beginners in the study
of music. There is something whimsical in the
thought of writing a sientific treatise in verse, yet
it is probable the author's views were, by that
means, the more forcibly to impress his instruc-

tions on the memory of those who were to profit by them.

JOHN KEPLER, a great astronomer and mathematician, was born at Wiel, in the Duchy of Wirtemburg, in the year 1751. His father, the desendant from an ancient family, had been an officer in the German army ; but, after a series of misfortunes, was reduced to the necessity of keeping an inn for the support of himself and his children. His needy circumstances would not permit him to afford them any other than a common school education ; but John, who had an early propensity to learning, found means, at his father's death, in 1590, to obtain admittance as a student into the University of Tubingen. Here, after having acquired a competent knowledge of physics, he began to study mathematics ; and, in this branch of science, he made so rapid a progress that he was soon afterwards invited to teach mathematics at Gratz, in Styria. In 1598, he was banished from Gratz, on account of his religious tenets, but was soon recalled. The troubles, however, that were fast involving that place, induced him to think of a residence elsewhere. Tycho Brahe solicited him to settle at Prague ; and, in 1600, he removed thither. On the decease of that celebrated astronomer, in the following year, Kepler received a command from the Emperor Rudolphus to finish the astronomical tables which Brahe had begun, and which have since been known by the name of the Rudolphine Tables.   He applied himself diligently to this undertaking ; but such difficulties arose, partly from the nature of the work, and partly from the neglect of the treasurers who were entrusted with the fund appropriated to the execution of it, that he was not able to complete the whole until the year 1672.   In 1613, he went to the Assembly at Ratisbon to assist in the reformation of the calendar, but returned to Lintz, where he had been stationed by the Emperor, and where he continued until the year 1626.   In November in that year he proceeded to Ulm, in order to publish his Tables ; and in the subsequent year he settled at Sagan, in Silesia, where he published the second part of his Ephemerides.   He went, in 1630, to Ratisbon, to solicit the payment of the arrears of his pension ; but being seized with a fever, he died, at that place, in the fifty-ninth year of his age.

We shall pass unnoticed all Kepler's astronomical and mathematical works, and speak only of that entitled " Harmonices Mundi."   The third book of this work treats of the subject of musical harmony ; several of the first chapters are confined entirely to discussions relative to the music of the ancients.   In the seventh chapter he treats of the proportions throughout all the eight usual sounds of the diapason.   He also speaks of the modern method of notation by lines and letters of the alphabet; and gives his opinion respecting the origin of the clefs. In the latter he has shown so much ingenuity, that we shall insert, as a specimen of the work, his conjectures relative to the origin of the present mode of marking the tenor or C clef: they are certainly curious.

He begins by asserting that the letter C, at the head of the musical stave, is thus marked, ⊟.

" This, I suppose," he continues, " arose from the distortion of the ancient letter C; for, as the writers used broad-pointed pens, most of the notes were made square, for dispatch in writing; nor could a round C be described with these pens: so that they were constrained to make it with three little lines, the one slender and the other two thick, in the room of the two horns, the pen being drawn broadways, thus ⊑. The fine little line, on account of their expeditious writing, was made longer, and was carried above and below, thus ⊨; but in order to terminate the horns, they drew little lines parallel to the first, thus ⊨; and at length these two lines were made one, and the whole character became of this form, ⊟; but by the gaping of the quill it was frequently, and at length generally, made hollow or open, thus ⊟."

Kepler endeavours also to account for the origin, and explains the use of the flat and sharp signatures. In the tenth chapter he compares the hexachords of the moderns with the tetrachords of the ancients, and clearly demonstrates the superior excellence of the hexachord system. He concludes his book with a fanciful analogy between the science of harmony and the different branches of civil government.

The singularities that are discoverable in the writings of Kepler, drew upon him the censures of many who were engaged in a similar course of study with himself. Martinus Schookius, who allows that he was an able astronomer and mathematician, says, that when he affects to reason upon physical principles no person can talk more absurdly. He expresses his concern that a man, in other respects so excellent, should have entertained such preposterous notions as he; for (he proceeds) " what could an old woman in a fever dream more ridiculous, than that the earth is a vast animal, which breathes out the winds through the holes of the mountains, as it were through a mouth and nostrils ?" and yet he has written expressly thus in his " *Harmonices Mundi*," and attempts also seriously to prove that the earth has a sympathy with the heavens, and by a natural instinct perceives the position of the stars.

The absurdities of Kepler were such as frequently to have exposed him to the ridicule of mathematicians much less learned than himself. Mr. Maclaurin has remarked that his whole life

seems to have been occupied in the pursuit of
fancied analogies; but he adds that it was to
this dispostion we owe discoveries of such importance, as are greatly more than sufficient to excuse
his conceits.

It may, however, with truth be observed, that
if Kepler had made no greater discoveries in mathematics than he did in music, it is probable that
his conceits might have remained, but his discoveries would all long since have been forgotten.

CHAP. IV.

ENGLISH
MUSICAL COMPOSERS AND WRITERS,

WHO FLOURISHED

From about the Year
1600 to 1650.

COPERARIO. — BEVIN. — BATESON. — TOMKINS. — BENNET. — JOHN FARMER. — ALLISON. — COSYN. — AMNER. — HUME. — BREWER. — CAMPION. — EST. — FORD. — HOOPER. — JONES. — LEIGHTON. — MAYNARD. — PIERSON. — DR. STONARD. — RAVENSCROFT. — DR. HEYTHER. — ORLANDO GIBBONS. — EDWARD GIBBONS. — ELLIS GIBBONS. — GILES. — BARNARD. — NICHOLSON. — DEERING. — HINGSTON. — HILTON. — WILLIAM AND HENRY LAWES. — DR. WILSON. — DR. ROGERS. — JENKINS. — BATTEN. — COLEMAN. — CRANFORD. — LOW. — PORTER. — WARWICK. DR. FLUD. — BUTLER. — CHILMEAD.

TOWARDS the beginning of the seventeenth century, the principles of harmony had become generally known, and the art of composition had arrived at a great degree of perfection. Something like what we now denominate *air*, is also discoverable in many of the melodies composed at this period.

The subsequent improvements consisted in an amendment of style and expression, and in the power which the composers began to attain of exciting the passions by an artful combination and succession of corresponding sounds, rendering, by this means, a more intimate connection between music and poetry than had before been known.

In most of the other countries of Europe the science still continued to receive encouragement and to flourish. The professors were supported by the patronage and countenance of the nobles and great men, and consequently exerted all their efforts and abilities in the study of it. The case was different in England. During the whole reign of James the First, the subject was so little regarded by any of those in whose power alone were the means of encouragement, that the professors complained, and not without reason, that the science was destitute of patronage, and was fast declining from that state which it had, not long before, attained.

At this period the recreations of the court were indeed of a dramatic kind, consisting of masques and interludes ; but, in the composition of these, the gentlemen of the Chapel were chiefly employed, and the gentlemen and children of the Chapel were oftentimes even the performers.

The composers of choral music found themselves so much neglected, that most of those who had not permanent situations in cathedrals or collegiate churches were compelled to seek a subsistence in other countries.

In the distracted reign of Charles the First, things went on still worse. The puritans having seized the reins of government, repealed, in 1644, the statutes of Edward the Sixth and Elizabeth for uniformity in the common prayer; and established a new form of worship, in which the singing of psalms was the only music allowed. They required that in these the whole congregation should join, and ordained, " That every one who could read was to have a psalm book, and others, not disabled by age or otherwise, were to be exhorted to learn to read. But for the present, where many of the congregation could not read, it was ordered that the minister, or some other fit person appointed by him and the other ruling officers, *do read the psalm line by line before the singing thereof.*"* It was even the opinion of these men, who, from the affected meekness and inoffensiveness of their dispositions, had assumed the name of *Puritans,* that the organs of all churches should be pulled down, and the choral music-books torn and destroyed: the churches and libraries were consequently ransacked for the service-books, and all, whether Latin or English, popish or

---

* Hence the origin of this barbarous custom in some of the parochial churches and in nearly all the conventicles of this kingdom.

protestant, were deemed equally superstitious and ungodly; and, as such, were committed to the flames.

Theatrical entertainments likewise of every description were looked upon by the puritans with abhorrence. Even so early as the year 1579, a little tract had been published by Stephen Gosson, the rector of St. Botolph's, entitled, " The School of " Abuse, containing a plesaunt Inuective against " Poets, Pipers, Plaiers, Jesters, and such like Cater- " pillars of a Common-wealth; setting up the " Flagge of Defiance to their mischievous Ex- " ercise, and overthrowing their Bulwarkes, by " profane Writers, natural Reason, and common " Experience." The same subject was afterwards furiously taken up by that hot-brained zealot, William Prynne, in his " Histrio-Mastyx, the " Player's Scourge, or Actor's Tragedie." The prosecution of Prynne for publishing this book, and the consequences of it, are known to every one conversant with English history. Its effect, however, on the minds of the people was such as to put a total stop to dramatic entertainments of every kind.

The first effort to reinstate these was made by Sir William Davenant, on the 23d of May, 1656, at Rutland House, in Charter-house Square, by an entertainment consisting of orations in prose, intermixed with vocal and instrumental music, composed by Coleman, Lawes, and Hudson. This was received with so much applause that others of

a similar kind were afterwards given, and met
with equal encouragement.

In the University of Oxford, the choral service,
in spite of all the efforts of the puritans, continued
still to be performed ; and occasional concerts were
held of vocal and instrumental music. But these
only lasted till the surrender of the garrison in
1656, when the king, who had taken shelter there,
was under the necessity of seeking refuge in some
other place. The spirit, however, that had been
excited in the university, contributed afterwards to
an association amongst its members, which was the
cause of a regular weekly concert being established.
At the restoration these concerts fell off, in some
degree, for a while, as almost all the professional
men who had resorted to Oxford during the usurpation were then called away to the cathedrals
and the collegiate choirs.

Of the eminent musical professors who flourished
in England betwixt the years 1600 and 1650, the
following memoirs are extant.

JOHN COPERARIO, a celebrated performer on the
viol da gamba, and a composer for that instrument
and the lute, was one of the musical preceptors to
the children of King James the First.

Some of his vocal compositions are to be found
in Sir William Leighton's Collection ; and there

are several others extant in manuscript. In conjunction with Laniere and another person, he composed the songs in a masque written by Dr. Campion, on the marriage of the Earl of Somerset with Lady Frances Howard (the divorced Countess of Essex), which was presented in the banqueting house at Whitehall, on St. Stephen's night, 1614. One of the songs in this masque, beginning with the words, "Come ashore," is inserted in Smith's "Musica Antiqua," as a specimen of the music of this composer.

Coperario was the author also of, "*Funeral* "*Tears for the Death of the Right Honourable* "*the Earle of Devonshire, figured in seaven* "*Songes, whereof sixe are soe set forthe that the* "*Wordes may be expressed by a Treble Voyce* "*alone to the Lute and Base Viol, or else that* "*the Meane Part may be added, if any shall* "*affect more Fulnesse of Parts. The seaventh is* "*made in Forme of a Dialogue, and cannot be* "*sung without two Voyces,*" printed in 1606; and "*Songs of Mourning, bewailing the un-* "*timely Death of Prince Henry,*" printed in 1613.

It has been supposed by some persons that Coperario was by birth an Italian. This, however, is an error, arising from the circumstance of his having Italianized his plain and genuine English name of John Cooper into *Giovanni Coperario.*

Elway Bevin, a man eminently skilled in the knowledge of practical composition, flourished towards the end of the reign of Queen Elizabeth. He was of Welsh extraction, and had been educated under Tallis. In 1589, four years after the death of his master, he was made a gentleman-extraordinary of the Chapel Royal. He was also organist of the Cathedral Church of Bristol; but he lost both these places in the year 1637, on its being discovered that he adhered to the Romish communion. Several of the *services* printed in Barnard's Collection were composed by him.

Before Bevin's time, the rules for the composition of canon were known to few, and these only such as were deeply skilled in the most abtruse parts of musical practice. This writer, however, with a view to the improvement of students, communicated to the world the result of many years study and experience, in a treatise that has been highly commended by all who have had occasion to speak of it. It was published in a thin quarto volume of fifty-two pages, in the year 1631, and entitled, " *A briefe and short Introduction to the Art of* " *Musicke, to teach how to make Discant of all* " *Proportions that are in use: very necessary* " *for all such as are desirous to attaine to Know-* " *ledge in the Art; and may, by Practice, if they* " *can sing, soon be able to compose three, foure,* " *and five Parts; and also to compose all Sorts of*

" *Canons that are usuall, by these Directions,*
" *of two or three Parts in one, upon a plain*
" *Song.*" The rules, as here laid down, are in
general very brief. For the composition of canon
there are a great variety of examples, of almost
all the possible forms in which it is capable of
being constructed, even to the number of sixty
parts.

Thomas Bateson, a good vocal composer, was,
about the year 1600, elected organist of the Cathedral Church of Chester.

He published a set of *English Madrigals for
three, four, five, and six Voices;* and, about 1618,
was appointed organist and master of the children
in Trinity Church, Dublin. He is supposed to
have obtained the degree of Bachelor of Music in
the university of that city.

Thomas Tomkins, the son of one of the chanters
in the choir of the Cathedral Church of Gloucester, received his musical education under Bird.
His abilities were such as very early in life to obtain for him the place of gentleman of the Chapel
Royal, and afterwards that of organist.

Some years subsequent to the latter promotion,
he became organist of the Cathedral of Worcester,
and in this city composed *Songs of three, four,
five, and six Parts,* which appear to have been
published about the year 1623. He was also the

author of a work, in ten books or parts, consisting of *anthems,* hymns, and other pieces adapted to the church service, entitled, "*Musica Deo sacra et* "*Ecclesiæ Anglicanæ; or, Music dedicated to* "*the Honour and Service of God, and to the Use* "*of Cathedrals and other Churches of England,* "*especially the Chapel Royal of King Charles* "*the First.*" The words of some others of his compositions are to be seen in Clifford's Collection. There is in the library of Magdalen College, Oxford, a manuscript of Tomkins, consisting of vocal church music in four and five parts. Some of the *madrigals* also in the "Triumphs of Oriana" are of his composition.

Dr. Burney has given us the following character of his works. "By the compositions I have scored, or examined in score, of Tomkins, he seems to me to have had more force and facility than Morley. In his songs there is much melody and accent, as well as pure harmony and ingenious contrivance."

The times of his birth and death are both unknown; and the principal data from which can be ascertained the period when he flourished are, that he was a pupil of Bird; that he was admitted to the degree of Bachelor of Music in the University of Oxford in 1607; and that, according to the assertion of Wood, he was living after the breaking out of the rebellion.*

* Fasti Oxon. vol. I. col. 176.

Tomkins had several brothers, all of whom were educated to the profession of music. Giles was organist of the Cathedral Church of Salisbury; John was organist of St. Paul's, and a gentleman of the Chapel; and Nicholas (one of the gentlemen of the privy-chamber to King Charles the First) was a person well acquainted with the practice of music.

John Bennet was a composer principally of *madrigals.* In 1599, he printed " *Madrigals to* " *four Voyces, being his first Works.*" There is a madrigal by him in the "Triumphs of Oriana," and some *songs* in a work published by Ravenscroft, hereafter mentioned. In the latter work he is said to be a gentleman " admirable for all kind of composures, either in art or ayre, simple or mixt."

Beyond this short eulogium we meet with no particulars respecting Bennet. It does not appear that he was a graduate of either of the universities.

His madrigals are finely studied, and abound with all the graces and elegance of vocal harmony; and of his collection of madrigals it may be said, in general terms, that it is an honour to our country, and in no respect inferior to any collection of the kind published by Italian or other foreign musicians.

JOHN FARMER published, in 1599, " *The first*
" *Sett of English Madrigals to four Voices.*"
In his preface he professes to have " fully linked
his music to *number,* as each gives to the other
its true effect, which is to move delight : a virtue
(he adds) so singular in the Italians, as under that
ensign only they hazard their honour." This assertion, however, is so far from being true, that
there appears, says Dr. Burney, " more false accent
in Farmer's songs than in those of any of his
contemporaries."

This person was likewise the author of a little
book entitled, " *Divers and sundrie Waies of two*
" *Parts in one, to the Number of Fourtie, upon*
" *one playn Song; sometimes placing the Ground*
" *above, and two Parts benethe, and otherwise*
" *the Ground benethe, and two Parts above; or*
" *againe, otherwise, the Ground sometimes in the*
" *Middest betweene both.   Likewise other Con-*
" *ceites, which are plainlie set downe for the*
" *Profite of those which would attain unto*
" *Knowledge.*"   Printed in London in the year
1591.

RICHARD ALLISON, a teacher of music in London in the reign of Queen Elizabeth, lived at a
house in Duke's Place, near Aldgate.   He was one
of the ten persons who composed parts to the
common psalm tunes printed by Thomas Est in
1594.   He also published a collection of psalms,

with this title, *"The Psalmes of David in Meter,"* &c. in 1599.

BENJAMIN COSYN, a celebrated composer of *lessons for the harpsichord,* and probably an excellent performer on that instrument, flourished about this time. There are many of his lessons extant, somewhat in the same style with those of Dr. Bull, and in no respect inferior to them.

JOHN AMNER, Bachelor of Music of the University of Oxford, in 1613, was organist of the Cathedral Church of Ely, and master of the choristers there. Of his composition there are extant, *" A Sacred Collection of Hymns, of three, four, " five, and six Parts, for Viols and Voices,* printed in 1615; and some anthems, the words of which are to be found in Clifford's Collection.

TOBIAS HUME, a soldier by profession, but an excellent performer on the viol da gamba, published in 1607, and dedicated to Anne, the queen of James the First, a collection of songs, entitled, *" Captain Hume's poeticall Musicke, principally " made for two Basse Violls, yet so construed " that it may be plaied eight several Waies, upon " sundrie Instruments, with much Facilitie."*

THOMAS BREWER, who was educated at Christ's Hospital, London, and brought up to the practice of the viol, composed several excellent *fantazias* for that instrument, and was the author of many of the rounds and catches inserted in Hilton's Collection. He was also the composer of a celebrated song, printed in two parts in the earlier editions of Playford's Introduction, and in his Musical Companion in three parts, to the words, " Turn, Amaryllis, to thy swain."

THOMAS CAMPION, a physician by profession, and, according to the assertion of Anthony Wood, an " admired poet and musician," was the composer of *Two Books of Airs, in two three, and four Parts.* He was the author of, " *A new Way* " *of making foure Parts in Counterpoint, by a* " *most familiar and infallible Rule,*" printed in octavo without a date. This tract, but under the title of the " *Art of Descant, or composing Mu-* " *sick in Parts, with Annotations thereon, by Mr.* " *Christopher Simpson,*" is published, by way of appendix, to the earlier edition of Playford's Introduction.

MICHAEL EST, Bachelor of Music, and master of the choristers of the Cathedral Church of Litchfield, was the author of several collections of *madrigals* and other vocal compositions.

His publications are much more numerous than those of any other composer of his time. One of these is entitled, " *The Sixt Set of Bookes,*

" wherein are *Anthemes for Verses, and Chorus*
" *of five and six Parts ; apt for Violls and*
" *Voices.*"   It is probable that this person was
the son of that Thomas Est who first published the
psalms in parts, and other works, assuming in
some of them the name of Snodham.   One of
Michael Est's three-part songs, " How merrily we
" live," has lately been revived, and honoured
with the public favour;   and there are several
others among his works which are equally deserving of notice.

THOMAS FORD, one of the musicians in the suite
of Prince Henry, the son of King James the First,
was the author of some canons and rounds printed
in Hilton's Collection, and also of a work entitled,
" *Musicke of sundre Kinds set forth in two*
" *Books, the first whereof are Aires for four*
" *Voices to the Lute, Orpherion, or Basse Viol;*
" *with a Dialogue for two Voices and two Basse*
" *Violls, in Parts, tunde the lute-way.   The*
" *second are Pavens, Galiards, Almaines, Toies,*
" *Jiggs, Thumpes,* and such like for two Basse*
" *Viols the liera-way, so made as the greatest*
" *Number may serve to play alone, very easy to*

---

* The word *dump*, besides sorrow and absence of mind
(the meanings affixed to it by Dr. Johnson), signifies a *melancholy tune;* and it was, according to Mr. Stevens, in a note on
a passage in Romeo and Juliet, an old Italian dance.   It re-

" *be performed.*" This work was published in folio, in the year 1607.

EDMUND HOOPER, organist of Westminster Abbey, and a gentleman of the Chapel Royal, (where he also acted as organist) was one of the composers of the *Psalms,* in four parts, published in 1594, and of some of the *anthems* in Barnard's Collection. He died in the month of July, 1621.

ROBERT JONES seems to have been a voluminous composer. Two of the works published by him are, " *A Musical Dreame, or the Fourth Book of* " *Ayres ; the first Part for the Lute, two Voices,* " *and the Viol da Gamba; the second Part is for* " *the Lute, the Viol, and four Voices to sing ;* " *the third Part is for one Voice alone to the* " *Lute, the Basse Viol, or to both if you please,* " *whereof two are Italian Ayres,*" printed in 1609; and " *The Muses' Gardin for Delights,* " *or the Fifth Booke of Ayres onely for the* " *Lute, the Bass Violl, and the Voice.*"

Two songs by this composer, " My love bound " me with a kiss," and " Farewell, dear love," are to be found in Smith's " Musica Antiqua."

---

mains a question whether the present word *thumpe* is not the same as this. Sir John Hawkins thinks it may have arisen from some particular air for the lute, in which the performer, when playing it, was directed in certain parts to *thump* one of the open strings as a kind of accompaniment.

Sir William Leighton, Knight, one of the honourable band of gentlemen-pensioners, published in 1614, in conjunction with some other persons, a work entitled, " *The Teares or Lamen-* " *tations of a sorrowful Soul, composed with* " *musical Ayres and Songs, both for Voices and* " *divers Instruments.*"

John Maynard, a performer on and composer for the lute, was the author of, " *The Twelve* " *Wonders of the World, set and composed for* " *the Violl de Gamba, the Lute, and the Voyce,* " *to sing the Verse, all three jointly, and none* " *several : also Lessons for the Lute and Basse* " *Violl to play alone : with some Lessons to play* " *lyra-wayes alone, or if you will, to fill up the* " *Parts with another Violl set lute-way,*" published in folio in the year 1611. These Twelve Wonders are so many songs exhibiting the characters of a courtier, divine, soldier, lawyer, physician, merchant, country gentleman, bachelor, married man, wife, widow, and maid.

Martin Pierson, or Pearson, was master of the choristers at St. Paul's. He took his degree of Bachelor of Music in the year 1613, and about sixteen years afterwards published a work with this singular title, " *Mottects, or grave Cham-* " *ber Musique, containing Songs of five Parts of* " *seuerall Sorts, some ful, and some Verse and*

" *Chorus, but all fit for Voyces and Vials, with*
" *an Organ Part ; which, for want of Organs,*
" *may be performed on Virginals, Base Lute,*
" *Bandora, or Irish Harpe.   Also a Mourning*
" *Song of sixe Parts for the Death of the late*
" *Right Honorable Sir Fulke Grevil, Knight."*
He died about the latter end of the year 1650, and
was buried in St. Faith's Church, London.

WILLIAM STONARD, organist of Christ Church,
Oxford, and created Doctor of Music in 1608, composed several *anthems,* the words of which are inserted in Clifford's Collection.   He was also the
composer of some pieces communicated by Walter
Porter to Dr. Wilson, the professor of music at
Oxford, which were directed to be preserved for
ever among the archives of the music-school.

THOMAS RAVENSCROFT was educated under Edward Pearce in the choir of the Cathedral Church
of St. Paul.   He was afterwards admitted to the
degree of Bachelor of Music at Oxford, and became well skilled both in the theory and practice of
this art.

In the year 1611, he printed a collection of songs
entitled, " *Melismata ; Musical Phansies, fitting*
" *the Court, Citie, and Country Humours, to three,*
" *four, and five Voices ;"* and, in 1614, " *A*
" *brief Discourse of the true (but neglected) Use*
" *of characterizing the Degrees by their Perfec-*

" *fection, Imperfection, and Diminution in mea-*
" *surable Musicke, against the common Practice*
" *and Custom of these Times.*" The intention of
this work was to revive the use of those musical
proportions which, on account of their intricacy,
had long been discontinued. In justification of
his attempt, he cites the authority of Franchinus,
Glareanus, and Morley. At the conclusion are
inserted several examples to illustrate the principles he has laid down. These are expressed in
the harmony of four voices on the " Pleasure of
" five usual recreations, 1. Hunting ; 2. Hawk-
" ing ; 3. Dancing ; 4. Drinking ; 5. Enamour-
" ing."

The work however by which the name of Ravenscroft is now best known to the world, is a collection of psalm tunes published in the years 1621 and
1623, in small octavo, and entitled, " *The whole*
" *Book of Psalms, with the Hymnes Evangelicall*
" *and Songs Spirituall, composed into four Parts by*
" *sundry Authors, to such severall Tunes as have*
" *beene and are usually sung in England, Scot-*
" *land, Wales, Germany, France, and the Ne-*
" *therlands.*" This work, which is one of the most
complete of the kind that ever appeared, contains
a melody to every one of the hundred and fifty
psalms. The names of the composers of the bass,
tenor, and counter-tenor parts are, Tallis, Dowland,
Morley, Farnaby, Thomas Tomkins, John Tomkins, Pierson, Parsons, Hooper, Kirbye, Blancks,

Allison, Farmer, Cavendish, Bennet, Palmer, Milton, Stubbs, Cranford, Harrison, and Ravenscroft. The harmonies were for the most part new, and several of the melodies are not to be found in any collection of earlier date.

In this book we have the origin of distinguishing our church tunes by the name of some town or city, such as Canterbury, York, Rochester, and many others. It was republished in the year 1633, and, since that time, it has passed through a great many editions. At the present day a genuine copy is considered a valuable acquisition.

About the conclusion of the reign of King James the First, music received a new and very suitable acquisition in the foundation of a music lecture in the University of Oxford by

WILLIAM HEYTHER, Mus. Doc.—The occasion of this was as follows:—William Camden, the justly celebrated antiquary, having, a few years previously to his decease, determined to found a history lecture in the above university, his friend Mr. Heyther was commissioned to wait on the vice-chancellor with the deed of endowment. This gentleman, having been very assiduous in the study of music, expressed a desire to be honoured with a musical degree; and accordingly that of Doctor was conferred upon him in the month of May, 1622, at the same time with his friend Orlando Gibbons. On this occasion it is supposed that he examined into the nature of musical instruction here, and found that although there was a professorship of music founded by King Alfred, yet the stipend was insufficient to induce any skilful man to become a candidate for the office; and the reading of an old lecture, over and over again, had long been considered a matter of form. He therefore proposed, in a convocation holden on the 5th of May, 1626, to found a new and more useful lecture. Having the permission of the university, he gave to them, by deed dated the 20th of February, 1627-8, an annual rent-charge of sixteen pounds, six shillings, and eight pence. Of this, thirteen pounds, six shillings, and eight pence, were to constitute the wages of the music-master, and the remaining three pounds were to be given to the reader of a lecture on the theory of music once every term, and of an English lecture on music at the time of keeping the acts. Dr. Heyther's endowment was increased by the addition of the ancient stipend, and was afterwards further augmented by Nathaniel Lord Crew, Bishop of Durham.

Dr. Heyther, for some time previously to the taking of his degree, was a member of the choir of Westminster, and a gentleman of the Chapel Royal. Camden and he were on so intimate a footing as to reside together in the same house: he was appointed executor in Camden's will, and upon his death came in for a considerable life-estate in his property.

Dr. Heyther's knowledge of music does not appear to have been very extensive. Wood informs us that the musical exercise performed as the act for his degree was composed by Orlando Gibbons.

He died in the month of July, 1627, and was interred in the broad or south aisle adjoining to the choir of Westminster Abbey.

ORLANDO GIBBONS, one of the most celebrated English musicians of his time, was a native of the town of Cambridge, and born in the year 1583. At the age of twenty-one he was appointed organist of the Chapel Royal, and in 1622, along with Dr. Heyther, as before stated, obtained the degree of Doctor of Music in the University of Oxford. Three years after this, being ordered to go to Canterbury for the purpose of attending the marriage solemnity between King Charles the First and Henrietta of France (for which he had composed the music), he was seized with the small-pox, and died there at the age of forty-five. He was buried in the cathedral church of that city.

In 1612, he published *Madrigals in five Parts for Voices and Viols;* but the most excellent of his works are his compositions for the church, namely, his *services* and *anthems,* of which there are many extant in the cathedral books. His anthem of *Hosanna* is one of the most perfect models for composition in the church style now extant. He composed the tunes to the *Hymns*

and Songs of the Church, translated by George
Withers; and some of his *lessons for the virginal*
are preserved in the collection before mentioned,
entitled " Parthenia."

The compositions of Orlando Gibbons are for
the most part truly excellent; and the study of
them cannot be too strongly recommended. The
characteristics of his music are fine harmony, un-
affected simplicity, and almost unexampled grandeur. For choice of subjects, for skill in the
management of them, and for flow of melody in
all the parts, this great master was inferior to none
of his contemporaries, and infinitely superior to
most of them. Specimens of his anthems are to
be found in nearly all the miscellaneous collections of ancient sacred music that are extant. His
five-part madrigal of " Silver Swan," which is a
remarkably fine specimen of this species of music,
is inserted in Dr. Crotch's publication; and there is
a preludium for the organ, and other organ pieces
of his composition, in Smith's " Musica Antiqua."

EDWARD GIBBONS, elder brother of the above-
mentioned composer, was a Bachelor of Music
of the University of Cambridge, and was incorporated at Oxford in July, 1592. He was organist of the Cathedral Church of Bristol, and was
also priest-vicar, sub-chanter, and master of the
choristers there. In 1604, he was appointed a
gentleman of the Chapel Royal. It is said that,

in the rebellion, he furnished the king with the sum of a thousand pounds, for which act of loyalty he was afterwards very severely treated by those in power, who deprived him of a considerable estate ; and though at that time more than eighty years of age, he and three grand-children which he maintained were actually turned out of their home.

He was the musical preceptor to Matthew Lock ; and Anthony Wood says that several of his compositions were deposited in the music-school at Oxford.

ELLIS GIBBONS was another brother of Orlando Gibbons. Of the compositions of this excellent musician, whom Wood has styled " the admired organist of Salisbury," two only are known; and these are *madrigals*, the one in five, and the other in six parts, printed in the " Triumphs of " Oriana."

NATHANIEL GILES was born either in or near the city of Worcester, and was admitted, in 1585, to the degree of Bachelor in Music, and, about forty years afterwards, to that of Doctor, in the University of Oxford. He was one of the orga- nists of St. George's Chapel at Windsor, and master of the boys there. In 1597, he was ap- pointed master of the children, and afterwards, in the reign of King Charles the First, organist of the Chapel Royal.   He died in the month of January, 1633, at the age of seventy-five, and was buried in one of the aisles adjoining to St. George's Chapel at Windsor.

His compositions are chiefly *services* and *anthems,* many of which are understood to possess considerable merit.

JOHN BARNARD, one of the minor canons of the Cathedral Church of St. Paul, London, published in parts, in the year 1641, one of the most valuable collections of church music which this country can boast.   It is entitled, " The first Book of selected " Church Music, consisting of Services and An-" thems, such as are now used in the Cathedral " and Collegiate Churches of this Kingdom, never " before printed, whereby such Books as were " heretofore, with much Difficulty and Charges, " transcribed for the Use of the Quire, are now, to " the saving of much Labour and Expense, " published for the general Good of all such as " shall desire them either for public or private " Exercise.   Collected out of divers approved " Authors."

The contents are, services for morning and evening, and the communion, preces and responses by Tallis, Rogers, Bevin, Bird, Orlando Gibbons, William Mundy, Parsons, Morley, Dr. Giles, and Woodson ; the litany by Tallis ; and anthems in four, five, and six parts, to a great number, by Tallis,

Hooper, Farrant, Shepheard, William Mundy, Gibbons, Batten, Tye, Morley, Hooper, White, Giles, Parsons, Weelkes, Bull, and Ward.*

This work unfortunately was not printed in score, and the consequence of the parts being separated is, that, at present, it is entirely lost to the world. Some years ago diligent search was made for a complete set of Barnard's books, and in all the kingdom there was not one to be found. The most perfect copy was that belonging to the choir of Hereford, but in this the boys' parts were wanting.

RICHARD NICHOLSON, organist of Magdalen College, Oxford, was admitted to the degree of music in that university in 1595. He was the first professor of music at Oxford under Dr. Heyther's endowment, and was the composer of many *madrigals*. He died in the year 1639.

RICHARD DEERING, the descendant of an ancient Kentish family, was educated in Italy; and when his education was completed, he returned to England with the character of an excellent musician. He resided in this country for some time, but, upon a very pressing invitation, went to Brussels, and be-

---

* The anthem, " O God, the Maker of all things," ascribed to Mundy, has been proved by Dr. Aldrich to have been the composition of King Henry the Eighth.

came organist to the monastery of English nuns there. From the marriage of Charles the First until the time when that monarch left England he was organist to the queen. He was admitted to the degree of Bachelor of Music at Oxford in 1610, and died in the communion of the Church of Rome about the year 1657.

He has left us, of his composition, " *Cantiones* " *Sacræ quinque Vocum, cum Basso continuo ad* " *Organum,*" printed at Antwerp in 1597; and others entitled, " *Cantica Sacra,*" published at the same place about nineteen years afterwards.

JOHN HINGSTON, a pupil of Orlando Gibbons, was organist to Oliver Cromwell, who, notwithstanding the rage of the puritans in general against it, was himself a great admirer of music. Hingston had been retained in the service of the king, but, being tempted by the offer of a hundred pounds a year, he went over to the party of the Protector, and instructed his daughters in music.

JOHN HILTON, Bachelor of Music of the University of Cambridge, was organist of the Church of St. Margaret, Westminster, and also clerk of that parish. He died during the time of the usurpation, and was buried in the cloister of Westminster Abbey.

He was the author of a *madrigal* in five parts,

printed in the " Triumphs of Oriana." In 1627, he published a set of *Fa-la's** for three voices, which are remarkable for the excellence of their melodies ; and in 1652, a valuable collection of *catches, rounds, and canons* for three and four voices, under the quaint title of " *Catch that catch " can,"* containing some of the best compositions of this kind any where to be found. Many of them were written by himself, and others by the most eminent of his contemporaries. In the books of some of the cathedrals, there are preserved a morning and evening *service* of his composition which were never printed.

WILLIAM LAWES, the son of Thomas Lawes, a vicar-choral of the Church of Salisbury, and a native of that city, having shewn an early propensity to music, was, at the expense of Edward Earl of Hereford, placed under the tuition of Coperario. He was a member of the choir of Chichester, and was called from thence, in 1602, to the office of gentleman of the Chapel Royal; but afterwards resigning that situation in favour of Ezekiel Wood, he became one of the private or chamber musicians to King Charles the First. Fuller says that " he was respected and beloved

---

* These were short songs set to music, with a repetition of those syllables in the second and fourth line, sometimes only at the end of every stanza.

by all who cast any looks towards virtue and honour." His gratitude and loyalty for his master were such that he took up arms in his cause; and although, to exempt him from danger, Lord Gerrard made him a commissary in the royal army, yet the activity of his spirit disdained this intended security, and at the siege of Chester, in 1645, he lost his life. The king is said to have been so much affected at his death, that he wore a particular mourning for him.

His compositions were, for the most part, *fantazias for viols and the organ*; but the chief of his printed works were, " *Choice Psalms put into* " *Music for three Voices*," with a thorough-bass, composed to the words of Mr. Sandys's paraphrase, in conjunction with his brother Henry, and published with nine of his canons (by the latter) in 1648. In the preface to this work he is said to have composed above thirty different kinds of music for voices and instruments; and we are informed that there was no instrument in use in his time, that he did not compose as appropriately to, as if he had studied it alone. Many of his songs are to be met with in the collections of the day, and several *catches* and *rounds,* and a few of his *canons,* are published in Hilton's Collection.

HENRY LAWES, the brother of the last-mentioned composer, was likewise a pupil of Coperario. He was a native of Salisbury, and born in the year

1600. In the month of January, 1625, he was made *pisteller*,* and in November following, a gentleman of the Chapel Royal. After this he was appointed clerk of the cheque, and a gentleman of the private music to King Charles the First.

He is celebrated for having introduced the Italian style of music into this kingdom; but this rests upon no better foundation than his having been educated under Coperario, and having composed a song on the story of Theseus and Ariadne, in which there are some passages that a superficial peruser might mistake for recitative. This song is published among his *Ayres and Dialogues for one, two, and three Voices*, printed in London in 1653. In the preface to this collection, the author mentions his having formerly composed some airs to Italian and Spanish words. He speaks of the Italians as being great masters of music, but, at the same time, contends that his own nation had produced as many able musicians as any in Europe. He censures the partiality of the age for songs sung in a language which the hearers do not understand, and, in ridicule of it, speaks of a song of his own composition, printed at the end of the book, which was nothing more than an index of the initial words of some old Italian

---

* All the lexicographers are silent concerning this word: it probably might imply *a reader of the Epistles. Pistel*, in Chaucer, implies not only an *epistle*, but a short *lesson*.

songs or madrigals. He says that this index, which he had set to a varied air, and, when read together, was a strange medley of nonsense, passed with a great part of the world as an Italian song.

The first composition in the above collection is " The Complaint of Ariadne," (before mentioned) the music to which is neither recitative nor air, but in such a medium betwixt the two that a name is wanting for it. The circumstance which contributed to recommend it to notice cannot now be discovered, but the applauses that attended the singing of it almost exceed belief.

In the year 1633, Henry Lawes and Simon Ives were ordered to compose the music to a masque, afterwards presented at Whitehall on Candlemas-night, before the king and queen, by the gentlemen of the four inns of court; for which task they received the sum of a hundred pounds.

Lawes also composed tunes to Mr. Sandys's paraphrase on the psalms, published in 1638, and afterwards in 1676. These tunes are different from those composed jointly by the two brothers, and published in 1648. They are for a single voice with a bass, and were intended for private devotion.

Milton's Comus was originally set to music by our author, and was first represented on Michaelmas-night, 1634, at Ludlow Castle, in Shropshire, for the entertainment of the family of the Earl of Bridgewater and others of the neighbourhood.

Lawes himself played in it the character of the attendant spirit, who towards the middle of the drama appears to the brothers habited like a shepherd. The music never appeared in print.

The songs of Lawes, to a very great number, are to be found in the collection entitled, " Select " musical Ayres and Dialogues," by Dr. Wilson, Dr. Charles Colman, Henry Lawes, and William Webb, published in 1652; " Ayres and Dia- " logues," published by himself in the year follow- ing; "The Treasury of Music," 1669; and seve- ral others printed about that time. In these are contained the songs of Waller, all or nearly all of which were set to music by Lawes, and, as an acknowledgment of the obligation, that poet has celebrated his skill in the following lines:

> " Let those who only warble long,
> And gargle in thei throats a song,
> Content themselves with UT, RE, MI;
> Let words of sense be set by thee."*

Lawes continued in the service of the king no longer than till the breaking out of the rebellion. From that time he employed himself in teaching ladies to sing. He however retained his place in

---

* This passage is in allusion to the custom that some musi- cians of the time had fallen into, of composing not to verse, but merely to the syllables of Guido's hexachord, which had no meaning.

the Chapel Royal, and composed the coronation
anthem for King Charles the Second. He died in
October, 1662, and was interred in Westminster
Abbey.

Were we to judge of the merits of Lawes as a
musician from the numerous testimonies of contemporary writers, we should be compelled to rank
him amongst the first which this country has ever
produced ; but if we examine his works, his title
to fame will not appear quite so well grounded.
He was engaged in the service of the church, but
contributed nothing towards the increase of its
stores. His talent lay chiefly in the composition
of songs for a single voice, and in these his greatest
excellence consisted in the correspondence which
he kept up between the accent of the music and
the quantity of the verse.

Dr. Burney says, that the greater part of his
productions are " languid and insipid, and equally
devoid of learning and genius."

John Wilson, a native of Feversham, in Kent,
was first a gentleman of the Chapel Royal, and
afterwards, in his faculty of music, a servant in
ordinary to the king. He is reported to have been
the best lute-player of his time ; and being a constant attendant on the king, frequently played to
him in private.

He was created Doctor in Music at Oxford in
1644, and he continued in that university about

two years; but on the surrender of the city, he went to reside in the family of Sir William Walter, of Sarsden, in Oxfordshire. In the year 1656, he obtained the musical professorship, and resided in Baliol College. After the Restoration he was made a gentleman of the private music of Charles the Second, and was also admitted a gentleman of the Chapel Royal. These preferments drew him from Oxford, and induced him to resign his professorship to Edward Low, who, for some time before, had officiated as his deputy.

He died in the year 1673, at the age of seventy-nine, and was interred in the cloister of St. Peter's Church, Westminster.

His compositions are, " *Psalterium Carolinum,* " *the Devotions of his Sacred Majestie, in his* " *Solitudes and Sufferings, rendered in Verse,* " *set to Musick for three Voices and an Organ or* " *Theorbo,*" published in 1657; " *Cheerful Airs* " *or Ballads; first composed for one single* " *Voice, and since set for three Voices,*" published at Oxford in 1660; " *Aires for a Voice* " *alone to a Theorbo or Bass Viol,*" printed in a collection entitled, " Select Airs and Dialogues," in 1653; and *Divine Services and Anthems,*" published in the year 1663. He also composed *Fantazias for Viols,* and music to several of the odes of Horace, and to some select passages in Ausonius, Claudian, Petronius Arbiter, and Statius. The latter was never published, but is extant in a manuscript volume, curiously bound in blue

turkey leather with silver clasps, which he presented to the university, with a strict injunction
that no one should be permitted to peruse it until
after his death.   It is now deposited among the
archives of the Bodleian library.

Dr. Burney says, that Wilson " seems to have
set words to music more clumsily than any composer of equal rank in the profession ;" and in
another place, that " his compositions will certainly not bear a severe scrutiny either as to genius
or knowledge."

BENJAMIN ROGERS was the son of Peter Rogers,
a gentleman of the Chapel of St. George at
Windsor.   He was first a chorister under the
tuition of Dr. Nathaniel Giles, and then a clerk
or singing man in the Chapel.   Afterwards he
was appointed organist of Christ-Church, Dublin, where he continued until the breaking out
of the rebellion in 1641, when he returned to
Windsor, and again became a clerk in the chapter.
The troubles during the rebellion soon deprived
him also of this situation ; and, aided by a small
annual allowance, which was paid to him in com-
pensation for his losses, he was compelled to earn
a subsistence by teaching music at Windsor.

In 1653, he composed *A Set of Airs in four
Parts for Violins,* which were presented to the
Archduke Leopold, afterwards Emperor of Ger-
many, and were often played before him.

Through the interest of Dr. Ingelo, chaplain to the Lord-Commissioner Whitelocke, Rogers was recommended to the University of Cambridge, and having received from Cromwell a mandate for that purpose, was admitted, in 1658, to the degree of Bachelor of Music.

In the year 1662, he was again appointed a clerk of St. George's Chapel at Windsor, with some addition of salary, and was also elected organist of Eton College. Both these places he held until, a vacancy occurring in Magdalen College, Oxford, he was chosen organist there. In 1669, upon the opening of the New Theatre at Oxford, he took the degree of Doctor in Music.

He continued in his latter station of organist until the year 1685, when he was formally ejected by order of King James the First. The college allowed him a small pension, on which he lived in the outskirts of the city to an old age, entirely neglected.

His works are not numerous. There are some of his detached compositions in a collection entitled, " Court Ayres, consisting of Pavans, Al-" magnes, Corants, and Sarabands, of two Parts," published by Playford in 1655; some *hymns* and *anthems* for two voices, in a collection entitled " *Cantica Sacra*," and others in the psalms and hymns in four parts, published by Playford. His *services* and *anthems*, of which there are several in our cathedral books, are the most celebrated of his works. They contain great sweetness of melody and correctness of harmony, One 'of his full anthems, " Lord, who shall " dwell in thy tabernacle," is inserted in Page's Harmonia Sacra; and another, for four voices, " Teach me, O Lord," amongst Dr. Crotch's Specimens.

As an evidence of the excellence of his music, Anthony Wood states, that " Dr. Wilson the professor, the greatest and most curious judge of music that ever was,* usually wept when he heard some parts of Rogers's music well performed, as being wrapt up in an extacy, or, if you will, melted down ; while others smiled, or had their hands and eyes lifted up at its excellency."

JOHN JENKINS, a native of Maidstone, in Kent, and born in the year 1592, was a celebrated composer of music for viols in the reigns of Charles the First and Second.

His compositions are chiefly *fantazias* in five and six parts, several of which have been greatly admired. He was also the author of many single *songs*, of which there are some specimens in Smith's Musica Antiqua ; and he set to music some part of a poem written by Edward Ben-

---

* If Dr. Wilson was not a better judge of music than he was a composer, his opinion will not carry much weight.

lowes, and entitled, " *Theophila, or Love's Sa-*
" *crifice.*" He also composed " *Twelve Sonatas*
" *for two Violins and a Bass, with a Thorough-*
" *Bass for the Organ,*" which were printed in
London about the year 1660, and reprinted at
Amsterdam in 1664. These were the first com-
positions of the kind that had been published in
England.

He died in the year 1678, at the great age of
eighty-six years ; and has been spoken of by several musical writers in terms of great respect.
Wood says of him that " he was a little man
with a great soul."

ADRIAN BATTEN, organist and vicar-choral of
St. Paul's, was a composer of *services* and *anthems,*
of which there are several inserted in Barnard's
Collection; and the words of many of his anthems are to be found in that of Clifford. He was
a good harmonist of the old school, without adding any thing to the common stock of ideas in
melody or modulation. Nor did he correct any
of the errors in accent with which former times
abounded. He seems to have jogged on in the
safe and beaten track, without looking much about
him.

DR. CHARLES COLEMAN was a gentleman of the
private music to King Charles the First. After
the rebellion he taught music in London. Dr.

Coleman, Henry Lawes, Capt. Cook, and George
Hudson, composed the music to an entertainment
written by Sir William D'Avenant, intended as
an imitation of the Italian opera, and performed
during the usurpation, at Rutland House, in Charter-house Yard.

WILLIAM CRANFORD, a singing man of St.
Paul's, was the author of many excellent *rounds*
and *catches* printed in Hilton's and Playford's Collections.   He composed that well-known catch,
to which Purcell afterwards adapted the words,
" Let's live good honest lives."

EDWARD LOW, originally a chorister in Salisbury Cathedral, was organist of Christ-Church,
Oxford, and professor of music in that university.
He died in July, 1682, and was buried in the divinity chapel adjoining to Christ-Church.
  He published, in 1661, " *Short Directions for*
" *the Performance of the Cathedral Service.*"

WALTER PORTER was a gentleman in the Chapel
Royal of Charles the First, and master of the
choristers at Westminster.   He was patronised
by Sir Edward Spencer, and was killed in the
rebellion.
  His works are, " *Aires and Madigrals for two,*
" *three, four, and five Voices, with a Thorough-*
" *Bass for the Organ or Theorbo-Lute, the*

" *Italian way*," printed in 1639 ; *Hymns and Motets for two Voices*, in 1657 ; and the psalms of George Sandys, set to music for two voices, with a thorough-bass for the organ, printed about the year 1670.

THOMAS WARWICK was organist of Westminster Abbey, and also one of the organists of the Chapel Royal. He composed *a song in forty parts*, which was performed, in 1635, by forty musicians, before King Charles the First. Sir Philip Warwick, secretary of the treasury in the reign of Charles the Second, was his son.

ENGLISH MUSICAL WRITERS,

Who flourished during the first half of the Seventeenth Century.

ROBERT FLUD, the son of Sir Thomas Flud, Knight, and some time treasurer of war to Queen Elizabeth, in France and the Low Countries, was born at Milgate, in the parish of Bearsted in Kent, in the year 1574. At the age of seventeen he was admitted a student of St. John's College, Oxford, and having taken the usual degrees in arts, he applied himself to the study of physic. He spent six years in travelling through France, Spain, Italy, and Germany; and not only became acquainted with several of the nobility of those countries, but even read lectures to them.   On his return to England, being celebrated for his knowledge in chemistry, he took the degree of Doctor in Physic, was admitted a fellow of the College of Physicians, and practised in London.   He was one of the fraternity of Rosicrucian philosophers, and dealt chiefly in the occult sciences.   It is asserted of his books, which are very numerous, that the reading of them turned the brain of Jacob Behmen. At present it is their only praise, that, for some time, they were greatly admired and anxiously read, not only by alchemists, astrologers, and searchers after the philosophers' stone, but by all the madmen in the republic of letters both at home and abroad.

He wrote against Kepler and Mersennus, and had the honour of replies from both.   Gassendus, who took up the cudgels for Mersennus, has examined and sifted his whimsical philosophy with great ingenuity.   In the dedication to Mersennus he remarks: " In the present dispute Flud will have one great advantage over you, namely, that whereas your philosophy is of a plain, open, intelligible kind, his, on the contrary, is so very obscure and mysterious, that he can at any time conceal himself, and, by diffusing a darkness round him, hinder you from discerning him so as to lay hold on him, much less to drag him forth to conviction."

Dr. Flud died in the year 1637, and was buried in the Church of Bearsted.

Among his numerous writings there is only one of which we shall have occasion to take any notice. This was published at Oppenheim, in the year 1617, in a thick folio volume, and entitled, " *Utri-* " *usque Cosmi, Majoris scilicet et Minoris, me-* " *physica, physica, atque technica Historia, in* " *duo Volumina, secundum Cosmi Differentiam* " *divisa. Tomus primus, de Macrocosmi His-* " *toria, in duos Tractatus divisa.*"

The third book of the first tract is on the subject of mundane music. In this discourse the author supposes that the elements of which the world is composed, (assigning to each a certain place according to the laws of gravitation) together with the planets and the heavens, make up a musical instrument, which he calls the *mundane monochord.* This he describes at some length, and has given a diagram in illustration of it. He also attempts to explain his whimsical hypothesis by the figure of a flute, from which, he says, it appears that the true proportion of the whole world may be collected.

It is scarcely possible for words to convey an idea of the folly and absurdity that are every where discoverable in the writings of this wild enthusiast, and his notions are so dark that they elude all investigation.

The second part of the second tract treats of

practical music, and of the musical instruments in use amongst the moderns. The remainder of the work, except the whimsical devices of musical dials, musical windows, musical colonnades, and some other extravagances, contains very little that is deserving of notice.

On the whole, it is evident that Flud was a man of disordered imagination, and an enthusiast in theology and philosophy. As such he is classed by Butler with Jacob Behmen and other mystical writers in the passage where, speaking of the learning of Ralph, he says that

> " He Anthroposcophus and Flud·
> And Jacob Behmen understood.

CHARLES BUTLER, Master of Arts of Magdalen College, Oxford, was a native of Wycombe, in the county of Buckingham. After he left the university, he was appointed master of the free-school at Basingstoke, Hants, and subsequently was vicar of Wootton St. Lawrence, in the same county.

In the year 1636, he published " *The Prin-* " *ciples of Music in Singing and Setting : with* " *the twofold Use thereof, ecclesiastical and* " *civil.*" This work abounds with a great variety of curious learning on the subject of music, selected from the best writers ancient and modern ; and it may be considered as an useful and judicious sup⸗ plement to Morley's Introduction.

The first chapter treats of the *modes* of the ancients, the second of singing, and the third of what the author denominates setting.   In the latter are discussed the subjects of melody, harmony, intervals, concords, and discords, with the consecution of each, and likewise the different ornaments of syncope, fugue, and formality.   The fourth chapter treats of counterpoint and descant.

In the first chapter of the second book, the author speaks of musical instruments and the voice ; in the second chapter, of the use of sacred music, of the continuance of church music, and the objections to it ; and in the third chapter he treats of the allowance of civil music, with its uses and abuses.

Mr. Butler was a man of great learning and ingenuity.   Among his other publications there is an English Grammar, in which he proposes a scheme of regular orthography, and makes use of characters, some of which are borrowed from the Saxon alphabet, and others are of his own invention.   All his works are printed in these strange characters.   His principles of music, by the assistance of the advertisement to the reader, may, however, be read without much difficulty.

He died in the year 1647.

EDMUND CHILMEAD, a deeply read mathematician, and well skilled both in the theory and practice of music, was the author of a tract

" *De Musicâ Antiquâ Grœcâ*," printed at the
end of the Oxford edition of Aratus in 1672.

He was born at Stow in the Wold, in Glouces-
tershire, and became one of the clerks of Magdalen
College, Oxford. About the year 1632, he was
one of the petty canons or chaplains of Christ-
Church ; but being ejected by the parliament
visitors, in 1648, he came to London, and took
lodgings in the house of Thomas Est, the musician, in Aldersgate Street. In a large room of this
house he held a weekly music meeting, from the
profits of which his chief subsistence was derived.

He was an excellent Greek scholar, and was
employed to draw up a catalogue of the Greek
manuscripts in the Bodleian library. Wood mentions a treatise of his, " *De Sonis*," which does
not appear to have been published. The rest of his
works seem chiefly to have been translations. He
died in the year 1654, in the forty-third year
of his age, having, for some years past, received
relief in his necessities from Edward Bysche, Esq.
Garter King at Arms, and Sir Harry Holbrook.
He was interred in the Church of St. Botolph,
without Aldersgate.

His tract " *De Musicâ Antiquâ Grœcâ*" contains a designation of the ancient genera, agreeably to the sentiments of Boëtius, with a general
enumeration of the modes ; after which follow
three odes of Dionysius, with the Greek musical
characters adapted to the notes of Guido's scale.

CHAP. V.

ITALIAN
MUSICAL COMPOSERS AND WRITERS,

WHO FLOURISHED

𝔉rom about the 𝔜ear

1600 TO 1650.

PALLAVICINO.— CACCINI. — VIADANA.— SORIANO.— ROMANO.—PERI.—PAOLO.— CIFRA.—AGOSTINO.— LANIERE. — MONTEVERDE. — VALENTINI. — ALLEGRI.—BERNARDI.—MERULA.—FERRARI.—SCACCHI.—CARISSIMI.—CESTI.—FRESCOBALDI. COLONNA.—DIRUTA.—DONI.

Towards the latter part of the sixteenth century, the principles of harmony had become generally known in many of the countries of the Continent, and, in the beginning of the seventeenth century, an unprecedented degree of emulation and rivalry took place betwixt the professors of different kingdoms and states, but particularly betwixt those of Italy and Germany. The former, having Palestrina at their head, had elevated church music to a pitch infinitely beyond what it had before attained; and in the composition of madrigals, for elegance of style, correctness of harmony, and sweetness and variety of modulation, they were unrivalled.

The Italian masters were the first who disseminated the principles of music throughout Europe; and, in most of the subsequent improvements, in the practice they seem to have given the rule.

There have been many opinions respecting the time when the *opera* was first attempted. That, however, which is now most generally assented to, is, that it had its origin with Rinuccini, a Florentine poet, who composed a musical pastoral called *Daphne*. The merit attributed to this piece induced its author to write the opera of *Euridice*, which was represented at the theatre of Florence in the year 1600, on the marriage of Mary de Medicis with King Henry the Fourth of France. The music to both these pieces was composed by Jacobi Peri.

An opera entitled " *L'Orfeo, Favola in Mu-*" *sica*," composed by Monteverde, was performed in 1607, and is supposed to have been the first that was ever printed. The structure of this drama is very unlike that of the modern opera. In the performance of it the accompaniment of the whole orchestra was seldom required, the airs sung by the performers being sustained by instruments of various kinds assigned to each character. To the overture, which is a short prelude, eight bars of breve time in length, and which is directed to be played thrice over before the drawing up of the curtain, succeeds the prologue, consisting of five speeches in recitative ; the purport of this is to declare the argument of the drama, to excite attention, and enjoin silence. The opera then begins with a speech in recitative by a shepherd, which is immediately succeeded by a chorus of five parts in counterpoint, directed to be sung to the sound of all the instruments. Other choruses are directed to be sung to guitars, violins, and flutes. There are no solo airs ; but recitatives, choruses, ritornellas or symphonies, trios, and duets, make up the whole of this opera, which concludes with a moresca, or Moorish dance.

What is called the *cantata spirituale,* or oratorio, is generally believed to have been indebted for its origin to San Filippo Neri, a priest, who, about the middle of the sixteenth century, was accustomed, after the sermons, to assemble such of his congregation as had musical voices, in the oratory of his chapel, for the purpose of singing various pieces of devotional and other sacred music. Regularly composed oratorios were not, however, in use till nearly a century afterwards. These, at their commencement, consisted of a mixture of dramatic and narrative parts, in which neither change of place nor unity of time were observed. They consisted of monologues, dialogues, duets, trios, and recitatives of four voices. The subject of one of them was the conversation of Christ with the Samaritan woman ; of another, the

prodigal son received into his father's house ; of
a third, Tobias with the angel, his father, and
wife ; and of a fourth, the angel Gabriel with the
Virgin Mary.

We now recur to our memoranda of the lives
and writings of eminent Italian musicians, com-
mencing with those of the seventeenth century.

BENEDETTO PALLAVICINO, a native of Cremona,
and a celebrated musical composer, was chapel-
master to the Duke of Mantua about the year 1600.

His works consist chiefly of *madrigals* for five
and six voices, and are in general good. They
contain, however, no great variety of style, melody,
harmony, or modulation.

GIULIO ROMANO CACCINI, a native of Italy, resided at Florence towards the beginning of the
seventeenth century. He composed the music to
several *canzonets* and sonnets, written by the best
poets of his time. These were adapted for a single
voice ; and he himself sung them in public, principally to the theorbo-lute played by Bardillo,
who was then eminent for his performance on that
instrument. Caccini also composed the music of
a drama entitled " *Euridice*," which was subsequently published at Florence.

LODOVICO VIADANA, chapel-master, first of the Cathedral of Fano, a small city in the Duchy of Urbino, and afterwards of the Cathedral in Mantua, is celebrated for having, about the year 1605, improved the science of music by the invention of the figured or thorough-bass. Dr. Burney says, indeed, that he has found instances of the minute beginnings of this expedient before the time of Viadana, but he allows that this musician was the first who drew up general rules for expressing harmony by figures inserted over the bass.

Of the works of Viadana, the two following are the chief : " *Opus Musicum sacrorum Concen-* " *tuum,*" published in the year 1612 ; and " *Opera* " *omnia sacrorum Concentuum,* 1, 2, 3, *et* 4 *Vo-* " *cum,*" in the year 1613, and again in 1620.

FRANCESCO SORIANO, chapel-master of St. Peter's Church at Rome, published, in 1610, *one hundred and ten canons* upon the chant to the hymn *Ave Maris Stella,* for three, four, five, six, seven, and eight voices, from which the musical reader will have a much higher opinion of his patience than his genius. Few masters except himself could perhaps have composed these canons, but many must have thought that the loss to music would not have been very great, if they had never had been composed.

MICHAELI ROMANO was a pupil of Soriano, and

afterwards chapel-master in the church called
Cathedrale de Concordia, at Venice. This person,
as well as his master, is celebrated for the composition of *canons*; a specimen of which, in one for
nine choirs or thirty-six voices, is inserted in
Kircher's Musurgia.

He is however best known by his work entitled,
" *Musica vaga et artificiosa*," published at
Venice in 1615, in which the subject of canon is
very learnedly discussed and explained by a variety
of examples. In the preface to this work are contained memoirs of the most celebrated Italian musicians who were living at the time when it was
written.

JACOBO PERI, a native of Florence, says Battista Doni, flourished about the beginning of the
seventeenth century, and had been a pupil of Christopher Malvezzi. He was not only a good composer, but a famous singer, and performer on
keyed instruments, and composed the principal
part of the music to a serious opera entitled
"*Euridice*," which had been written by Rinucci i,
for the Royal nuptials of Mary of Medicis with
Henry the Fourth of France, in the year 1600.

AGOSTINI PAOLO, a disciple of Bernardo Nanini,
was successively appointed organist of the Church
of Santa Maria, Trastevere, St. Lawrence in Da-
maso, and lastly of St. Peter's at Rome. For

invention he is supposed to have surpassed all his contemporaries, and his compositions for four, six, and eight choirs or choruses are said to have been the admiration of all Rome.

Agostino, after having held various professional situations of considerable eminence, at length succeeded Soriano in the office of chapel-master in the Pontifical Chapel at Rome, where he died in 1629, at the early age of thirty-six years. His remains were interred in the Church of St Michael in that city.

Dr. Burney states that Padre Martini has preserved an "*Agnus Dei,*" in eight parts, of this composer, which is a very extraordinary performance.

Antonio Cifra, a native of Rome, was educated in the music-school instituted by Palestrina and Nanini. After he had completed his studies he went into Germany, and was admitted into the service of the Archduke Charles, brother to the Emperor Ferdinand the Second. He afterwards became director of the music in the German College at Rome; and, about 1614, was appointed chapel-master of the Church at Loretto.

He was the author of a great number of *masses* and motets, which are as correct, artificial, and flowing, as the respect to the *canto fermo* and ancient rules would then admit. In the little secular music that he published he makes a wretched figure; for in this he is confused, uncouth, and in-elegant.

NICHOLAS LANIERE, LANIER, or LANEARE (for his name is spelt all these different ways), was born in Italy in the year 1568.   In the early part of his life, however, he came into England; and he continued to reside in this country until the time of his death.

He was the composer of a masque performed at Lord Hay's, mentioned in Ben Jonson's works; and also joint composer with Coperario, of another performed on the marriage of the Earl of Somerset with Lady Frances Howard.   Many of his songs are to be found in different collections published during the reign of King Charles the First; but they have in general very little merit.   Smith, in his Musica Antiqua, has inserted one of them, taken from the masque called "Luminalia, or the "Festival of Light," performed at court on the evening of Shrove-Tuesday, 1637, in which the queen and her ladies were the masquers.

Laniere, as well as a musician, was a painter and an engraver.   There is an excellent portrait of him, painted by himself, in the music-school at Oxford.

CLAUDIO MONTEVERDE, of Cremona, chapel-master of the Church of St. Mark at Venice, was a celebrated composer of *motets* and *madrigals*, who flourished about the beginning of the seventeenth century. He was also well.known for his skill in recitative, a style of music of which indeed he may be said to have been one of the inventors ; at least there are no examples of recitative extant more ancient than those in his opera of Orfeo.

There are several of his madrigals inserted in the collections published by Pietro Phalesio and others about the year 1600. As, in these compositions, Monteverde had dared to violate rules of counterpoint which had been long established, and were held sacred by orthodox professors, he drew upon himself many opponents, who treated him as an ignorant corrupter of the art, and inveighed with asperity against him. Musicians entered the lists on both sides, and the war became general. Monteverde defended himself in prefaces and letters prefixed to his works. But his best defence was the revolution he brought about in counterpoint ; for his licences, pleasing the public ear, were soon adopted not only by the dilettante, but by professors.

He was the first who used double discords, such as $\frac{9}{4}$, $\frac{9}{7}$, and $\frac{7}{2}$, as well as the flat fifth and the seventh unprepared. In his secular productions, by quitting ecclesiastical modulation, he determined the key of each movement, smoothed and phrased the melody, and made all his parts sing in a more natural and flowing manner than had been

done by any of his predecessors.   In his fifth and
last book of madrigals, almost every species of discord and modulation is hazarded, for the use of
which the boldest composers of modern times have
been often thought licentious.

PIETRO FRANCESCO VALENTINI, a Roman by
birth, and the descendant of a noble family, was
educated in the music-school in Rome instituted
by Palestrina and Nanino. He was an excellent
theorist.   Notwithstanding his high birth he was
so reduced in circumstances as to be necessitated
to make music his profession, and even to play for
hire.

He composed many pieces of great value, and
among the rest, a *canon* printed in Kircher's Musurgia, entitled " *Nodus Salomonis*," which may
be sung two thousand ways.   He was also the
author of a work, published in 1645, entitled,
" *La Transformatione di Dafne, Favola morale,*
" *con due Intermedii ; il primo contiene il Ratto*
" *di Proserpina, il secondo la Cattività nella rete*
" *di Venere e Marte.   La Metra Favola Græca*
" *versificata, con due Intermerdii ; il primo rap-*
" *presentante l' Uccisione di Orfeo, ed il secondo*
" *Pitagora, che ritrova la Musica.*"

GREGORIO ALLEGRI, a pupil of Nanino, was a
native of Rome, and admitted a singer in the Papal
Chapel in December, 1629.   He was distinguished

by his benevolent disposition. This he manifested in his compassion for the poor, and in his daily visits to the prisons of Rome, where he inquired into and relieved, to the utmost of his power, all whose distresses rendered them objects of compassion. He is said to have been an excellent contrapuntist.

His works are chiefly for the church. Among them there is a *Miserere* in five parts, in the minor key of G, which, on account of its excellence, was always reserved for the most solemn services, and was, for a long series of years, kept in the Pontifical Chapel with unprecedented care.

Of this composition we are informed by Padre Martini, that there were never more than three copies made by authority, one of which was for the Emperor Leopold, the second for the King of Portugal, and the third for himself. Respecting the former of these copies, the following anecdote has been related: "The Emperor, who was not only a lover and patron of music, but a good composer himself, ordered his ambassador at Rome to entreat the Pope to permit him to have it for the use of the Imperial Chapel at Vienna; which being granted, it was made by the Signor Maestro of the Pope's Chapel, and sent to the Emperor, who had then in his service some of the first singers of the age. But, notwithstanding the abilities of the performers, this composition was so far from answering the expectations of the Emperor and his court in the execution, that he concluded that the chapel-master, in order to keep it a mystery, had put a trick upon him, and sent him another composition. Upon which, in great wrath, he sent an express to his Holiness, with a complaint against Allegri, which occasioned his immediate disgrace and dismissal; and in so great a degree was the Pope offended at the supposed imposition of his composer, that, for a long time, he would neither see him nor hear his defence. However, at length, the poor man got one of the Cardinals to plead his cause, and to acquaint his Holiness that the style of singing in his Chapel, particularly in performing the Miserere, was such as could not be expressed by notes, nor taught nor transmitted to any other place, but by example; for which reason the piece in question, though faithfully transcribed, must fail in its effect when performed elsewhere. His Holiness did not understand music, and could hardly comprehend how the same notes should sound so differently in different places; however, he ordered his chapel-master to write down his defence, in order to be sent to Vienna, which was done; and the Emperor, seeing no other way of gratifying his wishes with respect to this composition, begged of the Pope that some of the musicians in the service of his Holiness might be sent to Vienna, to instruct the performers there in the service of his chapel how to perform the Miserere in the same expressive manner as at Rome, which was granted. But before they arrived, a war broke out with the Turks, which called the Emperor from Vienna ; and the Miserere has never yet, perhaps, been truly performed but in the Pope's Chapel.

Allegri died on the 18th of February, 1652, and was interred near the Chapel of St. Fileppo in the Chiesa Nuova, in the place appointed for the burial of the singers of the Pope's Chapel.

STEFFANO BERNARDI, says Dr. Burney, was a learned theorist, as well as a composer of *masses* and *madrigals* of a most elaborate and correct kind. He flourished from 1611 to about 1634 ; and in 1623 was chapel-master of the Duomo at Verona. He published a didactic work entitled " *Porta Musicale,*" the first part of which was printed at Verona in the year 1615. As an elementary tract, this has the merit of clearness and brevity.

TARQUINIO MERULA, a chevalier and student in the Academia Filomusi at Bologna, was chapel-master of the Cathedral of Bergamo in the year 1639.

His compositions are of various kinds, and consist both of vocal and intrumental music. One of his works, published in 1637, is entitled, "*Can-*" *zoni overo Sonate concertate par Chiesa e* " *Camera, à 2 e 3 Stromenti, lib.* 1, 2, 3, *e* 4."

It is deserving of remark, that Merula was the composer of sonatas thus early; and that beyond this period it will be difficult to carry the invention of this kind of music.

He was one of those who first introduced other instruments besides the organ, such as viols and violins, into the church service, in aid of choral singing. He published several collections of *psalms*, which he directs to be performed either with or without instruments.

Among the vocal compositions of Merula, there are two which are completely singular in their kind: the grammatical declension of the Latin pronoun, " *hic, hæc, hoc,*" set to music in the form of a fugue, or, as its generally called, canon in unison; and " *Quis vel qui; nominativo qui,* " *quæ, quod.*" The latter consists of several movements that are supported with great vivacity; and the imitations of the cant and stammering of school-boys, in repeating their lesson, are highly ludicrous.

Benedetto Ferrari, a native of Reggio, was both a poet and musician. He resided principally at Venice, where, about the year 1638, he established an opera, which he himself superintended; for which he was both poet and composer, and in which he was also a singer. His best known operas are those of "*Armida,*" composed in 1630; and " *Il Pastor Reggio,*" in 1640: but in these there are no airs, the dialogue only being carried on in recitative. Ferrari was himself so excellent a performer on the lute, that he has not unfrequently been styled Ferrari della Tiorba.

The period of his death is unknown.

MARCO SCACCHI, a native of Rome, was master of the chapel to Sigismund the Third and Uladislaus the Fourth, successively kings of Poland.

He was the author of a treatise published in 1643, entitled, " *Cribrum Musicum ad Triticum* " *Siferticum, seu Examinatio succincta Psal-* " *morum;*" of " *Cantilena* 5 *Voc. et Lachrymæ* " *sepulchrales,*" printed in 1647; and of a set of canons entitled, " *Canones, sive Lachrymæ se-* " *pulchrales ad Tumulum Johannis Stobæi.*"

The compositions of Scacchi are greatly esteemed by the Italians for the closeness of their contexture, and for the great ingenuity and contrivance that are to be found in them.

GIACOMO CARISSIMI, chapel-master of the Church of St. Apollinare in the German College at Rome, is celebrated by all the Italian writers as eminently the best musician of his time. He was alike successful in his compositions for the church, the oratorio, and the chamber; and is considered to have been the father of that more effeminate beauty which at this time peculiarly characterises the Italian vocal music.

Alberto delle Valle, speaking of the music which he had heard at Rome, says, that he had been present at the vespers on Easter-Monday, at the Church *Delle Spirito Santo*, where the music was performed by the nuns only, with such perfection as he never in his life had heard before; and on the Christmas-Eve, in attending the whole service at the Church of St. Apollinare, where every part of it was performed agreeably to so solemn an occasion, though, by arriving too late, he was obliged to stand the whole time in a very great crowd, he remained there with the utmost pleasure to hear the excellent music that was performed. He was particularly enchanted by the *Venite exultemus*, which was more exquisite than words can describe. " I know not," says Valle, " who was the author of it, but I suppose it to have been the production of the maestro di capella of that church." There was, observes Dr. Burney, no master in Italy at this time, 1640, whose compositions this description will so well suit, as those of the admirable Carissimi, who was now, in all probability, the maestro di capella in question, though so young that his fame was as yet unfledged ; however, it was in composing for this church that he acquired that great and extensive reputation which he enjoyed during a long life, and which his musical productions still deservedly enjoy.

Carissimi composed, for the use of the church,

a kind of dramatic dialogue, entiled *Jephtha.*
This consists of recitatives, airs, and chorus ; and,
for sweetness of melody, skilful modulation, and
original harmony, is esteemed one of the greatest
efforts of musical genius that has ever been given
to the world. Another work of the same kind,
and not less excellent, is his " *Judicium Salo-*
" *monis.*" He composed also a dialogue between
Heraclitus and Democritus, in which the affections of weeping and laughing are contrasted in
some of the most pleasing melodies that imagination ever suggested. Carissimi was truly excellent in imitating the inflections of the human
voice, and in uniting the charms of music with
the powers of oratory.

He brought the style of recitative to great perfection, and was the inventor of moving basses.
In the latter he was imitated by Agostino, Colonna, Bassani, and lastly by Corelli. He was
also among the first of those musicians who introduced the accompaniment of violins and other
instruments into the performance of motets.

Kircher, in the strongest expressions of gratitude, acknowledges his having received great assistance from Carissimi in the compilation of his
Musurgia, and particularly in those parts where
he treats of recitative. He highly eulogises his
compositions, informing us that he had the power
of exciting in his hearers whatever affection he
pleased. Respecting his oratorio of Jephtha, he

says that there were many new and admirable
effects produced in it by his knowledge of harmony, modulation, and happy expression of the
passions.

Dr. Aldrich has adapted English words to many
of Carissimi's motets.   One of them, " I am well
"pleased," is yet frequently sung in the cathedral
churches of England. It may be here remarked, that
Handel's celebrated chorus in Sampson, " Hear,
" Jacob's God," is taken from the chorus in Jephtha beginning, " *Plorate filiæ Israel*;" that, in
various other parts of his works, he copied from
Carissimi ; and that he did this with very slight
alterations, compared with those which he deemed
requisite when adopting the thoughts of other composers.

Specimens of his music are to be found in
Stevens's Sacred Music, and in Dr. Crotch's Selections.

Marc Antonio Cesti was first a pupil of Carissimi, and afterwards a monk in the monastery of
Arezzo in Tuscany. The Emperor Ferdinand the
Third made him his chapel-master. His compositions, however, were almost entirely confined to
the theatre ; and he is said to have been the first
who introduced the *cantata* upon the stage and
into secular performances. He composed five
operas, one of which, entitled " *Orontea,*" was
performed at Venice about the year 1649, and

another, " La Dori," a few years afterwards.
In 1660, he was admitted a tenor-singer in the
Pope's Chapel. Some of his airs were printed in
a collection published in London, about 1665, by
Pignani, entitled, " Scelta di Canzonette Italiane
" de piu Autori;" and one of them, " Dormi ben
" mio," in Dr. Crotch's publication.

The number of cantatas, says Dr. Burney, that
Cesti produced seems incalculable ; as in every
old library or collection of old Italian vocal music
that he had examined abroad and at home, he had
found more of Cesti's cantatas than of any other
author.   At Christ-Church, Oxford, in the collection of Dr. Aldrich, in the British Museum, in
the D'Arcy collection of the late Earl of Holder-
ness, in that of Lord Keeper North, of Sir Roger
l'Estrange, and of all the ancient families who
cultivated music in the seventeenth century, he had
found innumerable cantatas by Cesti ; and in
these cantatas it appears that he was a great improver of recitative.   The period of the death of
this composer is not known.

Girolamo Frescobaldi, a native of Ferrara,
was born in the year 1601, and, at the age of about
twenty-three, was appointed organist of the Church
of St. Peter's at Rome.

Frescobaldi is not less celebrated for his compositions for the organ than for his great powers
of execution on that instrument.   He was the first

of the Italians who composed for the organ in
fugue ; and in this species of composition, originally
invented by the Germans, he was without a rival.
He may be truly considered the father of that style
of organ-playing called by the Italians *toccatas*,
and by the English *voluntaries*.

In the year 1628, Bartolomo Grassi, organist of
St. Maria in Acquirio in Rome, published a
work of Frescobaldi, entitled, " *In Partitura il*
" *primo Libro delle Canzoni, à une, tre, e quatro*
" *Voci. Per sonare conogni Sorte di Stromenti.*"
From the title it seems that these were originally
vocal compositions, but that Grassi, for the improvement of those who were employed in the
study of composition, had rejected the words, and
published the music in score. In this form they
met with so favourable a reception from the public
as to be twice reprinted.

Another work of Frescobaldi was printed at
Rome in 1607, entitled, " *Il secondo Libro di*
" *Toccata, Canzone, Versi d'Hinni, Magnificat,*
" *Galiarde, Correnti, et altre Partite d'Intavola-*
" *tura di Cimbalo et Organo.*"

ITALIAN MUSICAL WRITERS,

Who flourished in the Beginning of the Sixteenth Century.

FABIO COLONNA, a descendant of an illustrious Roman family of that name, was born at Naples about the year 1567. In the early part of his life he became a member of the society called Accademia Lyncæi, established by the Duke de Aqua Sparta; the first of those institutions for the improvement of science and literature which are now so numerous throughout Europe. He applied himself with great assiduity to the study of philosophy, languages, mathematics, and the fine arts; but chiefly to that of physic, botany, and music.

In 1618, he published a work in three books, entitled, " *Della Sambuca Lincea, overo dell' In-* " *strumento Musico perfetto.*" This, which is now extremely scarce, could, however, at no time have been of much use to practical musicians; but at present, when there are extant so many better treatises on harmony, it is of no value whatever. He was also the inventor of a musical instrument called a pentachordon.

Colonna died about the year 1647, at the age of eighty.

GIROLAMO DIRUTA was a Franciscan friar, and the author of a work in dialogue, entitled, " *Il* " *Transilvano,*" printed at Venice in the year 1625. The design of this work is to teach the proper method of playing on the organ and harpsichord. After explaining the musical scale, and the characters used in mensurale music, the author gives many general directions respecting the position of the hand and the application of the fingers to the instrument. The book contains also several lessons on the ecclesiastical tones, written by himself and other masters. In the year 1622, he published a second part, in which he gives the rules of counterpoint, and the method of composing fantazias, with several examples. The third part treats of the ecclesiastical tones, and of the method of transposing them ; and the fourth contains the method of accompanying the choral service, and the use of the several stops of the organ.

GIOVANNI BATTISTA DONI, a native of the city of Florence, was born in the year 1594. He was the descendant of a noble family, and, though not by profession a musician, has been justly celebrated for his skill in this science. Early in life he was appointed professor of eloquence, and member of the Florentine Academy and that of Della Crusca. He was much favoured by Cardinal Barbarini, afterwards Pope Urban the Eighth, and at his recommendation was appointed secretary to the College of Cardinals. Being a man of extensive learning, and finding the attention required in this employment too great an interruption to his studies, he quitted it and retired to Florence, where he ended his days, at the age of about fifty.

From an account which he has given us of himself and his studies, it appears that, in the early part of his life, he was taught to play on the flageolet and the lute. He says that he also attained some proficiency on the harpsichord; and that, afterwards, notwithstanding the little time he had to spare from his more serious avocations, he applied himself with uncommon assiduity to the science of harmony.

In 1635 he published, at Rome, a discourse entitled, " *Compendio del Trattato de' Generi e* " *de' Modi della Musica, con un Discorso sopra* " *da Perfettione de' Concenti.*" This book is of a miscellaneous nature; but its avowed design is to shew that the music of the ancients was preferable to that of the moderns. It contains a tract entitled, " *Discorso sopra la Perfettione della Melodie,*" at the beginning of which the author treats of the madrigal style of composition, and of the particulars that distinguish the cantus figuratus from the cantus ecclesiasticus. The invention of the latter, he says, followed naturally from the use of the organ.

Five years afterwards Doni published his " *An-*

" *notazioni sopra il Compendio de' Generi, e de'*
" *Modi della Musica,*" and some other tracts.
In one of them he describes an instrument of his
own invention, called, after his patron, a Lira Car-
barini, resembling, in shape, the Spanish guitar,
but having three nicks, each of which was double,
like the theorbo or arch-lute.   The use of this instrument was to enable the performer to play either
in the Dorian, the Phrygian, or the Hypolydian
modes of the ancients.   All these tracts contain
curious particulars relative to the music and musicians of the author's time.

Doni published, in 1647, a treatise in three
books," *De Præstantia Musicæ veteris.*" The chief
arguments contained in it tend to shew the author's
opinion that the science of music was treated more
learnedly by the ancients than by the moderns ;
and that in the construction and use of such instruments as the cithara, lyre, and pipes of all kinds,
they were at least equal to the moderns, but in
such as were made to sound by mutual percussions,
as the cymbala and the crotala, they far excelled
them.   Doni is of opinion that the ancients were
so far acquainted with music in consonance that
they used the fourth, the fifth, and the diapason.

Of music in symphony he seems to entertain no
very high opinion ; and as to variety of motion
and difference in the length of notes, and all those
arts that constitute the distinction between figurate

and plain descant, he says that they produce nothing but confusion, and a false kind of music devoid of energy.

He laments that the music of modern songs did not express the words, and that music was no longer, as with the ancients, the sister of poetry. He then treats of the elements of music, in which he remarks that the practice of singing was much more expeditiously taught by the ancient Greeks than the modern Latins, with all the help of the six syllables of Guido, or the seven of other writers; and he asserts, with the greatest confidence, that students in music would be much eased by taking off two from Guido's six syllables.

At the conclusion of the above-mentioned work there is a catalogue of all Doni's tracts on music, to the number of twenty-four. Some of these, however, were never published, and others he did not even live to finish.

Notwithstanding the singularity of his opinions, it appears that Doni had perused the musical writings both of the ancients and moderns; and had he possessed somewhat more of judgment, and been better skilled in mathematics than he was, his assiduity and perseverance in research would have enabled him to have written much more sensibly than he has done on the subject.

CHAP. VI.

ENGLISH
MUSICAL COMPOSERS AND WRITERS,

WHO FLOURISHED

𝔉rom about the 𝔜ear

1650 to 1700.

CAPTAIN COOK.—TUCKER.—GREGORY.—DR. CHRIS-
TOPHER GIBBONS.—BRYNE.—DR. CHILD.—BANIS-
TER, SENIOR. — LOCK.—HUMPHREY. — WISE. —
ABELL.—PLAYFORD.—DR. STAGGINS.—DR. BLOW.
—HENRY PURCELL.—DANIEL PURCELL.—DR. ALD-
RICH. — THOMAS FARMER.—HALL.—IVES.—READ-
ING.

SIMPSON. — MACE. — WALLIS.— BIRKENSHA. — DR.
HOLDER.

On the restoration of the English government
under King Charles the Second, in the year 1660,
the manners af the country began to assume a new
character. Theatrical entertainments, which had
long been interdicted, were recommenced, and al
the arts of refinement were employed in order to
render them alluring to the public. The King's
Theatre in Drury Lane, and the Duke of York's

in Dorset Garden, were opened with performances of unexampled magnificence. Music was now rendered essential to the theatre, by the introduction of what were termed *act-tunes* (short compositions played betwixt the acts of the drama), for the relief not only of the actors, but likewise of the audience. Hence it was that the theatres became the nurseries of musicians. The state of dramatic music was indeed at a very low ebb, from the want of proper seminaries of instruction. All the most eminent composers for the theatre, for several years after the Restoration, were members of cathedral and collegiate churches : this circumstance occasioned Tom Brown to say, that " men of the musical profession hung betwixt the church and the playhouse, like Mahomet's tomb betwixt two loadstones." The consequence was, that previously to the time of Purcell, Lock, and Eccles, dramatic music had, in general, a grave and solemn character, ill adapted to the amusements of a theatre.

With respect to *choral music,* as soon as order had been re-established in the church, new organs were built in place of such as had been destroyed ; and skilful persons were appointed to superintend the revival of the several choirs of the kingdom. A few musicians of eminence, who had been organists of different cathedrals and collegiate churches during the reign of Charles the First, as Child, Christopher Gibbons, Law, Rogers, Wil-

son, and some others, were sought out and pro-
moted. The three former were appointed organists of the Royal Chapel; and to Gibbons were
also given the superintendance of the children
there, and the place of organist of Westminster
Abbey. Such, however, had been the effect of the
late confusions, that many months elapsed before
the children could be so far instructed as to be able
to sustain their parts in the service; and, during
all this time, the clergy of the several churches
were obliged to supply the want of boys by
cornets and men singing with feigned voices.

The salaries of the gentlemen of the Chapel
Royal, which had been augmented in each of the
preceding reigns, were increased by Charles the
Second to seventy pounds a year. The king likewise gave great countenance and encouragement
to the composers of sacred music, that had an
highly beneficial effect upon all the choirs of the
kingdom, as was obvious by the variation which,
not long afterwards, took place in the style of the
music. The natural gaiety of the king's disposition, and his want of sufficient judgment to enable
him to admire the compositions of Tye, Tallis,
Bird, Gibbons, and others, induced those who were
desirous of obtaining his particular notice or patronage to give a somewhat lighter cast to their
music. Amongst these were three persons, at that
time children of the Chapel, namely, Humphrey,
Blow, and Wise. They were all young men of

genius, and were equally distinguished for originality of style and well-grounded knowledge of the principles of harmony.

The advantages that music derived from the studies of the above composers, and of others, their contemporaries, were indeed very great; and from the numerous excellent compositions of Charles the Second's reign, that are now extant, it may be questioned whether the principles of harmony, or the science of composition, were ever better understood than in his time ?

The Italian opera, about the latter end of the seventeenth century, had arrived at considerable perfection.   It had been introduced at Paris; and some faint attempts to imitate it had been made in our theatres, by the introduction of vocal and instrumental music in some of our plays; such, particularly, as Macbeth and the Tempest, in which there were some airs and choruses, distributed at intervals, with a few short recitatives.   These were so well received by the public, that they were succeeded by several dramas written purposely as a vehicle for the music: they took the denomination of operas, but they were in fact nothing more than plays with songs intermixed in the scenes; and there could be no other pretence for calling them operas, than that music and dances were introduced in them, and that the French had given the name of operas to similar productions.

An English opera in the Italian style was not

attempted till the year 1707, when that of Arsinoë, adapted to Italian airs, was performed at
the theatre in Drury Lane. A succession of entertainments of this kind terminated in the establishment of an opera, in which the drama was
written in the Italian language, and the music was
in the Italian style of composition.

Before we proceed to give any further account
of the introduction of the opera into this country,
it will be necessary to continue our memoirs of the
lives and writings of English musicians, from the
Restoration to the conclusion of the seventeenth
century.

HENRY COOK was educated at the Chapel Royal
during the reign of King Charles the First; but at
the commencement of the rebellion he quitted it,
and entered the army. About the year 1642, he
had interest enough to obtain a captain's commission, and, from that time, he was always distinguished by the name of Captain Cook. The
loyalty and skill of this musical soldier recommended him to the notice and secured him the
patronage of Charles the Second; by whom he
was, not long afterwards, appointed master of the
children of the Royal Chapel.

A *hymn* in four parts, composed by Cook, was
performed instead of the litany, in the Chapel of
St. George at Windsor, by order of the Sovereign

and Knights of the Garter, on the 17th of April, 1661. None of his *church music* has hitherto been printed ; and, if we may judge from his few secular compositions that are to be found dispersed in the collections of the times, he seems to have by no means possessed the requisite qualifications for the high office to which he was appointed. In the second part of Playford's " Mu- " sical Companion," published 1667, there are two or three of his *songs*, which are in almost every respect dry and uninteresting.

He was the musical instructor of Humphrey, Blow, and Wise ; and, as Anthony Wood informs us, died of grief, in the year 1672, in consequence of the talents and musical reputation of his pupil Humphrey having been far superior to his own.

WILLIAM TUCKER was a gentleman of the Chapel Royal in the reign of Charles the Second at the time of the coronation, and also a minor canon in the Collegiate Church of St. Peter at Westminster.

He was a good church musician, and composed several *anthems*, the most celebrated of which are, " Praise the Lord, O ye his servants ;" " This is the " day the Lord hath made ;" " Unto thee, O " Lord ;" and " O give thanks unto the Lord." Of the latter, which is a full anthem, Mr. Mason very truly observes, that " every syllable has its just length, and each part of a sentence its proper pause : it admits no perplexing alterations or unmeaning repetitions, but proceeds in one full, yet distinct strain, harmonically, yet intelligibly." It is to be found in Page's Harmonia Sacra, and is also published separately.

This composer died in the year 1678.

WILLIAM GREGORY, a gentleman of the Chapel Royal in the same reign, was a composer of several anthems. The best are, " Out of the deep have I " called," and " O Lord, thou hast cast us out."

CHRISTOPHER GIBBONS, the son of the celebrated Orlando Gibbons, was, from his childhood, educated to the profession of music under his uncle, Ellis Gibbons, organist of Bristol. He had been a chorister in the Chapel of King Charles the First, and, at the Restoration, was appointed principal organist of the Chapel of Charles the Second, organist in private to his Majesty, and organist of Westminster Abbey. The king had so great a partiality for this musician that he was induced to give him a personal recommendation to the University of Oxford, requesting that he might be admitted to the degree of Doctor in Music. This he was, in consequence, honoured with in the month of July, 1664. He died in the parish of St. Margaret, Westminster, in the year 1676.

Christopher Gibbons was more celebrated for his skill in playing the organ than for his compositions. There are, however, many of his *anthems* extant, though we know of none that have been printed. Those most celebrated are, " God, be " merciful unto us ;" " Help me, O Lord ;" " Lord, " I am not high-minded ;" and " Teach me, O Lord." It is said that he assisted in the work entitled " *Cantica Sacra*," containing English and Latin hymns and anthems, published in 1674.

ALBERTUS BRYNE was a scholar of John Tomkins, and his successor as organist of St. Paul's Cathedral. He was the composer of many *services* and *anthems*. He died in the reign of Charles the Second, and was buried in the cloister of Westminster Abbey.

WILLIAM CHILD, MUS. DOC. a native of Bristol, was educated in music under Elway Bevin, organist of the cathedral church of that city. In the year 1631, he was admitted to the degree of Bachelor of Music in the University of Oxford ; and about five years afterwards was appointed one of the organists of the Chapel of St. George at Windsor, and one of the organists of the Royal Chapel at Whitehall. After the Restoration he became chanter in the King's Chapel, and was made a gentleman of the private music of Charles the Second. In 1663, he took his Doctor's degree.

His works are, " *Psalms for three Voices, with* " *a continued Bass either for the Organ or The-* " *orbo, composed after the Italian way,*" published in the year 1639 ; *catches and canons*, pub-

lished in Hilton's collection entitled, " Catch that
" catch can;" and some compositions of two parts
printed in a book entitled, " Court Ayres."

He composed also many *services* and *anthems*,
none of which however appear to have been printed,
except a service in the minor key of E, and that
famous one in the major key of D, both of which
are inserted in Dr. Boyce's " Cathedral Music." In
Smith's " Musica Antiqua" there is a full anthem
by Dr. Child, " O praise the Lord," which had
been composed in the year 1660, on the restoration
of the church and royal family.

His style was in general so unusually natural
and familiar, that it appears sometimes to have
given offence to those who had to sing his compositions. It is said that, at Windsor, he once called
the choir to practise a service he had composed,
and the choirmen found it so easy that they could
not refrain from ridiculing it. This circumstance
is supposed to have occasioned the composition of
his famous service in D, which, in some parts, is
remarkably intricate and difficult, but on the
whole extremely fine.

Dr. Child is celebrated for an act of beneficence
which could scarcely be expected from a person in
his station of life. It seems that he had been so
ill paid for his services at Windsor that a long
arrear of salary had incurred, which he could not
get discharged. After many fruitless aplications
to the Dean and Chapter, he at last told them,

that if they would pay him the sum in arrear, he would new-pave the choir of the Chapel. They paid him his money, and suffered the Doctor to perform his promise.

He died in March, 1696-7, in the ninety-first year of his age, and was interred in the Chapel of St. George at Windsor. On his grave-stone is the following epitaph :

" Go, happy soul, and in the seats above,
Sing endless hymns of thy great Maker's love.
How fit in heavenly songs to bear thy part,
Before well practis'd in the sacred art !
Whilst hearing us, sometimes the choir divine
Will sure descend, and in our concert join ;
So much the music thou to us hast given,
Has made our earth to represent their heaven."

JOHN BANISTER was the son of one of the waits of the parish of St. Giles, near London ; but having received from his father the rudiments of a musical education, he became in a short time such a proficient on the violin, that he was sent by King Charles the Second into France for improvement, and on his return was appointed one of the royal band. From this service he was dismissed for having told the king that the English performers on the violin were superior to those of France.

He set to music the opera of *Circe*, written by D'Avenant, and performed at the theatre in Dorset Garden in 1676 ; and was also the composer of several *songs* printed in the collections of his time.

He died in the month of October, 1679, and was interred in the cloister of Westminster Abbey.

Matthew Lock was originally a chorister in the Cathedral Church of Exeter, and a pupil of Edward Gibbons. Very early in life he attained a considerable degree of eminence in his profession. He was employed to compose the music for the public entry of King Charles the Second, and not long afterwards was appointed composer in ordinary to that monarch.

Dramatic music was that in which he chiefly excelled, but there are likewise extant by him many valuable compositions for the church. Amongst others is a morning service, composed for the Chapel Royal, in which the prayer after each of the commandments is set in a different way. This was deemed, by many persons, an inexcusable innovation, and, on the whole, was so much censured, that he was compelled to publish the entire service in score, with a vindication by way of preface.

Lock appears to have been a man of an unpleasant and quarrelsome disposition, and, consequently, he involved himself in almost continual broils. About the year 1672, he was engaged in a controversy with Thomas Salmon, A. M. of Trinity College, Oxford, on the subject of a book written by him, and entitled, " An Essay to the Ad-
" vancement of Music, by casting away the Per-
" plexity of different Cliffs, and uniting all Sorts

" of Music in one universal Character." Lock
could not refrain from attacking this work. Accordingly he published, " Observations upon a
" late Book, entitled an Essay," &c. which lying
immovable upon the bookseller's shelves, he after-
warks republished it with a new title. Salmon answered it in, " A Vindication of an Essay to the
" Advancement of Music, from Mr. Lock's Ob-
" servations." The subject matter of this dispute is
not of sufficient importance to demand from us
any detail of the arguments; suffice it to say, that,
under a studied affectation of wit and humour, the
pamphlets, on both sides, are replete with the most
scurrilous invective and abuse.

The musical world is indebted to Lock for the
first rules that were ever published in this kingdom
on the subject of thorough-bass. A collection of
these was inserted in a book entitled " Melo-
" thesia," which also contains some lessons for the
harpsichord and organ, by himself and other
masters. It is well known that Lock was the composer of the music to Shakspear's plays of Macbeth
and the Tempest, as altered by Sir William Davenant, and, in conjunction with Draghi, to Shadwell's
opera of Psyche. He was also the author of a
collection of airs published in 1657, entitled, " A
" little Consort of three Parts, for Viols or
" Violins," and of the music to several songs
printed in " The Treasury of Musick," " The
" Theatre of Musick," and other collections. In the

latter there is a dialogue by him, "When death shall
"part us from these kids," which may be ranked
among the best vocal compositions of the time.
The music in Macbeth has lately been arranged
for the voice and pianoforte, and published by
Jacobs, organist of the Surry Chapel.

Towards the latter part of his life Lock became a
Roman Catholic, and was appointed organist to
Catherine Queen of Portugal, the consort of King
Charles the Second.   He died in the year 1677.

PELHAM HUMPHREY was one of the first set of
children of the Chapel Royal after the Restoration,
and was educated at the same time with Blow and
Wise, under Captain Cook.   He was admitted
a gentleman of the Chapel in 1666; and he distinguished himself so eminently in the composition
of anthems, as to excite the envy of his master,
who, it has been reported, died of grief at seeing
paid to him that applause which was justly due to
his merit.   After Cook's death, Humphrey succeeded to his place of master of the children.   He
died in 1674, in the twenty-seventh year of his age,
and was interred in the east ambulatory, reaching
from north to south, of the cloister of Westminster
Abbey.

In Dr. Boyce's Collection of Cathedral Music there
are two very fine *anthems* of Humphrey's composition, "O Lord my God," and "Have mercy upon
me." In conjunction with Blow and Turner, he com-

posed the anthem, "I will alway give thanks."
He wrote also many of the tunes to the *songs* in
the "Theatre of Music," the "Treasury of
"Music," and other collections of his time, par-
ticularly that to the favourite song, "When
"Aurelia first I courted."

In Humphrey's verse anthems many new effects
are produced by modulation and notes of taste and
expression.

It is somewhat remarkable that all the seven
verse anthems which Dr. Boyce has inserted in his
collection, written by this plaintive composer,
should be in flat keys; most of them in C and F
minor, which are much out of tune on the organ
by the usual temperament of that instrument; if
well sung, however, these crude chords may add to
the melancholy cast of the compositions.

Several songs by Humphrey are inserted in
Smith's "Musica Antiqua."

MICHAEL WISE was a native of Salisbury, and
one of the first set of children of the Chapel Royal
after the Restoration. He became organist and
master of the choristers at Salisbury in 1668; and
in July, 1675, was appointed a gentleman of the
Chapel Royal. Eleven years after this last promotion, he was made almoner and master of the choristers of St. Paul's.

He was much favoured by Charles the Second;
and being appointed to attend the king in one of

his journeys, he claimed, as his organist for the
time being, the privilege of playing on the organ
in the church of whatever place the king stopped
at. It is said that in one place he had the pre-
sumption to begin his voluntary before the preacher
had finished the sermon ; and it is possible that
some such unwarrantable and indiscreet behaviour
as this might draw upon him the royal displeasure ;
for, on the King's decease, we find that he was
under a suspension, and at the coronation of James
the Second, Edward Morton officiated in his room.

He composed many fine *anthems*, " Awake up
" my glory," " Prepare ye the way of the Lord,"
" Awake, put on thy strength," and some others.
He composed also that well-known two-part *song*,
" Old Chiron thus preached to his pupil Achilles,"
and some *catches*, printed in the " Musical Com-
" panion."

He was a man of great pleasantry, but ended
his days unfortunately. Whilst he was at Salisbury,
in the year 1687, some harsh words took place
betwixt him and his wife, on which he rushed out
of the house in a violent rage, and (it being towards midnight) was stopped by one of the watch-
men ; with this man he began a new fray, and in
the contest received a dreadful blow on the head,
which fractured his skull and killed him.

John Abell, a gentleman of the Chapel Royal
in the reign of King Charles the Second, was celebrated for a fine counter-tenor voice, and for his

skill in playing the lute. The king admiring his
singing, had formed a resolution of sending him
and another English musician to the Carnival at
Venice, in order to shew the Italians that there
were good voices in England. But as the person
intended to accompany him, expressed an unwill-
ingness to take the journey, the king desisted
from his purpose. Abell continued in the Chapel
till the Revolution, in 1688, when he was discharged on account of his adherence to the Romish
communion. After this he went abroad, and greatly
distinguished himself by singing in public in several of the towns of Germany. In some of these
his receipts were enormously great; but, having
little foresight, he lived profusely, and entered into
all the expenses of a man of quality. At intervals
he was often so much reduced as to be under the
necessity of travelling through whole provinces
with his lute slung at his back, subject to all the
hardships and miseries of a strolling musician.

In his rambles he got as far as Poland; and on
his arrival at Warsaw, the king sent for him to the
court. Abell made some excuse to avoid going;
but, on being told that he had every thing to fear
from the king's resentment, he apologised for his
behaviour, and received a command to attend the
king the next day. On his arrival at the palace
he was seated in a chair in the middle of a spacious
hall, and immediately drawn up to a great height.
Soon afterwards the king and his attendants ap-

peared in a gallery opposite to him, and at the
same time a number of bears were let loose below.
The king gave him the choice whether he would sing
or be lowered among the bears. Abell chose the
former, and he declared afterwards that he never
sang so well in his life as he did in his cage.

Having rambled abroad for many years, it
seems that he returned to England ; for in 1701,
he published in London a collection of *songs* in
several languages, with a dedication to King William, in which he expresses a grateful sense of
his Majesty's favours abroad, but in particular of
his clemency in permitting him to return to his
native country.   Mention is also made of a work
of Abell, entitled, " *Les Airs d'Abell pour le Con-*
" *cert du Duole;*" and in the fourth volume of
Pills to Purge Melancholy, there are two songs
elegantly set to music by him.

JOHN PLAYFORD, born in the year 1613, was
by trade a music-seller and stationer in the Temple, near the church-door.

In the year 1665, he published " *An Intro-*
" *duction to the Skill of Music,*" which appears
to have been in a great measure extracted from
Morley's Introduction, Butler's Principles of Music, and other works on the subject.   It is divided
into three books, the first containing the principles of music, with directions for singing ; the
second, instructions for the bass, treble, and te-

nor viol, and also for the treble violin, with lessons for each; and the third, the art of descant, or of composing music in parts. This work, which is written in a plain and familiar style, succeeded so well, that before the year 1684 it had passed into ten editions. Of these the last is fuller than any of the former, and is also much more correct : in the preface there are many curious and interesting particulars relative to music and musical professors.

Playford appears to have possessed the friendship of most of the eminent musicians of his time, and, in consequence, was the publisher of a great number of musical works between the years 1650 and 1685. He was a good judge of music, and was very industrious in his trade, contributing not a little to the improvement of the art of printing music from letter-press types, by the use of what he, in some of his publications, calls the *new-tied note*. It must be here remarked, that the musical characters formerly in use in this kingdom were printed from metal types; the notes were distinct from each other, and the quavers and semiquavers were signified only by single or double tails, without any connection whatever. Matthew Lock, in his " *Melothesia*,' printed in 1673, from copper-plates, joined them together; and from hence it is supposed that Playford took the hint, and transferred the same improvement to letter-press types.

His skill in music was not so great as to entitle him to the appellation of a master. He knew nothing of the theory of the science, but was well versed in the practice, and understood the rules of composition well enough to write good harmony. Of this he has given proof in a great number of *songs* in two, three, and four parts, printed in the " Musical Companion," and also in his " *Psalms and Hymns in solemn Music,*" in four parts ; and in the collection entitled the " *Whole Book of Psalms, with the usual Hymns* " *and Spiritual Songs, composed in three Parts.*"

Playford lived to the age of fourscore, dying, as is generally supposed, about the year 1693. He was succeeded in business by his son HENRY, who, in 1701, published what he called the Second Book of the " Pleasant Musical Companion, being a " choice Collection of Catches for three and four " Voices ; published chiefly for the Encourage- " ment of Musical Societies, which will speedily " be set up in all the Cities and Towns in Eng- " land." The design of this work was to give to the public a scheme for instituting musical clubs in different places, with certain rules mentioned in the preface, and to afford them also an useful collection of music. It seems to have had some success in promoting the practice of catch-singing in London and Oxford, but it does not appear to have had that extensive influence which the compiler expected.

It is conjectured that Henry Playford outlived his father but a few years, for we meet with no publication by him subsequent to the year 1710.

NICHOLAS STAGGINS was educated under his father, a musician, but of no great eminence, who lived in London. He had interest enough to procure the place of composer to King Charles the Second, and afterwards to be made master of the band of William the Third. In the year 1644, he was admitted to the degree of Doctor in Music; but through the favour of Dr. James, the vice-chancellor of Cambridge, the most difficult part of the exercise for his act was dispensed with. This partiality occasioned great murmurings; notwithstanding which the university thought proper also to appoint him their public professor of music.

There was at Cambridge no endowment for a musical professorship, so that the appointment must have been merely intended as honorary : by virtue of it, however, Dr. Tudway succeeded to the title on the death of Staggins, and it has been continued ever since.

In a collection of " Choice Ayres, Songs, and " Dialogues to sing to the Theorbo-Lute, or " Bass-Viol," published in 1675, there is a *song* composed by Dr. Staggins to the words, " While Alexis;" and there is another, " How " unhappy a lover am I," in Smith's " Musica " Antiqua." It does not appear that he ever composed *anthems* or *services*, or indeed any works that could render him justly eminent in his profession.

JOHN BLOW, MUS. DOC. a native of North Collingham, in the county of Nottingham, and born about the year 1648, was one of the first set of children of the Chapel Royal after the Restoration. He was originally a pupil of Captain Cook, then of Hingeston, and finally of Christopher Gibbons. In the year 1673, he was appointed a gentleman of the Chapel Royal, and, in the following year, master of the children. In 1685, he was appointed one of the king's chamber musicians, and composer to his Majesty; a title which Lock enjoyed before him, but which seems to have been at that time merely honorary. He was also almoner and master of the choristers of the Cathedral of St. Paul, but he resigned these in 1693, in favour of his pupil Jeremiah Clark. Blow was not a graduate of either university; but Dr. Sancroft, by virtue of his authority, as Archbishop of Canterbury, conferred on him the degree of Doctor in Music at Lambeth. On the decease of Purcell in 1695, he became organist of Westminster Abbey, and, four years afterwards, was appointed composer to his Majesty, with a salary of forty pounds a year, under an establishment the origin of which was as follows :

After the Revolution, and while the king was in

Flanders, Dr. Tillotson, then Dean of St. Paul's, happened one day, in the course of conversation, to mention to Mr. Gosling, the sub-dean, that he thought church music much on the decline, and observed that the queen had expressed the same opinion. Mr. Gosling's answer was, that he thought Dr. Blow and Mr. Purcell capable of composing at least as good anthems as the greater part of those which had been so much admired, if they had only encouragement to do it. The Dean mentioned this to the queen. She approved of the idea, and said that they should have an appointment for the purpose, with a salary of forty pounds a year,* adding that each would be expected to produce a new anthem on the first Sunday of his month of waiting. A lapse of several years took place before the appointment was made, and in the mean time, in 1695, Purcell died. The situation of second composer was left open till the year 1715, when Mr. John Weldon was admitted and sworn into that place.

Blow, even while a Chapel boy, was a composer of anthems, as appears from Clifford's Collection; and, on account of his great merit, was eminently distinguished by King Charles the Second.

In consequence of the success of the "Orpheus

---

* These salaries have been since augmented to seventy pounds per annum; making them equal to those of the gentlemen of the Chapel.

" Britannicus" of Purcell, Dr. Blow was induced,
in the year 1700, to publish a similar work, entitled,
" *Amphion Anglicus ; containing Compositions*
" *for one, two, three, and four Voices, with*
" *Accompanyments of Instrumental Music, and*
" *a Thorough-Bass figured for the Organ,*
" *Harpsichord, or Theorbo-Lute.*"

   In the epistle dedicatory to the Princess Ann of
Denmark, the author informs her Royal Highness,
that he was preparing to publish his church-ser-
vices and divine compositions. It seems, however,
that he did not live to carry this design into
effect. From some verses prefixed to this collection, it appears that a canon composed by Dr.
Blow had been much admired at Rome.

> " His Gloria Patri long ago reach'd Rome ;
> Sung and rever'd too in St. Peter's dome :
> A canon will outlive her jubilees to come."

   This is that fine canon to which Gloria Patri,
in Dr. Blow's Gamut Service, is set.* That it
should be sung at Rome may seem strange, yet it
is true : for some compositions of Blow and Purcell had been sent to Cardinal Howard, at his particular request, from Dr. Ralph Battell, sub-dean
of the Chapel Royal.

---

   * The whole service is printed in the first volume of Dr.
Boyce's Cathedral Music, and the canon alone in the editions
of Playford's Introduction subsequent to the year 1700.

Of the merits of the " Amphion Anglicus," little that is favourable can be said. In the songs for two, three, and four voices, the harmony is frequently inaccurate, and in expression, melody, and all the graces and elegancies of this species of vocal composition, they are evidently defective.

Dr. Blow set to music an *Ode on St. Cecilia's Day,* written by Mr. Oldham, and performed in 1684. It was published along with one of Purcell, that was performed in the preceding year. He likewise composed and published a *Set of Lessons for the Harpsichord or Spinnet,* and an ode on the death of Purcell, written by Mr. Dryden. There are also extant of his composition several hymns, printed in the " *Harmonia Sacra,*" and a great number of catches in the later editions of the " Musical Companion."

This celebrated musician died in the year 1708, and was interred in the north aisle of Westminster Abbey.

His serious compositions, several of which are inserted in Boyce's " Cathedral Music," in general deserve encomium, but in many respects are liable to censure. Dr. Burney has given us the following character of them : " Some of Dr. Blow's choral productions are doubtless in a very bold and grand style ; however, he is unequal, and frequently unhappy in his attempts at new harmony and modulation."—" Though there are strokes of pathetic, and subjects of fugue in Blow's works, that are admirable ; yet I have examined no one of them that appears wholly unexceptionable and free from confusion and crudities in the counterpoint. Of the two-part anthem with choruses, " Lord, how are they increased," the first movement is very plaintive and expressive ; but there are licences in the harmony which look and sound quite barbarous. In an anthem, " Turn " thee unto me, O Lord," printed by Henry Playford in the second collection of *Divine Harmony*, there are so many wanton violations of rule, particularly in the last chorus, that it would be endless to point them out ; but they seem such as no rule, authority, or effect can justify ; 7ths resolved into the 8ths ascending and descending ; 2ds treated with as little ceremony as 3ds. Indeed, I never saw so slovenly a score in print ; and it may, in general, be said of his *faults* in counterpoint, that there are *unaccounted millions* of them to be found in his works."

Specimens of the compositions of Dr. Blow may be found in Page's " Harmonia Sacra," Stevens's " Sacred Music," and Smith's " Musica " Antiqua."

WE are now arrived at a period in which it is necessary to give some account of the labours of a man who, it has justly been observed, is as much the boast of an Englishman in music, as Shakespeare in the drama, Milton in epic poetry, Locke in metaphysics, or Sir Isaac Newton in philosophy and mathematics.   This is

HENRY PURCELL, who was born in Westminster in the year 1658.   His father Henry, and his uncle Thomas Purcell, were both musicians, and gentlemen of the Chapel Royal at the restoration of King Charles the Second.

From whom he received his first instructions in music, cannot now be ascertained with any degree of certainty.   But his father dying in 1664, when he was no more than six years old, it is probable he was qualified for a chorister by Captain Cook, who was master of the children from the Restoration till the year 1672; for, as Purcell was appointed organist of Westminster Abbey at eighteen years of age, he must have been taught the elements of his art before his fourteenth year, at which time Pelham Humphrey (brought up in the Royal Chapel under Cook) was appointed his successor as master of the boys.   Purcell certainly continued to sing in the Chapel, and to receive lessons from Humphrey, till the breaking of his voice.   After this he received lessons in composition from Dr. Blow.

Purcell is said to have profited so much from his first lessons and his close application, as to have composed (even during the time of his being a singing boy in the chapel) many of those anthems which have been constantly sung in our cathedrals since.

At the age of eighteen he was appointed organist of Westminster Abbey; and, in 1682, six years afterwards, was advanced to one of the three places of organist of the Chapel Royal, on the death of Edward Low.

After this he produced so many admirable compositions for the church, but particularly for the chapel of which he was organist, that his fame was soon extended to the remotest parts of the kingdom. His anthems were eagerly procured, and heard with rapture wherever they were performed; nor was he suffered long to devote himself exclusively to the service of the church. Very early in life he was solicited to compose for the stage and the chamber. In both of these undertakings he was so superior to all his predecessors, that his compositions seemed to speak a new language; yet, however different it was from that to which the public had long been accustomed, it was universally understood. His songs seem to contain in them whatever the ear could wish, or the heart could feel.

The unlimited powers of his genius embraced every species of composition that was then known with equal felicity. In writing for the *church*, whether he adhered to the elaborate and learned style of his great predecessors, Tallis, Bird, and

Gibbons, in which no instrument is employed but the organ, and the several parts are constantly moving in fugue, imitation, or plain counterpoint; or (giving way to feeling and imagination) whether he adopted the new and more expressive style, of which he was himself one of the principal inventors, accompanying the voice parts with instruments, to enrich the harmony, and enforce the melody and meaning of the words, he manifested equal abilities and resources. In compositions for the *theatre*, though the colouring and effects of an orchestra were then but little known, yet, as he employed them more than his predecessors, and gave to the voice a melody more interesting and impassioned than during the last century had been heard in this country, or perhaps in Italy itself, he soon became the delight and darling of the nation: and, in the several species of *chamber music* which he attempted, whether sonatas for instruments, or odes, cantatas, songs, ballads, or catches, for the voice, he so far surpassed whatever our country had produced or imported before, that all other musical productions seem to have been instantly consigned to contempt or oblivion.

As many of his numerous compositions for the church are still retained and admired in the King's Chapel and in our cathedrals, we shall in this place insert, from Dr. Burney, a short examination of the chief of them.

His four-part anthems, " O God, thou art my

" God," must certainly have been one of his juvenile productions, before he had sufficiently refined his ear, or exercised his judgment; as there are many crude harmonies and false accents in it, which, in riper years, he would not have tolerated.

Of his six-part anthem, " O God, thou hast cast " us out," the first movement (in which there are many bold harmonies) is extremely elaborate, but spirited and pleasing. The verse, " O, be thou " our help," is not only full of new and fine effects, but touching.

The first movement of his full anthem in eight parts, " O Lord God of Hosts," is a noble composition, *alla Palestrina,* in which all the laws of fugue upon two, and sometimes more subjects, are preserved inviolable; the harmony, though bold, is in general chaste, and the effect of the whole spirited and majestic. The second movement is extremely pathetic and expressive; but, both in that and the last movement, he seems trying experiments in harmony; and, in hazarding new combinations, he now and then gives the ear more pain than pleasure.

The two-part anthem, " Thy way, O God, is " holy," continues to be excellent music still in the slow movements; the quick movements, however, are somewhat *passes,* and the melody to these words, " The air thundered," &c. seems too light and dramatic for the church at any period.

The three-part anthem, " Be merciful unto me,

" O God," is throughout admirable; but the opening of this anthem, and the last movement in C natural, are in melody, harmony, and modulation, truly *divine music*.

The complete service of Purcell in B flat, printed by Boyce, is a most agreeable and excellent piece of counterpoint, of which the modulation frequently stimulates to attention by unexpected transitions, yet of so sober a kind as not to give the ear the least uneasiness till we come to the bottom of the sixth page, when some crudities of the sharp 3d, with the flat 6th and flat 3d, 4th, and 5th, occur; which it is to be hoped, in spite of our reverence for Purcell, the organists of our cathedrals scruple not to change for better harmony.

The *Benedictus*, as well as the *Te Deum*, and all the rest of the service, must be extremely pleasing in other respects to every ear sensible to harmony. The words are, in general, accented with great accuracy; and the few points of imitation are fragments of agreeable melody. Notwithstanding the exceptionable passages, the abilities of Purcell as a profound contrapuntist appear, upon the whole, perhaps more in the course of this service than elsewhere; as he has manifested deep study and meditation in a species of writing to which it was not likely that his creative and impetuous genius would submit, having had the patience, as well as abilities, to enrich it with no less than four different canons of the most difficult construction, as of 2, 3, and 4 in one, by inversion.

Besides the whole service, with three full and six verse anthems in Dr. Boyce's Collection, there are nine verse and full anthems, wholly different, still sung in the Cathedral at York; and in Dr. Tudway's Collection in the British Museum, there are, besides a whole service in B flat, different from that in Boyce, eight full and verse anthems, different from all the rest; four of which were composed for the Chapel Royal of Charles the Second, and are accompanied with instruments. And still, exclusive of these and the hymns printed in the two books of *Harmonia Sacra*, in a manuscript bequeathed to Christ-Church College, Oxford, by Dr. Aldrich, there are two motets and a *Gloria Patri* for four and five voices in Latin, with seven psalms and hymns for three and four voices, by our fertile and diligent composer, that have all their peculiar merit, but of which some may, without hyperbole, be said to reach the true sublime of sacred music.

To enter into a minute examination of these, would extend this article to too great a length; we shall, therefore, finish our account of his choral productions by a few remarks on his *Te Deum* and *Jubilate*, composed for St. Cecilia's day, 1694.

The custom, since the death of Purcell, of opening the *Te Deum* with an overture or symphony, which Handel and Graun have done so powerfully, renders the beginning of our countryman's composition somewhat abrupt, meagre, and inferior in dignity to the subject ; there is, however, a stroke of genius, boldness, and effect, in the four last bars of the first line, where the discords are struck by the trumpets, and resolved by the violins, which marks the great musician.

There is likewise a grandeur in the movement, and richness in the harmony of the chorus, " *All,* " *all the earth doth worship thee;*" and the distribution of the parts, in ascending after each other by the harmonic intervals of the perfect chord, has a beautiful effect. But it seems as if *all* the composers of this hymn had mistaken the cry of *joy* for that of *sorrow,* in setting " *To thee all* " *angels cry aloud.*" Here Purcell, as well as Handel, has changed the key from major to minor, and, in admirable modulation in itself, has given the movement a pathetic expression, which, in reading and considering the idea of that eternal laud and praise which the hierarchies and heavenly hosts offer up to the throne of God, it seems not to require.

The cherubin and seraphin singing in duo, and the universal acclamation of *holy,* are certainly most happily designed, and expressed with almost the energy of inspiration. The transient state of melody has, however, rendered this verse, " The glorious company of the apostles praise "thee," and, indeed, most of the solo parts, somewhat rude and inelegant; and it is chiefly in the choruses and disposition of the whole work, that Purcell is still admirable, and will continue so among Englishmen as long as the present language of this hymn shall remain intelligible.

"Also the Holy Ghost the Comforter," is a delightful fragment of harmony and melody, which time can never injure; and "Thou art the King "of glory," in double fugue, is grand and masterly.

"When thou tookest upon thee," and "When "thou hadst overcome the sharpness of death," have permanent beauties of melody, contrivance, and expression, that are wholly out of the reach of fashion. This praise, however, does not include the division upon the word *all*. Through the numberless mistakes of a bad copy,* very great beauties are manifest in looking over the score, from "Thou sittest at the right hand of God," to "Ever, world without end." We shall only instance the division on the word *glory;* indeed the whole movement of "O Lord, save thy people," in which the sound is truly an echo to the sense, and in the expression of the words, "Lift them "up for ever," is admirable.

---

* No composition of merit was ever worse engraved than this *Te Deum:* wrong notes, wrong cliffs, confusion and blunders of all kinds, disgrace every plate from the beginning to the end, which, without skill in composition, a reader would often ascribe to the author of the work.

The whole verse, " Vouchsafe, O Lord, to " keep us this day without sin," to " As our " trust is in thee," is so incorrectly printed, that it is scarcely possible to know the author's design with respect to harmony; much expression is, however, discoverable in the voice part, and the supplication at the words, " Have mercy upon us," is truly pathetic. The short fugues, " Let me never be con- " founded," though regular, might have been written by a man of less genius than Purcell.

The beginning of the *Jubilate* is well calculated to display a fine performer ; and therefore the military cast which is given to the whole air by pointed notes may be proper ; " But I must own," says Dr. Burney, " that I never was partial to that style of movement ; yet Purcell and all his contemporaries in England were so much of a different opinion, that it prevails too much in all their works."

" Be ye sure that the Lord he is God," if sung with taste and feeling, will always be good music, and so will the next movement, as long ss the art of music shall be had in reverence.

In the verse, " For the Lord is gracious," Purcell has displayed his uncommon powers of expression, particularly at " His mercy is everlasting," which seems exquisite composition. The *Gloria Patri, alla Palestrina*, but more animated, perhaps, than any movement that Palestrina ever composed, is full of such science and contrivance as musicians can alone properly estimate; but the general effect of the whole is so glorious and sublime, as must charm into rapture the most ignorant, as well as the most learned hearer.

This admirable composition was constantly performed at St. Paul's Church on the feast of the sons of the clergy, from the decease of the author, in 1695, till the year 1713, when Handel's *Te Deum* for the peace of Utrecht was produced by order of Queen Anne. From this period till 1743, when his second *Te Deum* for the battle of Dettingen was composed, they seem to have been alternately performed. But since that time Purcell's composition has been but seldom adopted, even at the triennial meetings of the three choirs of Hereford, Worcester, and Gloucester. Handel's superior knowledge and use of instruments, and more polished melody, and indeed the novelty of his productions, which, *cæteris paribus*, will always turn the public scale, took such full possession of the nation's favour, that Purcell's *Te Deum* is only now performed occasionally as an antique curiosity, even in the country.

Our author's *theatrical compositions*, if we take into consideration the number and excellence of his productions for the church, and the shortness of his life, will surprise by their multiplicity. The chief part of his instrumental music for the playhouse is included in a publication that appeared two years after his decease, under the title

of " *A Collection of Ayres composed for the*
" *Theatre and on other Occasions, by the late Mr.*
" *Henry Purcell. London, printed for Frances*
" *Purcell, Executrix of the Author,* 1697."
These airs are in four parts, for two violins, tenor
and bass, and were played as overtures and act-
tunes, till they were superseded by Handel's haut-
bois concertos.

Purcell seems to have composed introductory
and *entracte* music to most of the plays that were
brought on the stage during his time. The above-
mentioned publication contains his music to the
following dramas :

Abelazor, performed in 1677, when he was
only nineteen years of age. The music consists of
an overture and eight airs or tunes.

The virtuous Wife, 1680. Overture and seven
airs.

Indian Queen. The first movement of this
overture is equal to any of Handel's. There are
likewise two or three trumpet tunes, well calculated for that instrument, and a rondeau at the
end, which would now seem new, if played in a
concert by a good band.

Dioclesian, or the Prophetess, 1690. The
music of this opera consists of an overture of
two movements; the first excellent, in the style of
Lulli, and afterwards of Handel with better
fugues; *preludio,* accompaniment to a song ;

trumpet tune, air, hornpipe, country dance, and *canaries.**

King Arthur, 1691. Overture and twelve tunes.

Amphitrion, 1691. Overture and eight tunes.

Gordion Knot untied, 1691. Overture and seven tunes.

Distressed Innocence, or the Princess of Persia, 1691. Overture and seven tunes, all proofs of the author's original genius.

The Fairy Queen, 1692. Two overtures and sixteen tunes of different kinds. No. 12, an air, 4 in 2, is a very curious canon on two subjects ; the first treble and bass performing one, and the second and tenor the other. There is as much accent and spirit in this composition, as if it were in free counterpoint.

The Old Bachelor, 1693. Overture and eight tunes.

The Married Beau, 1694. Overture and eight tunes, among which is a very agreeable air for the trumpet, a march, and a hornpipe that are characteristic. This last is much in the style of a Spanish *fandango*.

The Double-Dealer, 1694. Overture and ten tunes. No. 6 and 9 are pretty and curious.

Bonduca, 1695. Overture and eight tunes,

---

* A French term for a rapid dance in jig time.

including *Britons, strike home,* and *To arms,* in four parts.

These are the contents of this posthumous publication ; but besides the music for these dramas, he composed overtures, act-tunes, and songs for *Timon of Athens,* 1678; for *Theodosius, or the Force of Love,* 1680 ; for Dryden's *Tempest,* 1690 ; and for *Don Quixote,* 1694.

Very few of Purcell's single songs seem to have been printed during his life. He published the music to a masque sung in the tragedy of Œdipus when it was revived in 1692; and " *A Musi-* " *cal Entertainment, performed November 22d,* " *1683, on St. Cecilia's day,*" printed in score by John Playford.

There are several of his songs in Playford's Collection entitled, " The Theatre of Music, 1687, " fourth and last Book ;" and though these are not in his best manner, they are more original and interesting than the rest. Among them, " A new " Song to a Scotch tune," by our author, seems more pleasing and less stolen than any imitation of the national melody of the northern inhabitants of this island that has been since produced. In the same collection there is an admirable piece of recitative in a truly grand style, " Amidst the " shades."

But the collection of his secular vocal music, which did him the greatest honour, and long rendered his name dear to the British nation, was published by his widow two years after his decease, under the title of " *Orpheus Britannicus.*" Here were treasured up the songs from which the natives of this island received their first great delight and impression from the vocal music of a *single voice.* Before that period we had cultivated madrigals and songs in parts with diligence and success ; but in all single songs, till those of Purcell appeared, the chief effects were produced from the words, not the melody. For the airs, till that time, were in general as unformed and misshapen, as if they had been made of notes scattered about by chance. Exclusive admirers of modern symmetry and elegance may call Purcell's taste barbarous ; yet, in spite of superior cultivation and refinement, in spite of all the vicissitudes of fashion, through all his rudeness and barbarism, original genius, feeling, and passion, are, and ever will be discoverable in his works by candid and competent judges of the art.

There are few songs in the Orpheus Britannicus but what contain some characteristic mark of the author's great and original genius. The following are such as seem to merit particular attention.

" Celia has a thousand charms ;" the first movement of this song, like many of those of Purcell, seems only *recitative* embellished with the fashionabe flourishes of the times, which are now become somewhat antiquated. The second movement, however, is plaintive and graceful ; and at, " I

" should my wretched, wretched fate deplore," is still new and pathetic.

" You twice ten hundred deities," opens with what is almost the best piece of recitative in our language. The words are admirably expressed throughout by modulation as well as melody ; and there is a propriety in the changes of movement, which does as much honour to Purcell's judgment, as the whole composition does to his genius.

The music of King Arthur has since his time been revived, well performed, and printed. The duet, " Two daughters of this aged stream," and " Fairest isle, all isles excelling," contain not a single passage that the best composers of the present times, if it presented itself to their imagination, would reject. The dialogue in the *Prophetess*, " Tell me why my charming Fair," is the most pleasing and ingenious of all the compositions of the kind, which the rage of fashion produced during fifty years. The first part of " O lead me " to some peaceful gloom," is truly elegant and pathetic.

" From rosy bowers," is said to have been set during his last sickness, and few of his productions are so elevated, so pleasing, so expressive, and throughout so perfect as this.

" When Mira sings," is a duet that will ever be captivating as long as the words remain intelligible ; of which he has augmented the force, particularly at the end, by notes the most select and expressive that the musical scale can furnish.

" Lost is my quiet," is another duet which still lives; and " Celebrate this festival," a birth-day song for Queen Mary, which is graceful and pleasing through all its old-fashioned thoughts and embellishments. " I'll sail upon the dog-star," has all the fire of Handel's prime.

" Mad Bess," is a song so much celebrated, that it needs no panegyric.

" 'Tis Nature's voice," is an enigmatical song, seemingly on music ; in which Purcell has crowded all the fashionable passages of taste and vocal difficulty of the times.

" Blow, Boreas, blow," was formerly in great favour among the admirers of Purcell ; but this seems now more superannuated than any of his popular songs.

" Let Cæsar and Urania live," was a duet in a birth-day ode, written during the reign of William and Mary, that continued long in favour. It is built on a *ground-bass* of only two bars, which are invariably repeated to different passages of the voice parts, that are in harmony with it throughout the movement. The latter part of this duet is extremely beautiful, and does not seem at all to have suffered from the voluntary restraint under which the composer laboured.

" I attempt from love's sickness," is an elegant little ballad, which, though it has been many years dead, would soon be recalled into existence and fashion by the voice of some favourite singer, who should think it worth animation.

" Let the dreadful engines," is the last song in the first volume of the *Orpheus Britannicus*, of which, though both the words and music of the first movement are wild and bombastic, yet the second and last discover a genius for the graceful comic, as well as the tender and sublime style of composition ; and there are several passages in this cantata sufficiently gay and new for a modern *burletta*.

In 1702, a second and more correct edition of the first volume of this work was published, with more than thirty songs that were not in the first impression ; but in order to make room for which, some of the former were omitted. The same year was likewise published a second volume of *Orpheus Britannicus*, by Henry Playford.

The song in this second volume beginning, " Ah ! cruel nymph," has great ingenuity in the first movement, and grace in the second ; and the next air, " Crown the altar," seems the most pleasing of any that Purcell has composed on a *ground-bass*. " May the god of wit inspire," for three voices, is natural and pleasing, and the *echoes* in the second part are very ingeniously contrived.

" Thus the gloomy world," accompanied with a trumpet and violin alternately, is masterly, and

well designed to display the truest and most brilliant notes of the trumpet.

Those who can relish good music of every age
and country, and have no exclusive partiality to in-
dividuals of either, will find amusement in the
performance or perusal of Purcell's *Four Seasons*,
in the *Fairy Queen*, which comprehend merit of
various kinds.

" To arms, to arms," is an admirable military
song, accompanied by a trumpet, which is so confined an instrument, that nearly the same passages
must be used in all ages, so that time has robbed
this song of but little of its novelty.   Indeed the
divisions of this air have been revived of late years,
and are now as fashionable in frivolous and unmeaning melody as ever.

There is a composition in Purcell's *Bonduca*, in
which he has anticipated a species of dramatic
music that has been thought of later invention;
the words are, " Hear, ye gods of Britain," which
he has set in an *accompanied recitative, à tempo*
or *ario parlante*.   The beginning, however, with
the bass *à pedale*, has the true characteristic of
recitative.   Afterwards, when the bass is put in
motion, the whole has the properties of an air,
ingeniously and spiritedly accompanied by two
violins and a bass.   Besides the true dramatic
cast of this composition, there are new harmonies
hazarded which have a very fine effect.

The song on St. Cecilia's day, 1692, has several

passages of which Handel made use, many years after, in his Allegro and Penseroso, and elsewhere.

" Genius of England," was long the favourite song of our theatres, though its passages are more common and vulgar now than those of any other of Purcell's capital songs.

It is said that Queen Mary, having expressed herself warmly in favour of the old Scots tune, " Cold and raw the wind doth blow," Purcell made it the perpetual bass to an air in the next birthday ode, 1692, beginning, "May her blest example " chase;" a piece of pleasantry which is likewise said to have been occasioned by her asking for this tune after Mr. Gostling, one of the gentlemen of the Royal Chapel, and the celebrated Mrs. Arabella Hunt, (with Purcell to accompany them on the harpsichord), had exerted all their talents and abilities to amuse so great a personage with compositions which they mistakenly thought of a superior class.

In the duet, " I spy Celia," the last we shall notice in the *Orpheus Britannicus,* the pleasing melody and harmony, the ingenious design, and variety of movement, will afford considerable entertainment to all the admirers of Purcell's compositions.

In *Bonduca,* the first song of the second act, which is for a ground-bass, and terminated by a chorus, has great merit in the richness of the harmony and the ingenuity of the accompaniment. The ballad air to "What shall I do to "shew how much I love her," became a favourite in the Beggar's Opera, where it was sung to the words, "Virgins are like the fair flower." "Sound, Fame, thy brazen trumpet," was, when composed, an excellent air for the display of a fine counter-tenor voice. The trio, "Triumph, "victorious Love," is free and masterly; yet there was a monotonous effect from the constant repetition of the same notes in the under part, which no variation of the harmony, even with Purcell's resources, can prevent.

The *sonatas* of Purcell, in which he himself says, he has endeavoured to imitate the style of the Italian masters, at the head of whom stood at that time Bassani and Torelli (Corelli's works not being then known in England), though they indicate no great knowledge of the bow or genius of the instrument, yet they are infinitely superior in fancy, modulation, design, and contrivance, to all the music of the kind anterior to that of Corelli.

" As to his models in vocal music," says Dr. Burney, " I think I can perceive obligations which he had to Carissimi in the best of his recitatives, and to Lully in the worst; it manifestly appears that he was fond of Stradella's *manner* of writing, though he does not seem to have pillaged his passages."

We must not quit his vocal music without an

honourable and grateful memorial of his CATCHES, ROUNDS, and GLEES, of which the humour, ingenuity, and melody, were so congenial with the national taste, as to render them almost the sole productions of that facetious kind which were in general use for near fourscore years : and though the countenance and premiums bestowed of late years upon this species of composition, as well as modern refinements in melody and performance, have given birth to many *glees* of a more elegant, graceful, and exalted kind than any which Purcell produced ; yet he seems hardly ever to have been equalled in the wit, pleasantry, and contrivance of his *catches*.

The following is an index to a folio volume of Purcell's compositions, in a collection of original manuscripts in his own hand-writing, now in the possession of his Majesty.

Anthems, with Symphonies and Instrumental Parts.

" It is a good thing," &c. in four vocal parts, with a symphony or prelude for two violins and bass. " O praise God in his holiness," with an overture or symphony, one violin and bass accompaniment to the first movement, and two violins and bass to the second, which is for eight voices. " Awake, put on thy strength," symphony, ritornels, solo verse, and chorus. " In thee, O Lord," with ditto. " The Lord is my light," &c. " I " was glad." " My heart is fixed on God," ri-

tornels. " Praise the Lord, O my soul," symphony, and for six voices, *à due cori.* " Rejoice
" in the Lord alway," for three voices with symphonies. " Why do the heathen so furiously
" rage," ditto. " Unto thee will I cry," ditto,
two violins. " I will give thanks," ditto, five
voices. One of the anthems performed at the coronation of King James the Second, two violins,
bass, and eight voices; an elaborate and fine composition. " O sing unto the Lord," symphony
and chorus for four and five voices, with two
violins and bass accompaniment; a long and
elaborate work. " Praise the Lord, O my soul,"
symphony for two violins and bass, solo verses
and duets.

Odes and Miscellaneous Songs.

A welcome song, in the year 1681, for the king;
symphony in four parts, solo verses, and chorus:
" Swifter Isis, swifter flow." A welcome song
for his Royal Highness, at his return from Scotland,
in the year 1680; symphony in four parts, solo
verses, trios, and chorus, *à* 4: " What shall be
" done in behalf of this man." A welcome song
for his Majesty at his return from Newmarket,
October 21, 1682: " The summer's absence un-
" concerned we bear," upon the same model as
the preceding compositions. " How pleasant in
" this flow'ry plain," a pastoral song, with a
symphony for two flutes and a bass, one and two
voices with a chorus, the last movement of which

is left unfinished. "Hark! how the wild musi-
" cians sing," another pastoral for three voices,
with two violins and bass accompaniment and
chorus. "Hark! Damon, what music's this?"
of the same kind—pastoral. "Above the tumults
" of a busy state," another pastoral duet. Ninth
ode of Horace imitated, in a dialogue between
the poet and Lydia: "While you for me alone
" had charms." Dialogue between Charon and
Orpheus;* a cantata for one and two voices. The
Epicure: "Underneath this myrtle shade," *à* 2.
The Concealment: "No, to what purpose should
" I speak?" a cantata with chorus. Job's Curse:
" Let the night perish." "Amidst the shades
" and cool refreshing streams," a song. Duet or
two-part song: "See where she sits, and in what
" comely wise," with two violins and bass; excellent. A song that was performed to Prince
George upon his marriage with the Lady Ann:
" From hardy climes and dangerous toils of
" war;" a long and capital production. Mr.
Cowley's Complaint: "In the deep vision's in-
" tellectual scene;" recitatives, airs, and chorus. Song out of Mr. Herbert: "With sick
" and famish'd eyes;" a lamentation. The welcome song performed to his Majesty in the year
1683; symphonies and five verses: "Fly, bold
" rebellion;" solo verses and finale for seven
voices. A Latin song made upon St. Cecilia:
" *Laudate Ceciliam.*" "Oh, oh, what a scene

" does entertain my sight ;" a two-part song.
" Though my mistress be fair ;" ditto. A sere-
nading song : " Sylvia, thou brighter eye of night ;"
a two-part song. " Go tell Aminta, gentle swain,"
for two voices. The welcome song performed to
his Majesty in the year 1684 : " From those se-
" rene and rapt'rous joys ;" a long composition,
consisting of many different airs and choruses.
Song on a ground : " Cease, anxious world, your
" fruitless pain." The Rich Rival, out of Mr.
Cowley : " They say you're angry ;" a kind of
cantata for one voice. " When Tucer from his
" father fled ;" a two-part song in Orpheus Britannicus. Sighs for our late sovereign King
Charles the Second : " If prayers and tears," &c.
printed. " In some kind dream upon her slum-
" bers steal ;" a two-part song. The thirty-fourth
chapter of Isaiah, paraphrased by Mr. Cowley :
" Awake, awake, and with attention hear ;" for
one voice. Welcome song, 1685 : " Why are all
" the Muses mute ?" consisting of many airs and
choruses. Two-part song, the words by Mr.
Cowley : " Here, here's to thee, Dick." Welcome
song, 1688, consisting of a symphony and many
airs and choruses, the largest work in the volume :
" Ye tuneful Muses, raise your heads." " If ever
" I more riches did desire ;" a long ode, with
airs, duets, and choruses. Anacreon's Defeat :
" This poet sings the Trojan wars," a single song.
Welcome song, 1687 : " Sound the trumpet, beat

" the drum," a very long composition. A Latin hymn for two voices : " *Crucia in hac flamma.*' A song performed at Mr. Maidwell's, a school-master, on the 5th of August, 1689 : " Celestial Muse " did the gods inspire." An overture and several airs and choruses. Birth-day ode for King William, a long symphony, airs, and choruses : " How does the glorious day appear." Another, " Of old when heroes thought it base." Another, " The bashful Thames for beauty so re-" nowned." " The pale and the purple rose." And, " In each truck," &c. two-part song, printed. " Sound the trumpet, beat the drum ;" another ode to King William, to which he sets his name and date, " Mr. H. Purcell, 1690." The beginning of an ode for Queen Mary, in the absence of King William, long symphony. " Arise, " my Muse, and to the tuneful lyre ;" left unfinished.

List of Purcell's Church Music.

In *Boyce's Collection.* Complete service in B flat. Full anthems : " O God, thou art my God." " O God, thou hast cast." " O Lord God of " hosts." Verse anthems : " Thy way, O God." " Be merciful." " Behold, I bring you glad " tidings." " They that go down to the sea in " ships." " Thy word is a lanthorn." " O " give thanks."

In use at York Cathedral : " Peace be within " thy walls." " Be merciful." " Lord, how

" long."   " Blessed are they."   " I was glad
" when."   " The way of God."   " O be joyful."
" Blessed is he."   " Blessed is the man."

In Dr. Tudway's Collection, British Museum :
Whole service in B flat, different from Boyce's,
with symphonies and ritornels.   " My beloved
" spake."   " My song shall be alway."   " Re-
" joice in the Lord alway."   (Bell anthem)
" Praise the Lord, O my soul."   Full anthems :
" Save me, O God."   " Thou knowest, Lord,"
for Queen Mary's funeral.   Verse anthems : " We
" give thanks."   " Behold I bring you."

In Dr. Aldrich's MS. Christ-Church College,
Oxon : A Latin *Gloria Patri*, in five parts. Two
Latin psalms, " *Jehovah, quam multi sunt beati*
" *omnes qui timent Dominum !*" and seven hymns
and psalms for three and four voices. Ten different compositions. *Te Deum.* Two whole services. Thirty-six psalms, hymns, and anthems,
besides what are in the *Harmonia Sacra.*

Having said so much of Purcell's extensive
genius and talents, it is but fair that we should
now speak of his defects.   There are in his works
grand designs and masterly strokes of composition, yet his melody frequently wants symmetry
and grace ; and by writing on a given bass,
which forced him to submit to a crude, and sometimes a licentious and unwarrantable use of pass-
ing-notes, his harmony is not always so pure as
it ought to be.   However, in all his music that

has been printed, except his compositions for the church, of which Dr. Boyce superintended the impression, the errors of the press are innumerable, and these must not be charged to his account.

An absurd custom prevailed in Purcell's time, which he carried to greater excess, perhaps, than any other composer, of repeating a word of one or two syllables an unlimited number of times, for the sake of the melody, and sometimes before the whole sentence has been heard.

He was so little acquainted with the powers of the violin, that there is scarcely a becoming passage for that instrument in any one of his works ; the symphonies and ritornels to his anthems and songs being equally deficient in force, invention, and effect ; and though his sonatas contain many ingenious, and, at the time they were composed, many new traits of melody and modulation ; yet, if they are compared with the productions of his contemporary Corelli, they will be called barbarous.

If Purcell, by travelling or by *living longer* at home, had heard the great instrumental performers, as well as great singers, that arrived in this country soon after his decease, and had had such to compose for, his productions would have been more regular, elegant, and graceful ; and he would certainly have set *English words* better than it was possible for any foreigner to do to our feelings, however great his genius, or excellent, in other respects, his productions. But Purcell, like his successor Arne, and others who have composed for the playhouse, had always an inferior band to the Italian opera composers, as well as inferior singers and an inferior audience to write for.

Music was manifestly on the decline in England during the seventeenth century, until it was revived and invigorated by Purcell, whose genius, though less cultivated and polished, was equal to that of the greatest masters on the Continent; and though his dramatic style and recitative were formed in a great measure on French models, there is a latent power and force in his expression of English words, whatever be the subject, that will make an unprejudiced native of this island feel more than all the elegance, grace, and refinement of modern music, less happily applied, can do. And this pleasure is communicated to us, not by the symmetry or rhythm of modern melody, but by his having fortified, lengthened, and tuned the true accents of our mother-tongue—those notes of passion which an inhabitant of this island would breathe in such situations as the words he has set describe; and these indigenous expressions of passion Purcell had the power to enforce by the energy of modulation, which, on some occasions, was bold, affecting, and sublime.

It has been extremely unfortunate for our national taste and our national honour, that Orlando Gibbons, Pelham Humphrey, and Henry Purcell, our three best composers during the seventeenth century, were not blessed with sufficient longevity for their genius to expand in all its branches, or to form a school which would have enabled us to proceed in the cultivation of music without foreign assistance.

Orlando Gibbons died, in 1625, at the age of forty-four ;

Pelham Humphrey died, in 1674, at twenty-seven ;

And Henry Purcell died, in 1605, at thirty-seven.

If a parallel were to be drawn, says Dr. Burney, between Purcell and any popular composer of a different country, reasons might be assigned for supposing him superior to every great and favourite contemporary musician in Europe.

Carissimi and Stradella, if more polished in their style, were certainly less varied, and knew still less of instruments than our countryman. They had both, perhaps, more grace and regularity, but infinitely less passion and fire.

The elder Scarlatti was more *recherché* and learned, but never so natural and affecting.

In Germany, if Keiser, during an active and much longer life, surpassed in the number and excellence of his dramatic compositions, his productions for the church, could they be found, would, I believe, bear no comparison.

Lulli, blest likewise with superior longevity,
composed also more operas than Purcell, and was
the idol of the nation for which he laboured; but
though his overtures long served as models, even
to Purcell, as well as to the composers of all the
rest of Europe, and his music was performed by
better singers and a more numerous band, supported by the patronage of a court, and all the
splendour of ingenious and costly exhibition ; it is
easy to see that even his theatrical works are more
manierées, monotonous, and uninteresting in themselves, than those of Purcell : but in relinquishing
the stage, and stepping on holy ground, we should
have found, even in France, during all his glory,
and the enthusiasm he raised, none of his votaries
who would attempt to put his sacred music in comparison with that of our countryman.

Rameau, the successor of Lulli in court and
popular favour, and who had more learning and
theoretical knowledge in the art than perhaps any
practical musician of modern times ; yet, in pathos
and expression of words and the passions, he was
Purcell's inferior, even upon the stage ; and in the
church he had no claim whatever to celebrity.

Handel, who flourished in a less barbarous age
for his art, has been acknowledged his superior in
many particulars; but in none more than the art
and grandeur of his choruses, the harmony and
texture of his organ fugues, as well as his great
style of playing that instrument; the majesty of

his hautboy and grand concertos, the ingenuity of the accompaniments to his songs and choruses, and even in the general melody of the airs themselves ; yet in the accent, passion, and expression of *English words*, " the vocal music of Purcell is sometimes, to my feelings," says Dr. Burney, " as superior to Handel's as an original poem is to a translation."

DANIEL PURCELL was a brother of Henry, and derived from him most of that little reputation which, as a musician, he obtained. He was, for some time, organist of Magdalen College, Oxford, and afterwards of St. Andrew's Church in Holborn. He offered himself a candidate for a prize payable out of a sum of two hundred pounds raised by a party of the nobility, to be given to the four best composers of music to Mr. Congreve's poem, the " Judgment of Paris." Weldon and Eccles obtained the two highest prizes, and he is supposed to have succeeded in one of the others.

Daniel Purcell composed the music to an opera called, " *Brutus of Alba, or Augusta's Triumph*," written by George Powell the comedian, and performed, in 1697, at the theatre in Dorset Garden ; and to another entitled, " The Grove, or Love's " Paradise." The latter, which was his chef-d'œuvre, appears to have been written either at Southwick, in Hants, the seat of Philip Norton, Esq. where, during the summer time, the friends of that gentleman were frequently entertained with dramatic representations; or else at the Grange, in the same county, the residence of his principal friend and patron, Anthony Henley, Esq. He was also the composer of many of the songs for different plays, several of which are inserted in the Pills to Purge Melancholy. These have in general but little to recommend them, and their author is at this day better known for his puns, with which the old jest-books abound, than for his musical compositions.

THE REV. DR. HENRY ALDRICH was an eminent scholar and an excellent divine; he was born in Westminster in the year 1647, and educated at Westminster school, under the famous Dr. Busby. In 1662, he was admitted a student on the foundation of Christ-Church College, Oxford; and he took his degree of Master of Arts in April, 1669. Entering, not long afterwards, into holy orders, he distinguished himself by his great proficiency in various branches of learning, and became a celebrated tutor in the college. On the 15th of February, 1681, he was installed a canon of Christ-Church, and, in May following, accumulated the degrees of Bachelor and Doctor in Divinity. In the controversy with the papists, in the reign of King James the Second, he bore a considerable share, and, by that means, rendered his merit so conspicious, that when, at the Revolution, Massy,

the popish Dean of Christ-Church, fled from the
country, his deanery was conferred on Dr. Aldrich.
In this eminent station he presided with a dignity
peculiar to his person and character, behaving with
great integrity and uprightness, attending assiduously to the interests of his college and to the
welfare of those under his care ; and promoting,
to the utmost of his abilities, learning, religion,
and virtue.

The learning of Dr. Aldrich, and his knowledge
of polite literature, were evinced by his numerous
publications ; but particularly by his editions of
several of the Greek Classics.   His skill in archi-
tecture and music was so great, that his excellence
in either of those sciences would alone have rendered him famous to posterity.   The three sides of
the quadrangle of Christ-Church College, called
Peck-Water Square, were designed by him, as
were also the Chapel of Trinity College, and the
Church of All-Saints in the High Street.

Amidst his variety of learned pursuits, and the
cares to which he was subjected in the government of his college, Dr. Aldrich found leisure to
study and cultivate, to a great extent, the science
of music, and that branch of it, in particular,
which related to his profession and office.   To this
end he made a noble collection of church music,
consisting of the works of Palestrina, Carissimi,
Vittoria, and other Italians, and, by adapting, with

great judgment, English words to many of their best motets, enriched the stores of our church, and, in some degree, made their works our own.

With a view to the advancement of music, and honour of its professors, Dr. Aldrich had formed the design of writing a History of Music, but he did not live to complete it. The materials from which he proposed to compile it, are yet extant in the library of his own college. From these it appears that he had carefully noted down every thing he had met with on the subject of music and musicians ; but no part of them had been put into any kind of form.

His abilities as a musician rank him among the first masters of the science. He composed many *services* for the church, which are well known, as are also near twenty of his *anthems.*

In the " Pleasant Musical Companion," printed in 1736, there are two of his *catches,* the one, " Hark, the bonny Christ-Church bells ;" the other entitled " A smoaking Catch," to be sung by four men smoking their pipes, which is not more difficult to sing than it is diverting to hear.

The Doctor himself possessed such an excessive love of smoking, that it became an entertaining subject of discourse in the university, and the following, among other stories, is related concerning it. A student of the college once finding it difficult to persuade a young gentleman, his chum, of the truth of this fact, laid him a wager that the Dean was smoking at that instant, ten o'clock in the morning. Away went the student to the deanery, where, on admission to the Dean in his study, he related to him the strange occasion of his visit. To this the Dean replied, in perfect good humour, "You see you have lost your wager, for I am not smoking, but filling my pipe."

That he was a lover of mirth and pleasantry may be inferred from the above, and from numberless other particulars which have been related of him. The following stanzas, of his composition, are a version of the well-known song, "A soldier and a " sailor," and exhibit traits of that singular vein of humour which he possessed in a very eminent degree:

> Miles et Navigator,
> Sartor et Arator,
> Jamdudum litigabant
> De pulchrâ quam amabant,
>   Nomen cui est Joanna.

> Jam tempus consummatum
> Ex quo determinatum
> Se non vexatum iri
> Præ desiderio viri,
>   Nec pernoctare solam.

> Miles dejerabat,
> Hanc præda plus amabat,
> Ostendens cicatrices,
> Quas æstimat felices
>   Dum vindicavit eam.

Sartor ait, Ne sis dura,
Mihi longa est mensura.
Instat æris fabricator,
Ut olla sarciatur,
   Rimaque obstipetur.

Dum hi tres altercantur,
Nauta vigilanter
Et calide moratur,
Dum prælium ordiatur,
   Ut agat suam rem.

Perinde ac speratur,
Deinceps compugnatur,
Et sæviente bello,
Transfixit eam telo
   Quod vulneravit cor.

The following epigram, entitled " Causæ bibendi," has usually been attributed to Dr. Aldrich :

" Si bene quid memini, causæ sunt quinque bibendi,
Hospitis adventus, præsens sitis, atque futura,
Aut vini bonitas, aut quælibet altera causa."

It has been thus translated :

" If on my theme I rightly think,
There are five reasons why men drink :
Good wine, a friend, because I'm dry,
Or lest I should be by and by,
Or any other reason why."

The publication of Lord Clarendon's History of
the Rebellion was committed to the care of Dr.
Aldrich and Dr. Sprat, the Bishop of Rochester ;

but, upon no better testimony than the hearsay evidence of a zealous patriot, Mr. John Old-mixon, they were falsely charged with having altered and interpolated that noble work.

In 1702, Dr. Aldrich was chosen prolocutor of the convocation; and on the 14th of December, 1710, to the unspeakable grief of the whole university, he died, at his college, in the sixty-third year of his age.   He lived in a state of celibacy; and as he rose in the world, he disposed of his income in works of hospitality and charity, and in the encouragement of learning.   Notwithstanding that modesty and humility for which he was remarkable, and which he shewed by withholding his name from his numerous publications, he exerted a firm and steady conduct in the government of his college.   Pursuant to the directions he gave previously to his death, he was buried in the Cathedral of Oxford, near the place where Bishop Fell lies; and his monument contains no other memorial than that character which he had justly acquired, of a deep scholar, a good churchman, and a devout Christian.

THOMAS FARMER, originally one of the waits in London, was nevertheless admitted to the degree of Bachelor of Music in the University of Cambridge in 1684.

He composed many *songs*, which are printed in the collections of his time, and particularly in the

" Theatre of Musick" and the " Treasury of Musick ;" and he was the composer of two fine collections of airs, the one printed in 1686, entitled, " *A Consort of Musick in four Parts, con-* " *taining thirty-three Lessons, beginning with an* " *Overture ;*" and the other in 1690, entitled, " *A* " *Second Consort of Musick in four Parts,* " *containing eleven Lessons, beginning with a* " *Ground.*" In the " Orpheus Britannicus" there is an elergy on his death written by Tate, and set by Purcell, from which it appears that he died young.

HENRY HALL, the son of Captain Henry Hall, of New Windsor, was born about the year 1655, and educated in the Royal Chapel, where he had for his last master Dr. Blow. His first promotion was to the place of organist of Exeter. After that he became organist of Hereford, and a vicar-choral in that church. He died in March, 1707, and was interred in the cloister of the college of the vicars of Hereford Cathedral.

He had a son named after himself, who was also organist of Hereford, and died in the year 1713.

The similar situation of these two persons, and the short distance of time betwixt their death, render it difficult to distinguish the one from the other; and this difficulty is increased by the additional circumstance that each had a taste for poetry. The elder was a sound musician, and composed many *anthems*, well known to those who are conversant in church music; and most of the musical compositions with the name Henry Hall are to be ascribed to him, for it has not been ascertained that the younger was the author of any; and indeed it seems that his character of a musician is lost in that of a poet.

SIMON IVES was a lay-vicar in the Cathedral of St. Paul, till driven thence by the usurpation, when he became a singing-master and a teacher of music in private families. He and Henry Lawes composed the airs, lessons, and songs of the masque presented at Whitehall on Candlemas night, 1633. Many of the *catches* and *rounds* of Ives are to be found in Hilton's Collection and in Playford's Musical Companion; as are also some of his *songs* among the " Ayres and Dialogues," published in his time; and a three-part elegy, " Lament and " mourn, he's dead and gone," in Smith's " Mu- " sica Antiqua."

He died in the parish of Christ-Church, London, in the year 1622. Whitelock, in his Memorials of English Affairs, gives him the character of having been a worthy man and an excellent musician.

JOHN READING, a pupil of Dr. Blow, was a lay-vicar and also master of the children in the Cathedral Church of Lincoln. Removing thence, he became organist of the parish-church of St. John at Hackney, and afterwards of St. Dunstan in the West, and St. Mary Woolnoth, London.

He published a collection of *anthems*, with this strange title : " *By Subscription, a Book of new* " *Anthems, containing a hundred Plates fairly* " *engraven, with a Thorough-Base figured for* " *the Organ or Harpsichord, with proper Re-* " *tornels. By John Reading, Organist of St.* " *John's, Hackney; educated in the Chapple* " *Royal under the late famous Dr. Blow.*"

ENGLISH MUSICAL WRITERS,

Who flourished from about the Year 1650 *to* 1700.

CHRISTOPHER SIMPSON, one of the most eminent English musicians of his time, was the author of two treatises on music, and was likewise much celebrated for his skill in playing on the viol.   Of his birth and education we meet with no records, nor are there any other particulars extant of him, except that, in his younger days, he was a soldier in the army raised by William Cavendish, Duke of Newcastle, for the service of King Charles the First against the Parliament ; that he was a member of the Romish communion, and was patronised by Sir Robert Bolles, whose son he taught to play on the viol. He lived for several years in the Turnstile, Holborn, and there ended his life.

In 1665, he published, in a thin folio volume, a work entitled, " *Chelys Minuritionum,*" that is, " The Division Viol," printed in columns, namely, in English with a Latin translation.

In the dedication to Sir John Bolles, the son of his patron, he asserts of him, that, as the book was written for his instruction, so it had made him not only the greatest artist, but the ablest judge of its contents of any unprofessional person in Europe; and for his authority, refers to a copy of verses printed at Rome, occasioned, as he says, by the excellent performance of his pupil on the viol, at a music meeting there. He concludes by intimating that the Latin translation was the work of a Mr. William Marsh.

The design of the treatise is to render familiar a practice which the performers on the viol da gamba, about the time of its publication, were emulous to excel in, the making of extemporary divisions on a ground-bass; but, as this required some previous knowledge of the principles of harmonies, the author here undertakes to unfold them.

It is divided into three parts: the first contains instructions at large for playing on the instrument; the second teaches the use of the concords and discords, and is, in truth, a compendium of descant; and the third part contains the method of managing the division to a ground, which is illustrated by many examples.

In 1667, Simpson published " *A Compendium* " *of Practical Musick*," in five parts, containing, 1. The rudiments of song; 2. The principles of composition; 3. The use of discord; 4. The form of figurate descant; 5. The contrivance of canon.

The first part contains little more than what is to be found in every book that professes to teach the precepts of singing.

The second part treats of the principles of composition, and of counterpoint, intervals, and concords, with their use and application; of the key or tone; and of closes or cadences belonging to the key. From the directions here given, it appears that it was the ancient practice to frame the bass part first.

He begins his rules for composition with directions how to frame a bass, and how to join a treble to a bass; after which he proceeds to composition of three, four, five, six, seven, and eight parts; and to compositions for two choirs or choruses each.

The third part of the book teaches the use of the discords, and shews the nature of syncopation, and of relation inharmonical. Here he takes notice of the three scales of music; the diatonic, the chromatic, and the enharmonic, of which he gives a concise, but clear definition.

He inclines to the opinion that the modern

scale, in which the octave is divided into twelve
semitones, is in fact a commixture of the diatonic
and chromatic.

The fourth part relates to the form of figurate
descant, and treats first, in a very concise and perspicuous manner, of the ancient modes or tones.
In his directions for figurate descant, the author
shews how they are made to pass through each
other, and speaks of the consecution of fourths
and fifths, thirds and sixths. He explains the
nature of fugue in general, and then gives directions for constructiong a fugue per arsin et thesin,
and also a double fugue.

He next treats of vocal music, which he says is
to be preferred to that of instruments, because, of
all sounds, that of the human voice is most grateful. He mentions the different kinds of vocal
music in use in his time, and afterwards speaks
of music composed for instruments. Of the latter
he observes, that it, no less than vocal music,
abounds in points, fugues, and all other figures of
descant.

The fifth part is on the subject of canon, a
species of composition in which the author says
our countrymen have been peculiarly excellent.
He explains the method of composing canon in two
and three parts, as also canon in the unison ;
syncopated or driving canon ; canon a note higher
or lower ; canon rising or falling a note each repetition ; retrogade canon, or canon *recte et retro ;*

double descant, in which the parts are so contrived that the treble may be the bass, and the bass
the treble ; and canon on a given plain song, with
examples of each.

Lastly, he gives direction for the composition
of the catch or round, called by some canon in the
unison.

THOMAS MACE, one of the clerks of Trinity
College, Cambridge, is distinguished, among the
writers on music, by a work entitled, " *Musick's*
" *Monument, or a Remembrancer of the best*
" *Practical Music, both Divine and Civil, that*
" *has ever been known to have been in the*
" *World ;*" published in folio in 1676.

He was born in the year 1613; but under
whom he was educated, or by what means he became possessed of so much skill in the science of
music as to be able to furnish matter for the above
work, he has no where informed us. We may collect
from it that he was enthusiastically fond of music,
and of a devout and serious disposition, though
cheerful and good-humoured even under the infirmities of age and the pressure of misfortunes.
His knowledge of music seems to have been
chiefly confined to the practice of the lute, (his
favourite instrument), and to so much of the principles of the science as enabled him to compose
for it.

As to the above book, a singular vein of dry

humour runs through it, which is far from being disgusting, since it exhibits a lively portrait of a good-natured old man. The four first chapters are an eulogium on psalmody and parochial music ; the fifth contains a recommendation of the organ for that purpose. The sixth chapter we shall transcribe as a specimen of the style and manner of the whole.

" *How to procure an organist.*

" 'The certain way I will propose shall be this ; namely, first, I will suppose you have a parish clark, and such an one as is able to set and lead a psalm, although it be never so indifferently.

" Now this being granted, I may say that I will, or any musick master will, or many more inferiors, as virginal players, or many organ makers, or the like, I say any of those will teach such a parish clark how to pulse or strike most of our common psalm tunes, usually sung in our churches, for a trifle, viz. twenty, thirty, or forty shillings, and so well that he need never bestow more cost to perform that duty sufficiently during his life.

" This I believe no judicious person in the art will doubt of. And then, when this clark is thus well accomplished, he will be so doated upon by all the pretty ingenious children and young men in the parish, that scarcely any of them but will be begging now and then a shilling or two of their parents to give the clark, that he may teach them to pulse a psalm tune ; the which any such child or youth will be able to do in a week or fortnight's time very well.

" And then, again, each youth will be as ambitious to pulse that psalm tune in publick to the congregation, and no doubt but shall do it sufficiently well.

" And thus by little and little the parish in a short time will swarm or abound with organists, and sufficient enough for that service.

" For you must know, and I entreat you to believe me, that seriously it is one of the most easy pieces of performances in all instrumental music to pulse one of our psalm tunes truly and well after a very little shewing upon the organ.

" The clark likewise will quickly get in his money by this means.

" And I suppose no parent will grudge it him, but rather rejoice in it.

" Thus you may perceive how easily and certainly these two great difficulties may be overcome, and with nothing so much as a willing mind.

" Therefore be but willingly resolved, and the work will soon be done.

" And now again methinks I see some of you tossing up your caps, and crying aloud, ' We will have an organ and an organist too ; for 'tis but laying out a little dirty money, and how can we lay it out better than in that service we offer up

unto God ?   And who should we better bestow it
upon, if not upon him and his service ?'

" This is a very right and an absolute good
resolve ; persist in it and you will do well, and
doubtless find much content and satisfaction in
your so doing.

" For there lies linked to this an unknown and
unapprehended great good benefit, which would
redound certainly to all or most young children,
who by this means would, in their minorities, be so
sweetly tinctured or seasoned, as I may say, or
brought into a kind of familiarity or acquaintance,
with the harmless innocent delights of such pure
and undefilable practices, as that it would be a
great means to win them to the love of virtue,
and to disdain, contemn, and slight those common, gross, ill practices which most children
are incident to fall into in their ordinary and accustomed pursuits."

But lest his arguments in favour of the general
use of the organ should fail, the author, in the
eighth chapter, shews how psalms may be performed in churches without that instrument.   In
the eleventh and twelfth chapters he treats of
cathedral music, and laments seriously its decline
in this kingdom.

In parochial psalmody the author recommends
what he calls *short - square - even and uniform
ayres*, and is " bold to say that many of our psalm
tunes are so *excellently good*, that art cannot

mend them or make them better." In speaking
of the difficulty of singing in tune, even with a
good voice, he observes, that " with an *unskilfull-
inharmonious-coarse-grained-harsh-voice*, it is impossible. 'Tis *sad* to hear what whining, toling,
yelling, or *screeking*, there is in our *country con-
gregations*, where, if there be no organ to com-
pel them to harmonical unity, the people seem
affrighted, or distracted." The liberal use of
compounds by the ingenious Master Mace, gives
his language a very Grecian appearance.

The second part of the work treats of the lute,
and professes to lay open all the secrets relating to
that instrument, which, till the author's time, had
only been known to the masters of the science.

The third part is on the viol and music in general ; and in this he censures the abuse of music,
in the disproportionate number of bass and treble instruments in the concerts of his time, in
which he says it was not unusual to have but one
small weak - sounding bass-viol to two or three
scolding violins, as he calls them.

He gives directions for procuring and maintain-
ing the best music imaginable, and exhibits first
the plan of a music-room contrived by himself for
concerts, with galleries for auditors, capable of
holding two hundred persons. The instruments
are a table-organ (an invention of his own) and a
chest of viols, two violins, and basses of strength
sufficient " that they may not out-cry the rest of

the music." To these he adds two theorboes, three " full-sized lyra-viols, lusty and smart-speaking; because that in consort they often retort against the treble, imitating, and often standing instead of that part, a second treble." " And being thus stored, you have a ready entertainment for the greatest prince in the world."

He afterwards gives directions for playing the viol, with a few lessons by way of example; and concludes with a chapter on music in general, which, however, contains nothing more than some reflections of the author on the mysteries of music, which, he says, have a tendency to *strengthen faith*, and are a security against *the sin of atheism.*

Mace does not appear to have held any considerable rank among musicians, nor is he celebrated either as a composer for, or a performer on the lute. His book, however, proves him to have been an excellent judge of the instrument, and contains such a variety of directions as to render it a work of great utility. We find in it many curious observations on the choice of stringed instruments, the various kinds of wood of which they are made, the method of preserving them, and the mode of choosing strings.

JOHN WALLIS, D.D. an eminent divine and mathematician, was born at Ashford, in Kent, in the year 1616. From the grammar-school at

Felsted, in Essex, he went to Emanuel College,
Cambridge, but was afterwards elected fellow of
Queen's.   About the year 1640, he was admitted
into holy orders, and, leaving the university, became domestic chaplain to Sir Richard Darley
and the Lady Vere.   Four years after his admission to orders, he was chosen one of the scribes
or secretaries to the Assembly of Divines at Westminster.   In 1649, he was made Savilian professor of geometry at Oxford ; on which occasion he entered himself at Exeter College, and
was admitted to the degree of Master of Arts, and
in 1654, to that of Doctor in Divinity. Soon after
this, on the decease of Dr. Gerard Langbaine,
he was appointed Custos Archivorum of the university.

He was one of those persons whose private
meetings for the improvement of philosophy by
experiments gave rise to the institution of the
Royal Society, and, after its establishment, he was
not only a constant attendant on, but a frequent
correspondent of this society.

His learning was not less deep than it was extensive ; and a singular degree of acuteness and
penetration is discoverable in all his writings ; the
only parts of which, necessary to be mentioned
in this place, are his edition of Ptolemy, with
the appendix entitled, " De veterum Harmonia
" ad hodiernam comparata;" his " Porphyrii
" in Harmonica Ptolmæi Commentarius, ex

" *Cod. MSS. Græce et Latine editus ;*" and " *Manuclis Bryennii Harmonica, ex Cod. MSS.*" all contained in the third volume of his works printed at Oxford in 1669.

Dr. Wallis was also the author of various musical papers inserted in the Philosophical Transactions, particularly a discourse on the trembling of consonant strings ; another on the division of the monochord ; another on the imperfection of the organ ; and a fourth on the strange effects reported of music in former times.

He died in October, 1703, in the eighty-eighth year of his age, and was interred in the Church of St. Mary at Oxford.

JOHN BIRKENSHA was probably a native of Ireland ; at least it is certain that he resided at Dublin, in the family of the Earl of Kildare, till the rebellion in 1641 drove him from thence to England. He lived in London many years after the Restoration, and taught the viol. We are informed by Sir John Hawkins, that he was remarkable for being a very genteel man in his person and behaviour.

In the Philosophical Transactions for the year 1672, there is a pompous advertisement by Birkensha, containing proposals for publishing by subscription a work on the theory and practice of music, entitled " *Syntagma Musicæ*," which, according to his account of it, was to be a book unequalled either in ancient or modern literature. It was, however, either never published, or is now become so scarce as seldom even to be heard of.

Berkinsha printed in 1664, " *Templum Musi-* " *cum, or the Musical Synopsis of Johannes* " *Henricus Alstedius ;"* a work resembling more a logical than a musical treatise ; and a small tract in one sheet, entitled, " *Rules and Directions for composing in Parts.*"

William Holder, D.D. a canon of Ely, residentiary of St. Paul's, and sub-dean of the Chapel Royal, was born in Nottinghamshire about the year 1614, and educated at Pembroke Hall, Cambridge. Shortly after the Restoration he was admitted to his Doctor's degree, and also became a fellow of the Royal Society and sub-almoner to the king. Amongst other works, he was the author of a treatise, " *On the natural Grounds* " *and Principles of Harmony,*" published in octavo in the year 1694. In this work the author first treats of sound in general, how it is produced and propagated ; then on the vibrations of sonorous bodies ; on the nature of concord, as consisting in the coincidence of the vibrations of two chords ; and on the three kinds of proportion, arithmetical, geometrical, and harmonical. In the chapter on " discords and degrees," he digresses to the music of the ancients, and assents with

Kircher in the opinion that they were unacquainted
with music in consonance.

This treatise is written with a remarkable degree of accuracy. There is in it no confusion of
terms. All that it teaches is rendered clear and
perspicuous, and the doctrines it contains are such
as every musician ought to be acquainted with.

Besides a profound knowledge of the theory of
music, it appears that Dr. Holder possessed much
skill in practical composition. In a manuscript
of church music of Dr. Tudway, in the British
Museum, there is an *anthem,* composed by him
for three voices in the major key of C, to the
words, " Praise our God, ye people."

Dr. Holder died at his house in Amen Corner,
London, on the 22d of January, 1696, aged
eighty-two years, and was buried in the vault
under the choir of St. Paul's Cathedral.

Dr. Holder attained great celebrity for skill in
teaching deaf and dumb persons to make themselves understood, on which subject he also published a treatise.

s

CHAP. VII.

===

ITALIAN
MUSICAL COMPOSERS AND WRITERS,

WHO FLOURISHED

𝔉rom about the 𝔜ear

1650 TO 1700.

===

DRAGHI. — STROZZI. — LORENZANI. — STRADELLA.—
SALVATOR ROSA. — SIMONELLI. — BENEVOLI. —
LEGRENZI.—BASSANI.—ERCOLE BERNABEI.—G. A.
BERNABEI.—G. P. COLONNA.—FOGGIA.—G. M. BO-
NONCINI.—A. BONONCINI. — LULLY.—THEOBALDO
GATTI.—CORELLI.—TORELLI.—CALDARA.

BARTOLI. — MENGOLI. — BONTEMPI.— PENNA.— LI-
BERATI.—BERARDI.

Giovanni Battista Draghi was an Italian by birth, and is supposed to have been one of those musicians who came into England with Mary d'Este, the Princess of Modena, and consort of King James the Second. He was a fine performer on the harpsichord, and composed and published, in England, many lessons for that instrument. He joined with Lock in composing the music to

Shadwell's English opera of *Psyche;* and, on his decease, in 1677, succeeded him in the place of organist to the queen.

Although Draghi was an Italian, and many of his compositions are entirely in the Italian style, yet, during his long residence in England, he seems, in a remarkable degree, to have assimilated his music to that of the old English masters. This is particularly apparent in his anthem, " This is " the day that the Lord hath made," and in many of the ballad airs and dance tunes composed by hm. The melodies of some of the latter are singularly excellent.

During the reigns of Charles the Second and James, Draghi was the favourite court musician ; and he is supposed to have been the musical preceptor to Queen Anne. Towards the latter end of his life he composed the music to a whimsical opera written by D'Urfey, entitled, " *The Won-* " *ders in the Sun, or the Kingdom of Birds,*" performed at the Queen's Theatre in the Haymarket, in 1706. Some of the music of this opera is extremely good ; but the piece proved unsuccessful, surviving only six nights, and scarcely paying half the expense which had attended the getting of it up.

In the printed collections of songs published towards the latter end of the seventeenth century, we meet with many that have the name of Signor

Baptist to them. This uniformly means Baptist Draghi, and not Baptist Lully, as some persons have supposed.

BARBARA STROZZI, or STROZZA, flourished about the middle of the seventeenth century, and was the author of some vocal compositions, containing an intermixture of air and recitative. These she published, in 1653, with the title of " *Cantate*, " *Ariette, e Duetti*," intimating, in the preface, that, having invented this mixed style, she had given a specimen of it to the public by way of trial. The style of the airs is too simple to be pleasing, yet the experiment succeeded. She is allowed to have been the inventor of that elegant species of vocal composition called the *cantata*.

PAOLO LORENZANI, a Roman by birth, and a pupil of Oratio Benevoli, was chapel-master first in the Jesuit's Church at Rome, and afterwards in the Cathedral of Messina, in Sicily, from whence he was invited by Louis the Fourteenth to Paris.

He composed and published, in this city, a collection of very excellent *motets*.

ALESSANDRO STRADELLA flourished about the middle of the seventeenth century. He was a fine singer and an excellent performer on the harp, an instrument in which he took much delight. For some years he held the situation of composer to the opera at Venice, under an appointment from the magistrates of that republic.

He was likewise a teacher of music there; and, amongst others, of whose instruction he had the superintendance, there was a young lady of rank, named Hortensia, who lived in a criminal intercourse with a Venetian nobleman. His frequent access to this lady produced a mutual affection, and they agreed to elope together. They embarked for Rome in a fine night, and, aided by a favourable wind, effected their escape.

On discovering the lady's flight, the Venetian had recourse to the usual methods of the country in obtaining satisfaction for real or supposed injuries. He dispatched two assassins, with instructions to murder both Stradella and the lady whereever they should be found, giving them a sum of money in hand, and making them the promise of a larger sum if they succeeded in the attempt. Being arrived at Naples, they were informed that those of whom they were in pursuit were at Rome, where the lady passed as Stradella's wife; on this intelligence they wrote to their employer, requesting letters of recommendation to the Venetian ambassador at Rome, in order to secure an asylum, to which they could fly as soon as the deed was perpetrated.

Having received these letters, they made the best of their way to Rome. At their arrival they

were informed that on the evening of the succeeding day, Stradella was to give an oratorio in the
Church of San Giovanni Laterano.   They attended
the performance, determining to follow the composer and his mistress out of the church, and,
seizing a convenient opportunity, to make the
fatal blow.   The music soon afterwards commenced ; but so exquisitely pathethic was it in some
parts, that, long before it was concluded, the sug-
gestions of humanity had begun to operate upon
them.   They were seized with remorse, and re-
flected with horror on the thought of depriving a
man of life who could give to his auditors so much
delight as they had felt.   In short, they entirely
desisted from their purpose, and determined, instead of taking away his life, to exert all their
efforts to preserve it.   They awaited his coming out
of the church, and, after first thanking him for the
pleasure they had received in hearing his music, informed him of the bloody errand on which they
had been sent ; expatiating on the irresistible
charms which, of savages, had made them men,
and had rendered it impossible for them to effect
their execrable purpose.   They concluded by
earnestly advising that he and the lady should
depart immediately from Rome, promising that
they would forego the remainder of the reward,
and would deceive their employer, by making him
believe they had quitted that city on the morning
of their arrival.

The lovers having thus escaped the malice of their enemy, fled to Turin. The assassins, on their return to Venice, reported to their employer that Stradella and Hortensia had fled from Rome and taken shelter in the city of Turin, a place where the laws were so severe as to afford no protection for murderers, except in the houses of ambassadors. They represented to him the difficulty of procuring any persons who would undertake their assassination in this place, and that they considered the thing so hazardous, that, notwithstanding their engagements, they were compelled to decline the enterprise.

This disappointment served but to sharpen the resentment of the Venetian. He had found means to attach to his interest the father of Hortensia, and he now formed the design of instigating the old man to become himself the murderer of his daughter. In this he at length succeeded, and, joining with him two others, they all three set out with a resolution of stabbing Stradella and Hortensia wherever they found them. They were furnished with letters to the French ambassador at Turin, recommending them to his protection as merchants.

The Duchess of Savoy was at that time regent. She had been informed of the arrival of Stradella and Hortensia, and of the occasion of their precipitate flight from Rome ; and, for better security, placed the lady in a convent, and retained Stradella in her palace as her principal musician. Thus secured, Stradella's fears began to abate, until one evening, strolling upon the ramparts of the city, he was attacked by the three assassins, who gave him each a stab in the breast with a dagger, and immediately fled to the house of the ambassador as a sanctuary.

The attack on Stradella, having been made publicly, and in the sight of a great number of persons, caused much uproar in the city. It soon reached the ears of the Duchess, who ordered the gates to be shut, and diligent search to be made for the assassins. Being informed that they had taken refuge in the French ambassador's house, she went thither in person to demand them. The ambassador insisted on his privilege, and refused to deliver them up. He however wrote to the person who had recommended them, to inquire the reason of the attack upon Stradella, and afterwards suffered them to escape.

From this time, finding himself disappointed in his revenge, but not in the least abated in his ardour to accomplish it, this implacable Venetian contented himself for a while with setting spies to watch the motions of Stradella, whose wounds, not proving so dangerous as had been at first supposed, had been cured. A year had elapsed after his recovery, and no fresh disturbance having been made, he thought himself free from any further attempts on his life. The Duchess, who was deeply interested for the honour of her sex, and for the happiness of two persons who had suffered so much, and who seemed so sincerely attached to each other, herself united their hands in marriage. After the ceremony, Stradella and his wife wishing to visit Genoa, went thither with a resolution of returning again to Turin ; but the assassins having intelligence of their departure from their place of security, immediately followed them. They reached Genoa, but, the moment after their arrival, the villains rushed into their chamber and stabbed each to the heart. The murderers had secured a vessel which lay in the port; to this they retreated, and thus escaping from the hands of justice, were never heard of more.

There is some doubt whether any of the entire compositions of Stradella were ever published, as no catalogue of them is to be met with in any of the accounts that have been given of him. Many of his pieces in manuscript are, however, deposited in the library of the Academy of Ancient Music, but in particular an oratorio entitled, " San Giovanni " Battista," and some madrigals. His compositions, specimens of which from his cantatas and canzonets are inserted in Dr. Crotch's publication, seem superior to any that were produced in the seventeenth century, except those of Carissimi ; and perhaps, if Stradella had enjoyed equal longevity, he would have been inferior in no respect to that great master.

SALVATOR ROSA has been ranked by Dr. Burney among the musical writers of this period. The Doctor is in possession of a manuscript music-book which belonged to this celebrated man, containing, amongst other music, eight entire *cantatas* composed by himself. One of his airs, " Vado " ben spesso," is to be found in Dr. Crotch's work.

Rosa, who has been chiefly celebrated as a painter and a poet, was born at Renessa, near Naples, in the year 1615. His youth was spent in dissipation; and he is even said to have associated himself with banditti. This course of life naturally led him, by way of retreat, into those wild scenes of nature which he afterwards so excellently described upon canvas.

He seems to have been one of the most miserable of men. The greater part of his cantatas are filled with the bitterest complaints either against his mistress, or against mankind in general. He says of himself, that he has had more misfortunes than there are stars in the firmament, and that he lived thirty years without the enjoyment of one happy day. This, when we consider his mode of life, we cannot feel surprised at.

He died at Rome in the year 1673, and was interred there, in the Church of Santa Maria degli Angeli de' PP. Certosini.

MATTEO SIMONELLI was a singer in the Pontifical Chapel in the year 1662, and was, in the language of the Italian writers, a grand contrapuntist; for which reason, and for his excellence in the church style, he has been called the Palestrina of his time. In teaching he was extremely successful, and he had the honour of being the first master to Corelli.

It does not appear that any of his compositions were ever published, but his works were preserved with great care in the College of the Pontifical Singers at Rome.

ORAZIO BENEVOLI was chapel-master to the Pope as early as the year 1648. In 1684, he was one of five candidates for the situation of chapel-master of the Metropolitical Church of Milan; and Antimo Liberati, who had been requested to give his opinion respecting the merits of these candidates, states, respecting Benevoli, that " he surpassed all the masters of his time in writing for four and even for six choirs ; in which, by the construction and order of the parts, the imitations, inverted fugues, double counterpoint, new contrivances, ligatures, preparations, and resolutions of discords, the texture, connection, and fluency of the whole, he so completely vanquished Envy herself as to obtain the applause of all."

After the cessation of the plague he was directed to compose a *mass* for the Cathedral Church of

St. Peter at Rome, which he did for six choirs of four parts each; and it was performed by a band of more than two hundred singers, arranged in different circles round the dome, the sixth choir occupying the summit of the cupola.

Benevoli appears to have died before the commencement of the eighteenth century.

GIOVANNI LEGRENZI was organist of the Church of Santa Maria Maggiore, in Bergamo, afterwards chapel-master in the Church della Spirito Santo, in Ferrara; and in his later years, chapel-master of the Church of St. Mark at Venice.

His works consist of *mases, motets, sonata per chiesa e de camera, psalms, litanies,* and *cantatas.*

GIOVANNI BATTISTA BASSANI, a native of Bologna, and chapel-master of the Cathedral Church and the Academia della Morte in that city, was a voluminous composer of music, having, at various times, given to the world as many as thirty-one different works. These consist of *masses, psalms, motets* with instrumental parts, and *sonatas* for *violins.* His Fifth Opera, containing twelve sonatas for two violins and a bass, is much admired; the style is grave and pathetic, and bears evidence of great learning and fine invention. The First and Third Operas of Corelli are apparently formed in imitation of this work.

Bassani was the tutor of Corelli, and one of the first of those musicians who composed motets for a single voice with accompaniments for violins. Two sets of these were published many years ago in London, some of which were much esteemed. Specimens of his music are to be found in Latrobe's Selections and Stevens's " Sacred Music."

He flourished from about the year 1675 to 1703.

ERCOLE BERNABEI, a Roman by birth, the pupil of Benevoli, and the master of Steffani, succeeded Kerl as chapel-master to Ferdinando Maria, the Elector of Bavaria, at Munich, about the year 1650. He was afterwards called to the same office in the Church of San Luigi de' Francesi at Rome, and at length to that of the Pontifical Chapel. He died about the year 1690.

In 1669, he published a fine collection of *madrigals* for three and four voices. At his decease a collection of his *motets* was published at Munich ; and some years afterwards another at Amsterdam. Bernabei was no doubt one of the finest composers of church music of his day. A specimen of his works may be seen in solo and duet, inserted in Stevens's " Sacred Music."

GIUSEPPE ANTONIO BERNABEI, the son of the above-mentioned Ercole, was also an ecclesiastical composer, but greatly surpassed his father both in melody and modulation. He succeeded his father as chapel-master to the Elector of Bavaria, by whom he was honoured with the title of *Conseiller Aulique*. There are extant several of his compositions, which are replete with musical science. He died in the year 1732, at the great age of eighty-nine years.

GIOVANNI PAOLO COLONNA, chapel-master of St. Petronio in Bologna, flourished at this time. He was the son of Antonio Colonna, a celebrated organ-builder of Brescia.

His compositions, which are very numerous, are almost wholly for the church, and consist of *motets, litanies, masses, psalms,* and *offices for the dead*. Many of these were published at Bologna between the years 1681 and 1694. His style is at once pathetic and sublime; and in the composition of church music he ranks among the first of the Italian masters. He was the composer of a few *operas,* one of which, "Amilcar in Cipro," is known to have been first performed at Bologna in the year 1692. The *psalms* of Colonna, which were published in 1694, have been much admired.

FRANCESCO FOGGIA is celebrated as one of the most eminent of the Italian musicians of the seventeenth century. He was born at Rome about the year 1604, and was a pupil of Paolo Agostini, whose daughter he afterwards married. Having distinguished himself very early in life by his skill in ecclesiastical music, he was appointed chapel-master of the Churches of St. John Lateran, Santa Maria Maggiore, San Lorenzo in Damasco, and other great churches in Rome. Kircher has spoken of him in terms of high commendation. He was living in 1684, the year in which Antimo Liberati published a letter containing a character of his writings. He says that Foggia " was the support and the father of music and true ecclesiastical harmony ; and that, both in his printed and manuscript productions, he had manifested such a variety in his manner of writing as had seldom been found in the works of one man, being equally excellent in the grand, the learned, the noble, the refined, the simple, and the pleasing style."

Padre Martini has preserved two *motets* from Foggia's Eighth Opera, in which, says Dr. Burney, " there is much ingenuity, and a greater variety of measure than is usual in the church music of this period, when a movement in triple time seldom had admission."

GIOVANNI MARIA BONONCINI, a disciple of Colonna, and chapel-master in the Church of St. Giovanni in Monte, was a celebrated composer, and the author of a treatise published at Bologna in the year 1673, a thin quarto volume, dedicated to the Emperor Leopold, entitled, " *Il Musico* " *prattico.*"

In the compilation of this treatise the author

appears to have availed himself of the writings and compositions of the most celebrated Italian musicians, as well theoretical as practical, of whom he has given a numerous list at the beginning of the book. A second part was afterwards published, which was translated into the German language. These volumes contain an introduction to the science of music, and likewise the precepts of musical composition. The author appears to have been deeply read in the science ; but, like most of the Italian writings of the same kind, from the time of Franchinus downward, the present work contains nothing that is either new or particularly interesting.

Of Bononcini's musical compositions there are extant, " *Cantate per Camera à* 5, 6, 7, *à* 8 *In-* " *stromenti, con alcune à una e due Trombe,* " *servendo ancora per Violini,*" at Bologna in 1685 ; and " *Sinfonie à tre Instromenti, col Basso* " *per l'Organo,*" at Bologna in 1686. These, like the First and Third Operas of Corelli, consist of slow movements, with fugues of various measures interspersed. Bononcini published also a set of *masses* for eight voices.

Three of his sons were eminent musicians, namely, Antonio Bononcini, Giovanni Battista Bononcini, who was settled at Venice, and was composer to the Emperor of Germany, and Giovanni Bononcini, (who spent several years of his life in England, and was for some time composer to the opera at London), of whom an account will hereafter be given. We shall in this place speak of the eldest of the three sons.

ANTONIO BONONCINI was settled at Modena, in Italy, and appears to have been first known as a composer towards the latter part of the seventeenth century. His attention was chiefly confined to secular music; and he was the author of several *operas*, which at that period obtained considerable celebrity.

JEAN BAPTISTE LULLY was born of obscure parents, at Florence, in the year 1734. Having whilst a child shewn a great taste for music, a cordelier, from no other consideration than the hope of his some time becoming eminent in the art, undertook to teach him the guitar.

While Lully was under the tuition of this benevolent ecclesiastic, a French gentleman, the Chevalier Guise, then on his travels, arrived at Florence. This person had been requested by Mademoiselle de Montpensier, a niece of Louis the Fourteenth, to find out for and bring her some pretty little Italian boy as a page. The countenance of Lully did not answer to the instructions, but his vivacity and ready wit, in addition to his skill on an instrument as much the favourite of the French as of the Italians, determined the Chevalier to engage him; and then, about ten

years of age, he was sent to Paris. On his arrival
he was presented to the lady, but his figure obtained for him so cool a reception, that, instead of
making him her page, she commanded the officers
of her household to enter his name in their books
as her under-scullion.

Neither the disappointment he experienced, nor
the employment to which he was destined, affected
the spirits of Lully. In the moments of his leisure
from the kitchen, he used to scrape upon a wretched
fiddle which he had contrived to procure. A
person employed about the court happening one
day to hear him, informed the Princess that the
youth had an excellent taste for music. She immediately directed that a master should be employed to teach him the violin ; and in the course
of a few months, he became so great a proficient
that he was elevated to the rank of court musician. In consequence of an unlucky accident
that took place, he was dismissed from this situation ; he afterwards, however, found means to get
admitted into the king's band of violins, and applied himself so closely to the study of music,
that in a little time he began to compose. Some
of his airs having been noticed by the king, the
author was sent for, and his performance of them
was thought so excellent, that a new band was
formed, called " *Les petits Violons,*" and he was
placed at the head of it. Under his direction
they soon surpassed the famous band of twenty-

four, till that time so much celebrated throughout
Europe. This was about the year 1660, at which
time the favourite entertainments at the French
court were dramatic representations, called *ballets*.
These consisted of dancing intermixed with acting
and speaking in recitative ; and to many of them
Lully was employed to compose the music.

An academy had been established at Venice
for the performance of operas, and Louis wished to
have one in France that should excel it. Accordingly, in 1669, he granted to the Abbé Perrin,
master of the ceremonies to the Duke of Orleans,
a privilege for the conducting of an opera after
the model of that at Venice, but to be performed in
the French language.

Cambert, the organist of St. Honoré, was engaged to compose the music; but after a little
while, Lully, who had risen high in the king's
favour, contrived to get him removed, and himself
appointed in his stead. Possessing now the situation of composer and joint-director of the opera,
he not only left his former band, and instituted
one of his own, but formed the design of building
a new theatre near the Luxemburg Palace, which
he afterwards accomplished. This was opened in
November, 1670, with a musical entertainment,
consisting of a variety of detached pieces included
under the title of " *Le Combat de l' Amour et de*
" *Bacchus.*"

Lully, some time previously to this, had been appointed superintendant of the king's private music, and had neglected almost entirely the practice of the violin; yet whenever he could be prevailed with to play, his excellence astonished all who heard him. For the guitar, though so trifling and insignificant an instrument, he, throughout his whole life, entertained the greatest partiality.

In the year 1686, the king was seized with an indisposition that threatened his life; but recovering from it; Lully was required to compose a *Te Deum*. Accordingly he wrote one which was not more remarkable for its excellence, than for the unhappy accident with which its performance was attended. Nothing had been neglected in the composition, nor in the preparations for the execution of it, and the more to demonstrate his zeal, he himself beat the time. With the cane that he used for this purpose, in the heat of action (from the difficulty of keeping the band together) he struck his foot; this caused a blister to arise, which increasing, his physician advised him immediately to have his little toe taken off, and after a delay of some days his foot, and at length the whole limb. At this dreadful juncture an empiric offered to perform a cure without amputation. Two thousand pistoles were promised to him if he should accomplish it; but all his efforts were in vain. Lully died on the 22d day of March, 1687, and was interred in the Church of the Discalceat Augustines at Paris, where an elegant monument was erected to his memory.

A singular story of a conversation betwixt Lully and his confessor, in his last illness, is related, which, even at so critical a moment, shews the natural archness of his disposition, at the same time that it exposes the weakness and folly of the priest. Having been for many years in the habit of composing for the opera, the priest, as a testimony of his sincere repentance, and the conditions of his absolution, required him to throw the last of his compositions into the fire. Lully, after some excuses, at length acquiesced, and pointing to a drawer in which the rough draft of *Achilles and Polixenes* was deposited, it was taken out and burnt, and the confessor went away satisfied. Lully grew better, and was thought out of danger, when one of the young princes came to visit him. " What, Baptiste," says he to him, " have you thrown your opera into the fire ? you were a fool for thus giving credit to a gloomy Jansenist, and burning good music."—" Hush, hush, my Lord (answered Lully in a whisper), I knew well what I was about, I have another copy of it !" Unhappily this ill-timed pleasantry was followed by a relapse ; the gangrene increased, and the prospect of inevitable death threw him into such pangs of remorse, that he submitted to be laid on a heap of ashes with a cord round his neck ; and, in this situation, he expressed a deep sense of his late transgression. On being replaced in his bed he became composed, and died shortly afterwards.

At the time when Lully was placed at the head of " *Les petits Violons*," not half the musicians in France were able to play at sight. A person was esteemed an excellent master who could play thorough-bass on the harpsichord or the theorbo in accompaniment to a scholar ; and, with respect to composition, nothing can be conceived more inartificial than most of the sonatas and airs for violins of that time. The treble part contained the whole of the melody ; the bass and the interior parts were mere accompaniment; and the whole was a gross and sullen counterpoint. The combinations of sounds then allowed were too few to admit of sufficient varity ; and the art of preparing and resolving discords was a secret confined to few. Lully contributed greatly to the improvement of French music. In his overtures he introduced fugues, and was the first who in the choruses made use of the side and kettle drums.

It is somewhat difficult to characterise his style. It seems however to have been completely original, and derived from no other source than the copious fountain of his own invention.

His compositions were chiefly *operas* and other dramatic entertaiments : these, though excellent in their kind, would give but little pleasure at the present day, the airs being short, formed of regular measures, and too frequently interrupted by recitatives. Louis the Fourteenth was fond of dancing, and had no taste for any music but airs, in the composition of which a stated number of bars was the chief rule to be observed. Of harmony or fine melody, or of the relation between poetry and music, he seems to have had no conception ; and these, of course, were a˥ so many restraints upon Lully's talents.

The merits of Lully ought to be estimated from his *overtures*, and works of a more serious nature than his operas. There are extant several of his *motets*, and some other good compositions for the church, though not in print. His operas and other theatrical performances, which were very numerous, have heen nearly all published. He composed *symphonies for violins* in three parts ; but these are not to be met with in print.

He is said to have been the inventor of that species of composition, the *overture*, and more particularly that spirited movement, the *largo*, which is the general introduction to the fugue ;* for though it may be said that the symphonies or preludes of Carissimi, Colonna, and others, are in effect overtures, yet the difference between

---

* It is asserted by Mattheson, that Handel, in the composition of his overtures, professed to imitate Lully ; and whoever will be at the trouble of making the comparison, will find some reason to be of this opinion.

them and those of Lully* is very evident: the
former were compositions of a mild and placid
kind, the latter are animated and full of energy.

J. THEOBALDE, called also THEOBALDO GATTI,
was a native of Florence. In all his compositions
be emulated the style and manner of Lully, and
he was by no means unsuccessful. Two of his
operas were represented at Paris, *Coronis*, a pastoral in three acts, and *Scylla*, a tragedy in five.

Theobalde died at Paris in the year 1727, at
a very advanced age, having, for more than fifty
years, been a performer on the bass-viol in the
orchestra of the opera there. He was interred in
the Church of St. Eustache,

ARCHANGELO CORELLI, a native of Fusigano,
a town situate near Imola, in the territory of
Bologna, was born in the month of February,
1653. His first instructor was Matteo Simonelli,
by whom he was taught the rudiments of music,
and the art of practical composition; but the
genius of Corelli leading him to prefer secular to
ecclesiastical music, he afterwards became a disciple of Bassani.

Corelli entertained an early propensity for the
violin, and, as he advanced in years, he laboured
incessantly in the practice of it. It has been said,
though without authority, that, in the y ear 1672

he went to Paris, and was driven from thence by
the jealousy and violence of Lully, who could
not brook so formidable a rival.

In 1680, he visited Germany, and met with a
reception suitable to his merit from most of the
German princes, but particularly from the Elector
of Bavaria, in whose service he was retained, and
continued for some time. After about five years'
residence abroad, he returned again to Rome, and
there pursued his studies with assiduity.

The proficiency of Corelli on his favourite instrument became so great, that his fame was extended throughout Europe. It does not appear
that he had attained a power of execution in any
degree comparable to that of later professors. The
style of his performance was, however, learned, elegant, and pathetic, and his tone firm and even.
Geminiani, who was well acquainted with it, used
to compare it with that of a sweet trumpet. A person who heard him perform says, that during the
whole time his countenance was distorted, his eyes
were as red as fire, and his eye-balls rolled as if
he were in agony.

About the year 1690, the opera had arrived
at great perfection in Rome under the direction
of Pasquini, the dramatic composer; and its excellence has been attributed to the circumstance
of Pasquini, Corelli, and Gaetani being performers in it; the first on the harpsichord, the se-

cond on the violin at the head of the band, and the third on the lute.

While thus engaged at Rome, Corelli was highly favoured by the patronage of Cardinal Ottoboni. Crescembini says that he regulated the musical academy held at the palace of the cardinal every Monday afternoon. Here it was that Mr. Handel became acquainted with him; and in this academy it was that a serenata of the latter was performed, the overture to which was so new and singular, that Corelli was completely confounded in his first attempt to play it.*

During his residence at Rome the number of his pupils was very great. Not only his own countrymen, but even persons from distant kingdoms, resorted to him for instruction, as the greatest master of the violin that had at that period had been heard of in the world.

At the time that Corelli enjoyed the highest reputation, his fame having reached the court of Naples, and excited a desire in the king to hear him perform, he was invited by order of his Majesty to that capital. Corelli, with some reluc-

---

* This serenata was entitled, "*Il Trionfo del Tempo*;" it was translated into English, and performed in London, in 1751, under the title of "The Triumph of Time and Truth." The overture is inserted in the printed collections of Handel's overtures; and it is conjectured that it was the first movement which appeared so difficult to Corelli.

tance, was at length prevailed with to accept the invitation ; but, lest he should not be well accompanied, he took with him his own second violin and violoncello players.   At Naples he found Alessandro Scarlatti and several other masters,* who entreated him to play some of his concertos before the king.   This he for a while declihed, on account of his whole band not being with him ; and there was no time, he said, for a rehearsal. At length, however, he consented, and, in great fear, performed the first of them. His astonishment was very great to find that the Neapolitan band executed his concertos almost as accurately at sight as his own band after repeated rehearsals, and when they had almost got them by art.   " *Sì* " *suona* (says he to Matteo, his second violin) " *à Napoli.*"

After this, being again admitted into his Majesty's presence, and desired to perform one of his sonatas, the king found the adagio so long and dry, that, being tired of it, he quitted the room, to the great mortification of Corelli.   Afterwards he was desired to lead in the performance of a masque composed by Scarlatti, which was to be executed before the king ; this he undertook, but, from

---

* This must have happened about the year 1708; as it appears that Scarlatti was settled at Rome from 1709 to the time of his decease.   Corelli's concertos therefore must have been composed many years before they were published.

Scarlatti's little knowledge of the violin, the part was somewhat awkward and difficult: in one place it went up to F; and, when they came to that passage, Corelli failed, and was unable to execute it; but he was astonished beyond measure to hear Petrillo, the Neapolitan leader, and the other violins, perform that which had baffled his skill. A song succeeded this in C minor, which Corelli led off in C major; " *ricomminciamo*," said Scarlatti good-naturedly. Still Corelli persisted in the major key, till Scarlatti was obliged to call out loudly to him and set him right. So mortified was poor Corelli with this disgrace, and the general bad figure which he imagined he had made at Naples, that he immediately afterwards stole back to Rome.

It was soon after this that a hautbois-player, whose name has not reached us, acquired such applause at Rome, that Corelli, in disgust, declared he would never again play in public. All these mortifications, joined to the success of Valentini, whose concertos and performance, though infinitely inferior to those of Corelli, were become fashionable, threw him into a state of melancholy and chagrin, which, as it is thought, tended greatly to hasten his death.

The preceding account of Corelli's journey to Naples, which has been extracted from Dr. Burney's History of Music, is not a mere personal anecdote. It throws a light upon the comparative state of music at Naples and at Rome in Corelli's time, and exhibits a curious contrast between the fiery genius of Neapolitans, and the meek, timid, and gentle character of Corelli, so analogous to the style of his music.

Corelli died at Rome in the month of January, 1713, and was interred in the Church of the Rotunda, otherwise called the Pantheon, in the first chapel on the left hand of the entrance. Over the place of his interment there is a sepulchral monument with a marble bust erected to his memory at the expense of Philip William, Count Palatine of the Rhine, under the direction of Cardinal Ottoboni.*

For many years after the death of this excellent musician, the anniversary of the day was commemorated by a solemn musical performance in the Pantheon. In the year 1730, Sir John Hawkins says, that an eminent master of his acquaintance was present at the solemnity, who related that the third and eighth of the concertos were performed by a numerous band, in which there were many persons who had been pupils of the composer. He added also that these two pieces were played in a slow, distinct, and firm manner, without graces, and just as they are written; and

---

* The bust represents him with a music-paper in his hand, on which are engraven a few bars of that celebrated air, the Jig, in his fifth sonata.

thence he concluded that this was the style in which they were always played by the author himself.

At the time of his death, Corelli is said to have been possessed of a sum of money equal to about six thousand pounds sterling. He was a passionate admirer of pictures, and lived in great intimacy with Carlo Cignani and Carlo Marat. His collection of paintings, with the sum just mentioned, he bequeathed to his friend and patron Cardinal Ottoboni. This nobleman reserved the pictures, but generously distributed the rest of the effects among the relations of the testator.

It is related of Corelli that he was remarkable for the general mildness of his temper, and the modesty and propriety of his demeanour; yet it appears that he was not insensible of that respect which was due to his skill and exquisite performance. It is said that, when he was once playing a solo at Cardinal Ottoboni's house, he observed the Cardinal and another person in discourse, on which he laid down his instrument; and, being asked the reason, answered that " he feared the music interrupted the conversation." He is related also to have been a man of humour and pleasantry. Some who were acquainted with him have censured him for parsimonious habits, but on no better ground than his accustomed plainness of dress, and his disinclination to the use of a carriage.

The works of Corelli are solely compositions for instruments, and consist of Six Operas,* originally entitled as follows:

Suonate à trè, due Violini, e Violone, col Basso per l' Organo. Opera Prima.

Suonate da Camera à trè, due Violini, e Violone ò Cimbalo. Opera Seconda.

Suonate à trè, doi Violini, e Violone ò Arcileuto, col Basso per l' Organo. Opera Terza.

Suonate da Camera à trè, doi Violini, e Violone ò Cimbalo. Opera Quarta.

Suonate à Violono e Violone ò Cimbalo. Opera Quinta, Parte prima, Parte seconda, Preludii, Allemande, Correnti, Gighe, Sarabande, Gavotte, e Follia.

Concerti Grossi con duoi Violini e Violoncello di concertino obligati, e duoi altri Violini, Viola e Basso di Concerto Grosso ad arbitrio che si potranno radoppiare.

The Four Operas of Corelli's sonatas were published, as they were completed, at different times. The first edition of the First Opera is not known; that of the Second Opera was printed at Rome in 1685; that of the Third at Bologna in 1690; and that of the Fourth, at Bologna in 1694. The first

---

* Two collections of sonatas printed at Amsterdam, and not enumerated in this list, have every evidence of being the composition of some other person, though printed in the name of Corelli.

edition of the Fifth Opera was published at Rome in 1700. These early editions were printed in the old lozenge-headed note, with the quavers and semiquavers disjoined from each other, forming a very obscure and illegible character.

Of the concertos, the first edition is that beautiful one printed at Amsterdam, for Estienne Roger and Michael Charles le Cene, in 1712.

All the works of Corelli are said to have been composed with great deliberation, to have been corrected by him at many different times, and to have been submitted to the inspection of the most skilful musicians of his day. Of the sonatas it may be remarked, that the First and Third Operas consist of fugues and slow movements without any intermixture of airs; and these are said by Mattheson to have been usually played in the churches abroad after divine service. The whole Four Operas, for many years, furnished the second music before the play at both the theatres in London. The Fifth Opera consists of those solo-sonatas which the author himself was accustomed to perform on particular occasions. The last of the twelve is a set of divisions, twenty-four in number, on a favourite air, known in England by the name of Farinell's Ground, and called by Corelli, *Follia*.

As to the peculiar excellences of the works of Corelli, we may observe that the First Opera is but an essay towards the perfection to which he afterwards arrived. There is comparatively but little art, and less invention in it; its third, eighth, and ninth sonatas are almost the only ones in practice. The Second Opera carries with it the evidence of a genius matured by exercise; the second, fifth, eighth, and eleventh sonatas are both learned and elegant. The Third Opera, the most elaborate of the four, abounds in fugues; its first, fourth, sixth, and ninth sonatas are the most celebrated, the latter has drawn tears from many an eye; but the whole are so excellent, that, exclusive of mere fancy, there is scarcely any motive for preference. The Fourth Opera is, in its kind, equal to either of the former two; the second and the eleventh sonatas excite melancholy, and soothe the mind in a most pathetic manner; the third, sixth, and tenth are chearful and lively in an eminent degree.

Of his solos, the second, third, fifth, and sixth are admirable; as are the ninth, tenth, and, for the elegant sweetness of its second movement, the eleventh.

The Sixth Opera, containing his concertos, though composed at a time when the faculties of the author might be supposed to have been on the decline, affords the strongest proof of the contrary. Nothing can exceed, in dignity and majesty, the opening of the first concerto, nor, for its plaintive sweetness, the whole of the third; and that person must have no feeling of the power of harmony, or the effects of modulation, who can listen to the eighth without rapture.

The compositions of Corelli are celebrated for
the harmony resulting from the union of all the
parts; but the fineness of the airs is another dis.
tinguishing characteristic of them. The allemande
in the tenth solo is as remarkable for spirit and
force, as that in the eleventh is for its charming
delicacy. His jigs are in a style peculiarly his
own; and that in the fifth solo was never equalled.
In the gavot movements in the Second and Fourth
Operas, the melody is distributed with great judgment among the several parts. In his minuets
alone he seems to fail; Bononcini, Handel, and
Martini, have all excelled him in this kind of air.

The music of Corelli is, generally speaking, the
language of nature. It is equally intelligible to the
learned and to the unlearned; and the impression that
it makes is almost indelible. For a long series of
years all who heard it became sensible of its effects;
for amidst the numerous innovations which the
love of change had introduced, it still continued
to be performed, and was heard with delight in
churches, in theatres, and at public solemnities and
festivals, in all the cities of Europe for nearly forty
years. Persons remembered and would refer to
passages of it, as to a classic author; and even at
this day, the masters of the science do not hesitate
to pronounce, of the compositions of Corelli, that,
for correct harmony, and for elegant modulation,
they are scarcely to be exceeded.

The natural and familiar style of Corelli's music

betrayed many persons into an opinion that it was easy to be imitated; and it almost seems, that, from harmonies such as his are, a canon might be drawn which would give to any music, composed in conformity to it, a similar appearance. The experiment, however, has been tried, and has failed. Ravenscroft and many other persons attempted to imitate the style of Corelli, but their compositions are immediately distinguishable by any accurate judge of music.

GIUSEPPE TORELLI, a native, says Dr. Burney, of Verona, Academico Filarmonico di Bologna, and a celebrated performer on the violin, was concert-master at Anspach about the year 1703. Afterwards he removed to Bologna, and was appointed chapel-master of the Church of San Petronio in that city. He is supposed to have died about the year 1708.

Torelli composed and published several collections of *airs and sonatas for violins;* but the most considerable, and the best of his works, is his Eighth Opera, printed at Bologna a short time after his death, entitled, " *Concerti grossi con una* " *Pastorale per il santissimo natale."* He is said to have been the inventor of that species of instrumental composition, the *concerto grosso.* His productions for the violin are now so superannuated as almost to cease to be music; for, having little original melody, and no uncommon stock

of harmony or modulation, there is nothing left
to make amends for the want of novelty and elegance.

ANTONIO CALDARA was born at Venice about
the year 1660. Under whom he had his musical
tuition is not now known. During the early part
of his life he resided almost wholly in his native
city, and in other parts of Italy. His first opera,
which was that of *Argine,* was composed at
Venice in 1689. About sixteen years after this
period he was invited into Germany, and was appointed one of the vice-chapel-masters to the imperial court at Vienna, under Fux. The celebrity
of Caldara, as a composer of the old school, for
sublimity of style, and for the depth and variety of
his harmony, was very great. These are eminently
conspicuous in his *oratorios* and his *masses.* Of
the former there were two which he composed
about the year 1722, entitled, " *Giuseppo,*" and
" *Il Ré del Dolore, in Giesu Cristo, Signor nos-*
" *tro, coronato di Spine.*" In 1731, he also set
an oratorio written by Metastasio, entitled, " *Sant'*
" *Elena in Calvario.*" But these were by no
means the whole of his compositions of this description : as many as twelve or fourteen others
have been enumerated.

Caldara was also the composer of several *operas,*
two sets of sonatas for two violins and a bass,
printed at Amsterdam, and " *Cantate da Camera*

" à. *Voce sola*," published at Venice. Some specimens of his music are inserted in the first volume of Latrobe's Selection.

He died in the year 1736.

Antonio Lotti was organist of the Chapel of St. Mark at Venice, and flourished betwixt the years 1670 and 1730. He was a pupil of Legrenzi, who was his predecessor in the Chapel of St. Mark, and the master of Marcello and other eminent composers. Lotti justly acquired great celebrity on the Continent. His music, it has been observed, combines the art and regularity of the old school with, at the same time, all the gracefulness, richness, and brilliancy of the modern. Hasse, who saw him in 1727, says of him : " Mark what expression, what variety, what correctness, what truth, in all his ideas."

In the year 1705, Lotti published at Venice, and dedicated to the Emperor Joseph, a work entitled, " *Duetti, Terzetti, e Madrigali* ;" and there are still extant, in manuscript, many of his compositions for the church. From one of his masses there is a fine chorus, " Qui tollis," inserted in the second volume of Latrobe's Selection of Sacred Music.

Lotti married Signora Santini, a well-known singer of that day, and was living at Venice in the year 1731.

ITALIAN MUSICAL WRITERS,

Who flourished from about 1650 *to* 1700.

DANIEL BARTOLI, a Jesuit, and a native of Ferrara, born in the year 1608, published at Bologna,
in 1680, a treatise " *Del Suono de' Tremori*
" *Armonici e dell' Udito.*" In this truly scientific and ingenious work are to be found several
discoveries in harmonics, that were pursued by
subsequent writers on the subject. It contains
four dissertations; the first treats of the similarity
betwixt certain undulations occasioned in still
water when a stone is thrown into it, and the pro-
pagation and motion of sound; the second treats
of the motion of sound compared with that of light;
of echoes or reflection of sound, and of its augmentation in a whispering room or gallery; the third,
of harmonic vibrations and ratios of sound, of
sympathetic sounds, of the breaking of a glass
with the voice; and the fourth, of the mixture of
sounds; of consonance, harmonics, and the immense increase of sounds in a vessel, or inclosed
place, by repercussion. It concludes with a description of the anatomy of the ear. He was the
author of many other profound and learned works,
and died at Rome in the year 1685.

Pietro Mengoli was a native of Bologna, and born about the year 1626. In the early part of his life he read public lectures on music in several of the schools of Bologna, for the purpose chiefly of explaining the doctrines of Zarlino and Galileo.

He published there, in the year 1670, a treatise entitled, " *Speculationi di Musica.*" In that part of the work which he denominates the Natural History of Music, he treats of the anatomy of the ear, of its capability of receiving sounds, and of the power of the air in conveying them. He then speaks of the combination of sounds, in which he lays down some new principles, that are, in fact, the chief foundation of the whole work. After this he explains, at considerable length, the nature of the musical intervals, shewing between what numbers the species of each interval are most perfect. He treats of the chords; then of singing and modulations of tune. The latter he distinguishes from singing in general, by observing that modulation is a succession of sounds so strongly impressed upon the senses that we are not able to repeat them. The author next discourses fully on the subjects of consonance and harmonical proportions, and also on the passions of the soul, endeavouring to show how they are concerned in and affected by music. Towards the conclusion he gives a table of the several musical chords that are suited to the different affections.

Some of the speculations contained in this work are specious and ingenious, but the philosophy of sound has been so much more scientifically and clearly treated since the time of its publication, that the difficulty of obtaining the book, which is now become scarce, is no great impediment to the advancement of music.

GIOVANNI ANDREA ANGELINI BONTEMPI, a native of Perugia, was chapel-master to the Elector of Saxony.

In the year 1695, he published, at Perugia, a work in small folio, entitled " *Historia Musica,*" the first part of which treats of the theory of music, the second of the practice of the ancients, and the third of that of the moderns.

In this work the author enters into the subject of the ancient music ; and in a tolerably concise manner gives the substance of what preceding writers had stated respecting it. That part which relates to the practice of the moderns contains, amongst other things, an account of the reformation of the scale by Guido, and of a person (with whose name he was not acquainted) who discovered the method of qualifying the fifths in the musical scale, in such manner as not to give offence to the ear. He informs us that this same person invented also the characters of ♯ and ♭, and by this means formed a system of sounds, separated from each other by the interval of a semitone ;

thus, he says, " uniting the chromatic with the
diatonic genus, and of the- two forming one."
The practice of counterpoint is traced from the
supposed time of its invention by Guido, down to
the time of De Muris.   On the authority of
Franchinus, Vanneo, and Kircher, he ascribes to
De Muris the invention of the cantus mensurabilis.

The Historia Musica of Bontempi is a work of
some merit ; but it seems little calculated for instruction.   The author had probably read much
on the subject of music, but it appears, in various
instances, that the knowledge he had attained was
not derived from its genuine source.   That he
had perused the Greek writers in the edition of
Meibomius cannot be doubted ; but his great
fault is in relying with too ready an acquiescence
on the authorities of Franchinus, Steffano, Vanneo,
and Kircher, in matters relating both to the theory
and practice of music.   A general character may
be given of this work by saying, that it is just
such as to be sufficient to, awaken that curiosity
which it is the end of history to gratify.   In those
who are ignorant of the subject it may excite
approbation ; but it falls short of affording satisfaction to a learned and curious inquirer.

There is another publication extant written by
Bontempi, in which it is said much learning is
displayed.   This is entitled, " *Nova quatuor*
" *Vocibus componendi Methodus.*"

LORENZO PENNA, of Bologna, a Carmelite monk, and a professor of music, was the author of a work entitled, " *Albori Musicale*," printed at Bologna in 1672. This is divided into three parts. The first treats of the elements of the canto figurato ; the second of counterpoint ; and the third of thorough-bass, or the art of accompaniment.

In this, which is one of the best of the Italian works on the subject, the scale of Guido, with the use of the syllables and cliffs, and the nature of the mutations, are explained in a very concise, intelligible manner, as are also the characters employed in the cantus mensurabilis. Of the rules of counterpoint little can be said further than that they are perfectly consistent with the laws of harmony. The third part of the work is taken from the writings of Luzzaschi, Merula, Frescobaldi, and other celebrated Italian organists.

A continuation of the " *Albori Musicale*" was published at Venice in the year 1678.

ANTIMO LIBERATI, during his youth, was a singer in the Imperial Chapel of Ferdinand the Third, and afterwards in the Pontifical Chapel. When arrived at manhood he was appointed maestro di capella and organist of the Church Della Santissima Trinità de Pellegrini, and chapel-master and organist of the Church Di Santi Maria dell' Anima della Natione Teutonica, at Rome. During the time he held the latter station, the place of chapel-master of the Metropolitical Church of Milan became vacant, and Liberati was requested to give his opinion of the respective merits of five persons who were candidates for it. In consequence of this request he wrote a letter, dated the 15th of October, 1684, which he afterwards published, with the title of " *Lettera scritta dal Sig.* " *Antimo Liberati, in risposta ad una del Sig.* " *Ovidio Persapegi.*" In this he discusses the merits of the compositions presented by the candidates in evidence of their abilities ; and then traces the rise and progress of music from the time of Pythagoras downwards, and gives his opinion respecting most of the eminent musicians who had lived both before and during his own time. This letter contains many curious particulars of musical history, but is written in such a vein of general panegyric, that it is much more likely to produce scepticism than conviction in the minds of modern readers.

Angelo Berardi, a canon of the Collegiate Church of St. Angelo di Viterbo, was the author of many musical tracts, and among the rest of one entitled, " *Documenti Armonici,*" in the composition of which he was assisted by Scacchi, chapel-master to the king of Poland. It was printed at Bologna in 1687, and is divided into three books, containing the precepts of counterpoint, fugue, and canon, illustrated by many examples; and is well deserving the attention of the curious.

In the year 1689, Berardi published at Bologna a work entitled, " *Miscellania Musicale*," in three parts. The first and second parts, selected from the writings of Boëtius, Zarlino, Vincentino, and others, contain little else than what is to be found in every treatise on the subject that has been written within the last hundred and fifty years. In the third part there are several examples of counterpoint, and a series of exercises on the twelve tones.

Four years after the publication of the above work, Berardi printed at Bologna, " *Il Perche Musicale, overo Staffetta Armonica;*" and in 1706, " *Arcani Musicali.*"

CHAP. VIII.

GERMAN
MUSICAL COMPOSERS AND WRITERS,

WHO FLOURISHED

During the Seventeenth Century.

1600 to 1700.

PRÆTORIUS. — SCHUTZ. — KLEMME. — HERBST. — HAMMERSCHMIDT.—FROBERGER. — KAPSBERGER. —ROSENMULLER.—WERKMEISTER.—JOHN AND ANDREW THIEL.—ZACHAU.—KRIEGER.—PACHELBEL.—BUTTSTETT.—KERL.—BIBER.—MUFFATT.—BUXTEHUDE.

CRÜGER. — ALSTEDIUS. — JOHN GERARD VOSSIUS.— KIRCHER.—MEIBOMIUS.—ISAAC VOSSIUS.—MEYER. —KUHNAU.—PRINTZ.

THE Emperor Leopold, who succeeded to the throne of Germany in the year 1657, was a great lover of music. He discovered an early propensity to the Italian style. The recitative of Carissimi appeared to him to be a species of musical composition, in which the powers of eloquence derived new force by the association to speech of sounds that corresponded with the sense. As soon therefore as a cessation from the toils of war gave him leisure to cultivate the arts of peace, he determined upon the introduction of Italian music into Germany. Accordingly we find, that shortly afterwards, he invited Italian composers to his court, and gave pensions and rewards to the most excellent of them, but particularly to Caldara, Ziani, Lotti, and Bononcini. He had also representations of Italian operas, and some of the most celebrated singers performed in them.

It was not, however, at Vienna alone that Italian music was thus introduced. The same passion influenced other princes ; and in other cities, as Berlin, Hanover, and Hamburgh, we find that Italian musicians were greatly caressed and encouraged. The works of some of the most eminent of them were published in Germany, and dedicated to German princes. Operas were represented in the principal cities ; and at length the German musicians became themselves the composers of operas. From these circumstances we are enabled satisfactorily to ascertain the origin of dramatic music in Germany and its adjacent countries.

MICHAEL PRÆTORIUS, a native of Cruetzberg, a city on the river Wena, in Thuringia, belonging to the Duke of Saxe Eisenach, was born in the year 1571. Having made great proficiency in music, he was appointed, by Henry-Julius Duke

of Brunswick, chapel-master and chamber-organist
of his court, and also private secretary to his
consort Elizabeth. Being an ecclesiastic by profession, he afterwards became prior of the Benedictine monastery of Ringheln, in the bishopric of
Hildesheim. He was also, but in what part of his
life it is not known, chapel-master to the Electoral
court of Dresden. He died at Wolfenbuttle on
the day of his nativity, 1621, having just completed
his fiftieth year.

The musical compositions of Prætorius are numerous, and consist of *motets, masses, hymns,* and
other church offices. He wrote also a treatise, intended to consist of four volumes in quarto, but only
three were printed, entitled " *Syntagma Musi-*
" *cum.*" This work contains a deduction of the
progress of ecclesiastical music from the period of
its origin to his own time.

HEINRICH SCHUTZ was born in the year 1585
at Hosteritz, a village on the river Elster, in
Voightland. His grandfather was a privy-coun-
sellor, and his father a burgomaster of Weissenfels.
In 1599, he was introduced to the Count Palatine
Moritz, at his court of Hesse Cassel, and was, by
the direction of that prince, instructed in languages
and the arts. Having perfected himself in the
rudiments of literature, he was admitted, about
eight years afterwards, into the University of
Marpurg, and began to study the law. In this he

made great proficiency ; but his patron finding that he had an invincible propensity to music, generously offered to take him from the university, and, at his own expense, to place him under the tuition of Gabriello, at that time a celebrated musician at Venice. This offer was so entirely accordant to the wishes and inclination of the young man, that it was immediately accepted. Schutz went to Venice, and continued there until the death of his master, which took place in the year 1612.

He then returned to Hesse Cassel, and the Count Palatine settled on him an annual pension of two hundred guilders. Hitherto he had not resolved to adopt the profession of music, but continued to study the law until the year 1615, when the Elector of Saxony invited him to his court, and invested him with the dignity of director of his music, and at the same time honoured him with a gold chain and medal. In 1628, having a desire to revisit Italy, he obtained permission for that purpose, and during his abode at Venice, in the year following, he published a collection of *motets*, with the title of " Sigillarius."

Soon after his return to Dresden the Electorate of Saxony became the seat of war. Not choosing therefore to make that city the place of his residence, he accepted an invitation from his Danish Majesty to reside at Copenhagen. From thence he afterwards removed to Brunswick-Lunenburgh, and in 1642 returned to Denmark, where he was appointed director of the king's music. Towards the latter end of his life he became very deaf, and employed much of his time in reading the Scriptures, and in the study of theology. He did not however renounce the study of music, for in his retirement he composed many noble works. He set to music several of the *psalms*, and the history of the passion as it is recorded by three of the Evangelists. He died in November, 1672, in the eighty-eighth year of his age.

His principal works are, " *Historie der Au-* " *ferstehung Jesu Christi,"* in seven books, published at Dresden in 1623 ; " *Kleinen geistlichen* " *Concerten,"* for one, two, three, four, and five voices, at Leipsig, 1636 ; and " *Symphoniarum* " *Sacrarum,"* the first part of which was published at Friburg in 1629 ; the second at Dresden in 1647 ; and the third in 1650. Eleven years after this all the works of Schutz were reprinted together at Dresden.

JOHN KLEMME, a Saxon by birth, and a celebrated organist and church musician, was patronised, for his early proficiency in music, by Christian the Second, Elector of Saxony. That prince committed him to the tuition of the ablest masters in the court of Dresden ; and he was instructed and maintained at his expense for nearly six years, when the Elector died. Fortunately for

Klemme, the succeeding Elector was also a lover
of music; and observing his desire for improvement, he placed him, for further instruction, under
Christian Erbach, an organist and composer at
Augsburg, with whom he studied three years. At
the expiration of this term he returned to Dresden,
and was soon afterwards appointed master of the
Electoral Chapel, and organist to the Elector.

The works of Klemme are thirty-six *fugues*
for the organ, composed after the manner of voluntaries, and published at Dresden in the year
1631. He was likewise the author of a set of
spiritual madrigals, in the German language, for
four, five, and six voices; and he assisted in the
publication of the second part of the *Symphonia-*
rum Sacrarum of Schutz. Klemme is considered
to have been one of the most skilful harmonists of
his time.

John Andreas Herbst was born at Nuremberg in the year 1588. At the age of forty he
was appointed chapel-master at Franckfort on the
Maine. He continued in that station about thirteen years, when he was called to the same office
at Nuremberg. In 1650, at the solicitation of
his friends, he returned to Franckfort, and kept his
former place until the time of his death, in 1660.

He was deeply read in the theory of music, and
in composition he had few equals. Like most of
the Germans, he was a sound and judicious orga-

nist.   In the year 1643 he published, in the German language, a work entitled *"Musica Poetica;"* and ten years afterwards, a translation into the same language of the *" Arte Prattica e Poetica"* of Giovanni Chiodino. He was also the author of a tract entitled, *"Musica Moderna Prattica, overo " Maniere del buon Canto,"* printed at Franckfort in 1658, in which he strongly recommends the Italian manner of singing.   His other works are, *A small Tract on Thorough-Bass,* and *A Discourse on Counterpoint.*

Of his musical compositions there are only extant, *" Meletemata sacra Davidis,"* and *" Sus- " piria S. Gregorii ad Christum,"* for three voices. These were printed in the year 1619, at the same time with another of his compositions for six voices.

ANDREW HAMMERSCHMIDT,   a Bohemian, born in 1611, was organist first of the Church of St. Peter at Friburg, and afterwards of that of St. John at Zittaw.   He is chiefly celebrated for his assiduity in the improvement of the church music in Saxony, and some of the other German provinces.   He died in 1675, at the age of sixty-four, and was interred in the great church of Zittaw.   The inscription on his tomb styles him the *"* German Orpheus.*"*

His compositions were chiefly *motets* for four, five, and six voices.

JOHN JACOB FROBERGER, a pupil of Frescobaldi, and organist to the Emperor Ferdinand the
Third, flourished about the year 1650. He was
an excellent performer on the organ and harpsichord, and his compositions for those instruments
have been highly applauded. He is said to have
been partial to imitations in music of different
occurences in life, to which he had the power of
giving great expression. In writing his compositions he used a stave of six lines for the right, and
one of seven lines for the left hand.

JOHN JEROME KAPSBERGER, a German of noble extraction, is well known not only for the
number and variety of his compositions, but also
for his great skill and execution on almost all instruments, but in particular on the theorbo-lute,
an instrument invented by a Neapolitan musician,
whose name is not now known. Kapsberger rendered essential assistance to Kircher in the compilation of his Musurgia.

A mean jealousy of the reputation of Palestrina
induced him, in conjunction with some others,
to make several nefarious attempts to destroy the
popularity of that great musician. The conspi-
racy failed, and the conspirators reaped for their
trouble only odium and disgrace.

Many of the compositions of Kapsberger are
for the lute. He wrote some *masses*, *litanies*,
motets, and other pieces for the church, and a

considerable portion of vocal music for the theatre and for public solemnities. He published at Rome a work entitled, "*Coro Musicale in* "*Nuptiis D. D. Thaddei Barberini et. Annæ* "*Columnæ.*"

JOHN ROSENMULLER was a Saxon by birth, and joint-professor of music with Tobias Michaelis in the Academy of St. Thomas at Leipsic, until he was imprisoned on suspicion of having committed a heinous crime. He found means to escape from prison, and fled to Hamburgh. After some stay there he went to Italy, where his skill on the organ was universally admired. At length he obtained the situation of chapel-master in the great church at Wolfenbuttle. He died in the year 1685.

The most celebrated of his compositions are, "*Sonate da Camera à 5 Stromenti,*" and *a collection of airs* of various kinds.

ANDREW WERKMEISTER, the son of a brewer at Bennickenstein, a small town in Thuringia, was born in the month of November, 1645. After the usual school education, he was sent to the college of Quidlenburg, and, having much improved himself in music, was, some time afterwards, invited, by the council of Hasselfelde, a city in the principality of Blankenburg, to become their organist. While in this employment he was sent

for, to the same office, at Elrich, but was prevented
from going thither by the Duke Rudolphus Augustus, who wished to keep him within his own
district. Being however invited, in the year 1674,
to Elbingerod, with the offer of the places of
organist and recorder of the town, he was permitted to accept them. He was some time afterwards appointed organist of the Church of St.
Martin at Hallerstadt, in which station he died in
the year 1706.

His works are, " Orgel-Probe," printed in
1681 ; " Musicæ Mathematicæ," in 1687 ; " So-
" natas for a Violin with a Thorough-Bass," in
1689 ; " Musicalische Temperatur," in 1691 ;
" A Treatise in German on the Use and Abuse
" of Music," printed in the same year ; " Hy-
" pomnemata Musica," in 1697 ; " Ereweiterte
" Orgel-Probe," in 1698 ; "Cribrum Musicum,'
in 1700 ; " A Translation of Steffani's Letters,
" with Notes," in 1700 ; " Reflections on Tho-
" rough-Bass," in German without a date ; "Har-
" monologiam Musicam," in 1702 ; " Organum
" Gruningense redivivum," in 1705 ; and "Mu-
" sicalische Paradoxal Discurse," published the
year after his death.

JOHN THIEL was the son of a tailor of Naumburg, and born in year 1646. He studied in the
universities of Halle and Leipsic. From thence
he went to Weissenfels, in Saxony ; and under

Schutz, the chapel-master there, perfected himself in the art of composition. Thus qualified, he removed to Stettin, in Pomerania, and became a teacher of music. In 1673, he was made chapel-master at Gottorp; but being driven from thence by the wars, he settled at Hamburgh. He was subsequently elected to the office of chapel-master at Wolfenbuttle, in the room of Rosenmuller. After holding this place for some years, he entered the service of Christian, the Second Duke of Merseburg, in which he continued until the death of that prince.

During this time he composed many pieces for the church; and in some of them professes to imitate the style of Palestrina. He was the composer of an highly valuable work, the title to which begins thus: " *Novæ Sonatæ rarissimæ Artis et* " *Suavitatis Musicæ, partim 2 Vocum, cum sim-* " *plis et duplo-inversis Fugis; partim 3 Vocum,* " *cum simplis et duplo et triplo inversis Fugis;* " *partim 4 Vocum, cum,*" &c.

From the evidences of deep learning contained in his works, Thiel is justly ranked among the first of the German musicians. He died at Naumburg in the year 1724.

ANDREW THIEL was a celebrated musician, a contemporary with, and, as it has been generally supposed, the brother of the last-mentioned composer.

He was the author of a collection of *lessons* published in the year 1696, entitled " *Neuer* " *Clavier Ubung.*"

FRIEDRICH WILHELM ZACHAU, the son of a musician of Leipsic, was born in that town in the year 1663. He was placed at the public school there, and became a deeply skilled proficient in the science of music, and likewise attained some excellence as a performer on the organ and other instruments. He studied under Thiel at Stettin, and in 1684 was appointed organist of the Church of the Virgin Mary at Halle, in Saxony, where he continued until his death in the year 1721.

He composed several pieces for the *church,* and some *lessons for the clavier or harpsichord.* His professional celebrity occasioned him to have many pupils, and it is no small addition to his character, that he was the musical preceptor of Handel.

JOHN PHILIP KRIEGER, the son of a merchant of Nuremberg, was born in the year 1649, and, very early in life, began the practice of music. After being under the care of several masters, he went into Holland, and from thence to Bareith, where he became first chamber-organist to the Margrave, and afterwards chapel-master in that city. In 1672 he travelled into Italy; and at

Rome he considerably improved himself by the instructions of Abbatini and of Pasquini, the famous performer on the harpsichord. On his return homeward, he continued some time at Naples, and took lessons from Rovetta, the organist of the Church of St. Mark in that city. He no sooner arrived at Vienna than he was invited to play before the Emperor, who was so highly delighted with his performance, that he presented him with a purse of ducats, a gold medal and chain. He continued in the service of the Emperor for some years, retaining, during all this time, his place of chapel-master at Bareith. Afterwards, being invited to Halle, he went thither, and at length became chapel-master to the Elector of Saxony at the court of Weissenfels, which function he exercised for nearly forty years. He died in the month of February, 1727.

The works of Krieger are of various kinds: they consist of *Sonatas for the Violin* and *Viol da Gamba; of Field Music,* or overtures for trumpets and other military instruments ; of Latin and German *psalms* set to music ; and *songs* in the several dramatic entertainments composed by him, entitled *Flora, Cecrops,* and *Procris. Several lessons for the harpsichord* by Krieger are also to be met with in manuscript, which appear to be written in a masterly style ; but it is no where said

that he published any compositions for that instrument.

JOHN PACHELBEL, a celebrated organist and
composer, was born at Nuremberg in the year
1653. Discovering in his youth a strong inclination for science, he was provided, by his parents,
with the ablest instructors that could be procured.
He studied for some time at Altdorff; but finding
himself straitened in circumstances, he removed
to the Gymnasium Poeticum in Regensburgh.
Here he continued three years, prosecuting his
studies, particularly in music, with so much diligence that the fame of his proficiency was spread
throughout all Germany. On his quitting Regens-
burg, he went to Vienna, and became deputy to
the organist of St. Stephen's Church in that city.
This situation, though attended with little profit,
he found very agreeable, as it procured him the
friendship and acquaintance of Kerl, at that time
chapel-master at Vienna. In 1675, Pachelbel
was sent for to Eisenach, and was there preferred
to the dignity of court-organist. Three years
afterwards he removed to Erfurth, where his abilities caused him to be eminently distinguished.
In 1690, he was invited to Stutgard, but, that
city being threatened with invasion by the French,
he quitted it and settled at Gotha. Not long after
this, on the death of Wecker, he succeeded to his

place as organist of Nuremberg, in which he continued till his own death, about the year 1706.

Pachelbel is celebrated as one of the most excellent of those German organists of whom Kerl is
accounted the father.   He studied the grand and
full styles, which he laboured much to improve.

The works of Pachelbel, that are known, are
very few, being only four *Funeral Hymns*, composed at Erfurth during the time that a violent
pestilence raged there; and *Seven Sonatas for two
Violins and a Bass*, and *Airs with Variations*,
printed at Nuremberg.

JOHN HENRY BUTTSTETT, born in 1666, a scholar
of Pachelbel, and organist of the principal church
at Erfurth, the capital of Thuringia, is numbered
among the great organ-players and composers for
that instrument of his time.

JOHN CASPER KERL was a native of Saxony.
Having, during his youth, shewn a great taste for
music, he was sent to Vienna, and, at the expense
of the Archduke Leopold, placed under the tuition
of Giovanni Valentini, chapel-master at the Imperial court.   His patron afterwards ordered him
to be sent to Rome, in order to complete his musical
studies under Carissimi.   At his return he had an
highly advantageous offer from the Elector Palatine; but he refused it, and settled in Bavaria,

where he became. chapel-master to the Elector Ferdinando Maria.

Kerl's principal work is his *" Modulatio orga-* *" nica super Magnificat octo Tonis ecclesiasticis* *" respondens,"* printed at Munich in 1686. He is justly esteemed one of the most celebrated organists that the world ever produced. In a competition that he had with some Italian musicians, at the court of the Elector of Bavaria, he composed a piece for the organ so difficult that none but himself could execute it.

HENRY JOHN FRANCIS BIBER, vice-chapel-master to the Bishop of Saltzburg, published, in 1681, a set of *Solos for a Violin and Bass.* He seems to have been amongst the first violin-players of his time ; and his solos are the most difficult and the most fanciful, says Dr. Burney, of any music of the same period. One of the. pieces is written on three staves, as if a score for two violins and a bass, but meant to be played in double stops. Others are played in different turnings of fourths and fifths, as for a treble viol. A second work by this musician, entitled *" Fidicinum sacro-prophanum,"* consists of twelve sonatas, in four and five parts, to be played on three instruments ; and a third, *" Harmonia artificioso-arioso,"* published at Nuremberg, consisting of pieces of seven parts to be played on three instruments.

GEORGE MUFFATT was an eminent organist, composer, and fughist, and one of the great harmonists of Germany, at the latter end of the seventeenth century. After having been, for some time, organist of the Cathedral Church of Strasburg, he went to Vienna, Rome, and Paris. At the latter place he continued six years, during which time he made himself, in a particular manner, acquainted with Lully's style of composition.

In 1690, he published his " *Apparatus musico-* " *organistus ;*" a work consisting of twelve *toccate,* which he performed at Augsburg on the day that the consort of the Emperor Leopold was crowned Empress, and his son Joseph, King of the Romans.

DIETRICH BUXTEHUDE, the son of John Buxtehude, organist of the Church of St. Olaus at Elsineur, was a pupil of Thiel, and celebrated for his skilful performance on the organ, and as a composer for that instrument and the harpsichord. He was organist of the Church of St. Mary at Lubeck.

He published *Six Suites of Lessons for the Harpsichord,* in which the nature and course of the planets is intended to be represented. With these is printed a *choral composition,* to German words, on the death of his father. In 1696, he published two operas of " *Sonatas à Violino,* " *Viola da Gamba, e Cembalo.*"

In Mattheson's Account of Handel, it is stated
that Buxtehude and he travelled together to Lubeck,
respecting a vacancy which there was in an organist's place there, and in the *waggon* composed
several double fugues *da monte*, not *da penna*.

GERMAN MUSICAL WRITERS,

Who flourished during the Seventeenth Century.

JOHN CRÜGER, director of the music in the
Church of St Nicholas, Berlin, published, in 1624,
a work entitled, " *Synopsin Musices, continen-*
" *tem Rationem constituendi et componendi Melos*
" *Harmonicorum,*" which went through several
editions.   He was likewise the author of a treatise on singing, " *Præcepta Musicæ practicæ*
" *figuralis,*" printed in 1625; of " *Quæstiones*
" *Musicæ practicæ ;*" and a hymn-book with
tunes, entitled, " *Praxis Pietatis Melica.*"   The
latter attained so much celebrity as to pass through
thirty editions at Berlin in the beginning of the
eighteenth century.

JOHN HENRY ALSTEDIUS, a German protestant
divine, was born about the year 1588, and attained
so high a degree of celebrity for learning and
talents, that he was successively appointed pro-

fessor of philosophy and divinity at Herborn, in the county of Nassau, and at Waissemburgh, in Transylvania. He was one of the most voluminous writers of his time. Amongst other works, he published "Templum Musicum," or a Musical Synopsis, which is stated to have béen so formal as to resemble a logical, rather than a musical treatise.

He died at Waissemburgh in the year 1638.

GERARD JOHN VOSSIUS, born at a small town in the neighbourhood of Heidelberg, was a man of universal learning and abilities. He commenced his studies at Dort about the year 1590; and, ten years afterwards, was chosen director of the college in that place, though at the time only twenty-three years of age. In 1614, he was appointed director of the Theological College which the States of Holland had then lately founded in the University of Leyden. Before he received this latter appointment, Vossius had attached himself to the profession of divinity, and had warmly espoused the side of Arminius at the famous synod of Dort. These principles, and his History of the Pelagian Controversy, recommended him to the notice of Archbishop Laud, who procured for him a prebendal stall in the Church of Canterbury, with permission to hold it notwithstanding his residence at Leyden. On this promotion he came over to England to be installed; and, having received an

honorary degree of Doctor of Laws at Oxford, returned to Leyden; from whence, in 1633, he removed to Amsterdam, and became the first professor of history in the college then newly founded
in that city. He died, at this place, in the year
1649, a the age of seventy-two.

Vossius published at Amsterdam, in 1650, a
work " *De quatuor Artibus popularibus;*" and
afterwards another, " *De Universæ Mathesios*
" *Natura et Compositione;*" in each of which
are contained many curious particulars relative to
music and musicians.

ATHANASIUS KIRCHER, a native of Fulda, was
born in the year 1601. At the age of eighteen
he was admitted into the society of Jesuits; and
after having passed through a regular course of
study, became a teacher of philosophy, mathematics, and languages, in the University of Wurts-
berg. In the year 1631, when the Swedes, under
Gustavus Adolphus, entered Germany, he retired
into France, and settled in the Jesuits' College at
Avignon, where he continued four years. He
was then called to Rome to teach mathematics in
the Roman College; and he afterwards became
professor of the Hebrew language in that city.
He died in the month of November, 1680, having
written and published different works to the number of twenty-two volumes in folio, eleven in
quarto, and three in octavo.

The chief of Kircher's musical works is his " *Musurgia Universalis.*" This is divided into ten books. ' In the preface the author states that he was aided in the compilation of it by Antonio Maria Abbatini, chapel-master of the Churches of St. Maria Maggiore and Pietro Heredia in Rome, by Kapsberger, and Carissimi.

He apologises for his attempting to write on the subject of music, who was not a professed musician ; but he states, in his defence, that from his youth he had assiduously applied himself to the study of this science.

In the first book he treats of the anatomy of the ear, not only in man, but in various kinds of quadrupeds and birds. From this he passes to a description of the voice in the human race, and of the vocal organs also of several species of animals.

In the second book he speaks of the music of the Hebrews, and gives the forms of some of their instruments. He then proceeds to the music of the Greeks, of which he gives a general and superficial account.

The next book enters deeply into the doctrine of harmonics, first explaining the several kinds of proportion, and afterwards demonstrating the ratios of the intervals. This book contains a system of musical arithmetic, taken from the writings of Boëtius and others, in which are contained rules for the addition, subtraction, multiplication, and division of intervals, by means of characters adapted to the purpose.

The fourth book is entirely on the division of the monochord, and the method of finding the intervals by various geometric and algebraic processes.

The fifth book contains directions for the composition of music in consonance. In this he explains the nature of counterpoint, both simple and figurate, and also of fugue ; and gives some general rules for composition in one, two, three, and more parts. Towards the close of the book he speaks of that spurious kind of fugue called *fuga in nomine ;* and not only explains the nature of canon, but gives examples of canons, some of which are very wonderful in their contrivance. He mentions one, which he says might be sung by twelve millions two hundred thousand voices.

In the sixth book he treats of instrumental music, and of the various instruments in use among the moderns. Nearly the whole of this book is taken from the Latin work of Mersennus. At the conclusion he gives a particular description of the great bell at Erfurth.

The seventh book contains a comparison between the ancient and modern music, with some specimens of the ancient Greek musical characters, taken from Alypius. This book is of a miscellaneous nature, and, amongst other things,

comprises a general enumeration of the most eminent musicians of the author's time, and contains
a great variety of fine compositions selected from
their works.

The second volume begins with the eighth
book. In this are inserted tables of all the possible combinations of numbers, as they relate to
musical intervals ; as also some minute investigations into the various kinds of metre used in
poetry, and particularly in Greek and Latin poetry,
which are illustrated by musical characters.

In the ninth book there is a chapter " De
" Sympathiâ et Antipathiâ Sonorum Ratione,"
and an experiment here mentioned is truly curious. The author says, if five glasses of the
same magnitude are filled, one with aquavitæ,
the second with wine, the third with aqua subtilis,
the fourth with a thickish fluid, such as sea water
or oil, and the fifth or middle one with common
water, and a finger be wetted and rubbed round
the edge of the water glass, the following effects
will be produced : The aquavitæ will be much
agitated, the wine gently shaken, the aqua subtilis
less shaken, and the sea water or other fluid not
moved at all. From this experiment we may
probably date the invention of *musical glasses.*
He then produces instances of the surprising effects
wrought by music, beginning with the dispos-
session of Saul, as recorded in sacred writ, which
he endeavours to account for mechanically ; and

he concludes by relating the whole process for the reputed cure of the bite of a tarantula.

In treating of echoes, he relates an interesting story, from Cardan, which we shall give in his own words. "A friend of mine having set out on a journey, had a river to cross, and not knowing the ford, cried out, *Oh;* to which an echo answered, *Oh:* he, imagining it to be a man, called out in Italian, *onde devo passar?* it answered, *passa;* and when he asked, *qui?* it replied, *qui.* But as the waters formed a deep whirlpool there, and made a great noise, he was terrified, and again asked, *devo passar qui?* the echo returned, *passa qui.* He repeated the same question often, and still had the same answer. Terrified with the fear of being obliged to swim, in case he attempted to pass, and it being a dark and tempestuous night, he concluded that his respondent was some evil spirit that wanted to entice him into the torrent. He therefore returned, and on relating his story to Cardan, was convinced by him that it was no demon, but only the sport of nature."

The author next proceeds to the description of such instruments as produce music by the rotation of a cylinder; and mentions one, in the form of a star, in the church of a monastery of St. Fulda, so contrived, as, by the motion of a cylinder round its axis, to produce music from a number of small bells. He then describes an instrument contrived to resemble, in its sound, a concert of viols. This was in fact a harpsichord with a circular belly, under which was a wheel, one-sixth part of which rose above the belly : the strings, which were of the intestines of animals, (like those of the harp) were strained into contact with the edge of this wheel, and being rubbed with powdered rosin, produced the tone he speaks of.

Kircher mentions, as a contrivance of his own, the *Æolian harp,* which he describes at considerable length. But although he might have been gnorant of the fact, St. Dunstan is said by Fuller to have had one which must have been of a nature very similar to Kircher's.* In this book it is that he gives an account of the celebrated hydraulic organ of Vitruvius, which no one has hitherto been able to comprehend.

The tenth book is on the subject of analogical music, as Kircher has termed it, and the chief intention of it is to demonstrate the harmony of the four elements and of the planetary system. The author endeavours to prove that the principles of harmony are discoverable in the proportions of our bodies, in the passions of the mind, and even in the seven sacraments of the Church of Rome. From these he proceeds to the consideration of political and metaphysical harmony ; and, in conclusion, to that harmony, if any one can understand what

---

* Fuller's Church Hist. p. 128.

he means by it, which subsists in the several orders of intellectual beings, and which is consummated in the union between God and the universe.

In the year 1673, Kircher published his " *Pho-* " *nurgia Nova,"* a work in which he explains the nature, properties, and effects of sound.

In this work the author gives a very circumstantial account of that useful instrument called by us the speaking trumpet, the invention of which he claims as his own. Of the power of this trumpet, he says, that with one of fifteen palms in length he and some companions made themselves heard from different stations at the distance of two, three, four, and five Italian miles.

To speak in general terms of the works of Kircher; they are chiefly either on subjects of the most remote antiquity, or on such as, from their nature, seem to elude all inquiry : notwithstanding this the world is under great obligation to him for the *Musurgia Universalis.* In availing himself of the researches of other learned men, and of all the assistance that he could possibly derive from an extensive correspondence, and the communications of persons eminent both in the theory and practice of music, he has been able to exhibit such a fund of instruction and entertainment, such a variety of curious particulars relative to the principles and gradual progress of the science, and such a number of curious anecdotes respecting the professors of his own time, and the opinions entertained of their works, that we know not which to admire most, his ingenuity or his industry.

Notwithstanding the merits of Kircher, his Musurgia, soon after its publication, underwent some severe censures from Meibomius, a German writer of considerable celebrity, of whom we shall next speak.

MARCUS MEIBOMIUS, a well-known philologist and critic, was a native of Tonningen, in Holstein. When advanced in years he settled at Stockholm, and became a favourite of Christina, Queen of Sweden. Having searched deeply into the writings of the Greeks, he contracted an enthusiastic partiality for the music of the ancients, and not only entertained an opinion of its superiority over that of the moderns, but also that *he* was able to restore and to introduce it into practice. The queen who, from frequent conversations with him, had been induced to entertain the same sentiments on the subject as himself, was prevailed with to listen to a proposal that he made. This was to exhibit a musical performance that should be strictly conformable to the practice of the ancients; and, to crown all, he, who had but a bad voice, and never in his youth had been taught the exercise of it, engaged to sing one of the principal parts. Instruments of various kinds were prepared under the direction of Meibomius, at the expense of the queen ; and public notice was given of a musical exhibition that should astonish the world, and enchant all who should be happy enough to be present. On the appointed day Meibomius appeared, and beginning to sing, was heard for a short time with patience, but his performance and that of his assistants soon became past enduring. Neither the chromatic nor the enharmonic genus was suited to the ears of his illiterate audience, and the Lydian mode had lost its power. In short, his hearers, unable to resist the impulses of nature, at length expressed their opinions of the perform- ance by a general and long-continued burst of laughter.

Whatever might be the feelings of the people, Meibomius was but little disposed to sympathise with them. Their mirth was his disgrace, and he felt it but too sensibly. Seeing in the gallery M. Bourdelot the younger, a physician, and his rival in the queen's favour, he imputed the behaviour of the people to some insinuations of this person. He therefore immediately ran up to him, and struck him a violent blow on the neck. To avoid the consequences of this rashness, he quitted the city before he could be called to account for it, and took up his residence at Copenhagen. In this place he was well received, and became a professor at Sora, a college in Denmark, for the instruction of the nobility. Here he was honoured with the title of counsellor to the king; and was soon afterwards called to Elsineur, and advanced to the dignity of president of the Board of Maritime Taxes or Customs ; but neglecting his employment, he was dismissed from his office, and he soon afterwards quitted Denmark. He now settled at Amsterdam, and became professor of history in the college there ; but, on refusing to give private instruction to the son of a burgo-master, alleging as his excuse, that he was not accustomed to instruct *boys*, he was dismissed from that station. On this he quitted Amsterdam, and visited France and England ; but afterwards returning, he died at Amsterdam about the year 1710.

The great work of Meibomius was his edition of the seven Greek musical writers, Aristoxenus, Euclid, Nicomachus, Alypius, Gaudentius, Bacchius, and Aristides Quintilianus. This was published at Amsterdam in the year 1652, and contains a general preface to the whole, and also a particular preface to each of the treatises as they occur ; and a Latin translation of the Greek text, with copious notes, tending to reconcile various readings, and to explain the meaning of the several authors.

To this edition Meibomius has added a treatise, *" De Musica,"* of Martianus Felix Capella ; that is to say, the ninth book of the work of that author, *" De Nuptiis Philologiæ et Mei curii,"* which contains a kind of abridgment of Aristides Quintilianus.

Notwithstanding all the industry and abilities of
Meibomius, his manner of introducing the Greek
authors is extremely reprehensible. His general
preface abounds with invectives against all who
presumed to think less highly of the ancient music
than himself, but especially against Kircher. His
abuse of the Musurgia of Kircher is in a great
measure directed against its style and the want of
accuracy in the language ; yet, in spite of all his
efforts to injure its reputation with the world, it
will ever be considered as an original work that
contains much information and much scientific
disquisition. Mersennus, who possessed more musical erudition than any man of his time, has not
escaped his censure. Indeed, little less than such
behaviour to those who differed from him in opinion, could be expected from a man so bigoted
as Meibomius appears to have been, and whose
irascible disposition seems so often to have led him
beyond the bounds of decency.

Isaac Vossius was the son of Gerard John
Vossius, who has already been mentioned. He
was born at Leyden in the year 1618, and, under
the instruction of his father, soon became distinguished for his proficiency in academical learning.
He was honoured by the patronage of Christina,
Queen of Sweden, who invited him to her court, and
was taught by him the Greek language. About the
year 1652, having, however, formed a design of

writing against Salmasius, who at that time stood high in her favour, the queen withdrew her regard and dismissed him from any farther attendance.

At the death of his father, Vossius was offered the situation of professor of history in the University of Leyden, but he thought proper to decline it. In 1670, he came into England ; and at Oxford was admitted to an honorary degree of Doctor of Laws. Three years afterwards he was made a canon of Windsor by order of King Charles the Second, who permitted him to reside in the Castle, where he died in the year 1688.

Of his works the most popular is his treatise " De Poëmatum Cantu, et Viribus Rhythmi," printed at Oxford in 1673. This he begins by a remark, that music is of two kinds, namely, such as consists of sounds only, and such as consists of sounds joined to words. He then gives an account of the rhythmus of the ancient Greeks and of the various kinds of metrical feet used in their verses, all of which he affects to admire with rapture. His contempt of modern music and musicians he freely expresses, and says that all the powers of exciting the passions by music had ceased above a thousand years before his time. On the controverted question, whether the ancients were acquainted with music in consonance ? he, with the utmost confidence, gives it as his decided opinion that they were. The improvement of the musical scale has, he says, erroneously been ascribed to Guido, since, in forming his scale, he derived all his ideas from the organs and harps of his time, which consisted, the one of twenty pipes, and the other of twenty strings. As to the application of the syllables, he considers that to be an invention of no use whatever. The invention of the *cantus mensurabilis,* the substitute for the ancient rhythmus, he holds in the utmost contempt. The arguments against the imperfection of the ancient music, arising from the form of the instruments, he endeavours, but in vain, to refute.

In the course of this work the author is lavish of his censures on the ignorance and folly of other writers on music ; though his own enthusiasm and bigotry have laid him widely open to the latter imputation. In short, it abounds with evidence of that gross credulity for which its author is well known to have been remarkable. This, however, is by no means the only weakness with which he is charged ; his partiality for the ancients, his bold and hasty conclusions, his affected contempt of all modern improvements, his insolent treatment of such persons as differed from him in opinion, and, above all, his vanity, have placed him in the foremost rank of literary coxcombs. As to his work, its general character may be given in few words : it is a futile, unsatisfactory, and, for the most part, unintelligible disquisition.

Joachim Meyer was a Doctor of Laws and professor in the University of Gottingen, where, in 1686, he was also appointed professor of music and cantor figuralis.   He held these places for about ten years, when, retaining only the *title* of professor of music, he relinquished the practice of it, and gave public lectures on history and law. He afterwards became rector of the college, but at the end of three years quitted that honourable station, on account of his age and infirmities, when, as a reward for his merit, he was still permitted to enjoy all his salaries, with the addition of a pension.

In the year 1726, he published a tract entitled, " *Unvorgreiffsiche Gedanchen uber die Neuliche* " *ingerissene Theatrilische-Kirchen-Music ;*" in which he severely censures many of his contemporaries, who, by the levity of their compositions, had confounded the ecclesiastic with the theatrical style.

John Kuhnau was the son of a fisherman of Geysinghen, a town near Altenburgh, on the borders of Bohemia.   In the year 1684, he was appointed organist of the Church of St. Thomas at Leipsic. Whilst he resided at this place, he wrote and published a dissertation " *De Juribus circa* " *Musicos Ecclesiasticos,*" which he afterwards defended against the censures of his adversaries. In 1689, he published two sets of *lessons for the harpsichord ;* and some years afterwards, two other sets, the one consisting of six, and the other of seven lessons.   About 1700, he was appointed director of music in the University of Leipsic.   In this station he died in the year 1722, and in the sixty-third year of his age.

Kuhnau left behind him two musical manuscripts in Latin, which have never been published: " *Tractatus de Monochordo, seu Musica Antiqua* " *ac Hodierna,*" and " *Disputatio de Triade* " *Harmonica.*"

WOLFGANG CASPAR PRINTZ was born at Weild⁻thurn, a small city in the Upper Palatinate, in the year 1664.   His father was a magistrate, and a receiver of the public revenues there, till, on account of his religion, he quitted his station and removed to Vohenstraus, a small town in the territory of Furstenburgh.   Young Printz discovering a taste for music, was instructed in the principles of composition, and in the practice of the harpsichord, violin, and other instruments. He was admitted a student in the University at Altdorff, where he continued three years ; and from thence he was taken into the service of Count Promnitz at Dresden, as director of his music and the court composer.   With this nobleman he travelled through Silesia, Moravia, and Austria. On the decease of the Count, Printz was invited to the office of chanter in the church of a town

named Triebel, where he married; but, after a
year's continuance in that employment, being called
to the same office in the church at Sarau, in
Upper Saxony, he entered upon it in the year
1665. Some years afterwards he was appointed
to the direction of the choir in the same church,
and, as it is supposed, continued in that station
until the time of his death, in the year 1717.

His works are numerous. Among them there
is a history of vocal and instumental music, which
was published at Dresden, in the year 1690, with
the title of " *Historiche Beschreibung der edelen*
" *Sing-und, Kling-kunst.*" This is written in
chronological order, and the author begins it with
an account of the invention of the harp by Jubal.
He has delineated the Hebrew instruments chiefly
from the authority of Joannes Schutterus, the
author of *Collectaneis Philologicis.* The Grecian
and Hebrew music are treated at some length ;
and the history is continued through all the later
writers to his own time, concluding with an account of himself and his studies.

He dates the invention of music in consonance
from the year 940, and ascribes it to St. Dunstan,
who, he says, composed songs, in different parts,
for " bass, tenor, descant, and vagant or alt."
He asserts, however, that Dunstan proceeded no
further in it than to the *contrapuntus simplex,*
and that it was not till some years after its invention, that the practice of singing in consonance became general.

Printz appears to have been an able man in his profession, and to have bestowed great pains in the compilation of his work, the brevity of which is its only fault.   Another work by him has been mentioned, " *De Instrumentis in toto Orbe mu-* " *sicis,*" which is said to have been written only a short time before his death.

CHAP. IX.

FRENCH
MUSICAL COMPOSERS AND WRITERS,

WHO FLOURISHED DURING

The Sixteenth and Seventeenth Centuries,

1500 to 1700.

LE JEUNE.—CAURROY.—FEUM OR FEVIN.—MAITON.
— FRANC.—GOUDIMEL.—VERDELOT.—DUMONT.—
DE BROSSARD. — MOREAU. — LAMBERT. — GAU-
THIER THE ELDER.—PIERRE GAUTHIER.—CHAR-
PENTIER. — COLASSE. — MINORET. — CAMPRA. —
GILLES.—LALANDE.—LA LOUETTE. — MARAIS.—
ELIZABETH DE LA GUERRE. — SALOMON.—MAR-
CHAND.—LOUIS COUPERIN.—FRANÇOIS COUPERIN.

MERSENNUS. — DES CARTES. — MENESTRIER. —
NIVERS.—LOULIE.—BURETTE.

AT the first introduction of music into the church
service in France, it met with considerable opposition; and it was not till nearly the conclusion
of the eighth century, that it became so settled as
to be employed without interruption. About the
beginning of the tenth century, we find that it had

attained a firm and permanent establishment. At
this period, there was at Corbie, in Picardy, a
musical institution of such celebrity that young
ecclesiastics were sent thither for instruction even
from foreign countries.   Public lectures were also
read in the University of Paris on those parts of
the writings of St. Augustine which treat of
music.

After the introduction of the system of Guido,
it is observable that in France the progress of the art
was remarkably slow. One improvement only seems
to have had its rise in that country.   This was the
fauxbourdon, or what the English termed *faburden*, a species of descant, the first notion of which
seems to have been taken from the bag-pipe.*
The French people became so extremely partial to
the fauxbourdon, that, for many years, they rejected all idea of any other kind of accompaniment.

Before the conclusion of the seventeenth century,
the Italian opera, having undergone a gradual refinement, had arrived at great perfection, and had
even found its way to Paris.   The establishment
of the Royal Academy in this city contributed

---

* *Faburden* was applied, in the early days of descant, to
such counterpoint as had either a drone bass *(bourdon)*, or
some part moving constantly in the same intervals with it; as,
in three parts, when the treble moves in sixths with the bass,
the middle part will consist of no other intervals than thirds.

greatly to the improvement of French music ; but
it failed to answer the ultimate end of its institution. It had been the design of Cardinal Maza-
rine and Louis the Fourteenth, to fix in France
a style corresponding with that of the Italians ;
but, from the natural temper and genius of the
people and other causes, it gradually deflected
from its original character, and, in the course of a
short time, assumed another so different as to afford ground for dispute whether the French or
Italian music was entitled to the preference. On
the part of the French, it was contended that their
operas were, in respect of poetry, regular compositions, perfectly consistent with the laws of the
drama. It was asserted of the music, that they
had the advantage of bass voices ; that the French
masters excelled those of Italy in their performance on the violin, the hautboy, and the flute ; and,
in conclusion, that their opera had an essential
superiority in the choruses and dances. In defence
of the Italian opera, it was said that, in the first
place, the language of Italy, as abounding more in
sonorous vowels than the French language, was
more naturally adapted to music ; that, in their
musical compositions, the invention of the Italian
masters appeared to be inexhaustible, whilst that
of the French composers was extremely narrow
and constrained. It was granted that the French
airs were in general soft, easy, and flowing ; but
that the Italians had an infinite superiority in pass-

ing boldly from the different keys, venturing on the most unexpected dissonances and the boldest cadences. With respect to compositions in several parts, it was remarked, that in the French music the melody of the upper part only was regarded, but that in the Italian music the melody was equally excellent in all the parts.

At the first introduction of the opera into France, Louis the Fourteenth granted to the Abbé Perrin, master of the ceremonies to the Duke of Orleans, the privilege of conducting; and Cambert, the organist of St. Honoré, was appointed to compose the music. The latter however was soon removed, and Lully was engaged not only to fill his place, but likewise to become a joint director with Perrin.

——————

CLAUDE LE JEUNE, a native of Valenciennes, and composer of the chamber to King Henry the Fourth of France, was one of the most celebrated of the early French musicians. The following singular anecdote, respecting a piece of music of Le Jeune's composition, is cited by Bayle from the Sieur d'Embry's Commentary on the French translation of Apollonius Tyanæus.

" I have sometimes heard the Sieur Claudin the Younger say, (who, without disrespect to any one, far excelled all the musicians of the preceding ages) that an air which he had composed, with its parts, was sung at the solemnity of the Duke of Joyeuse's marriage, in the time of Henry the Third, King of France and Poland, of happy memory, whom God absolve ; which, as it was sung, made a gentleman take his sword in his hand and swear aloud, that it was impossible for him to forbear fighting with somebody. Where-upon they began to sing another air of the sub-phrygian mode, which made him peaceable as before. This I have had since confirmed by some that were present. Such power and force have the modulation, motion, and management of the voice, when joined together upon the minds of men !"*

Le Jeune was the author of a work entitled " *Meslanges*," consisting of vocal compositions for four, five, six, eight, and ten voices, to Latin, Italian, and French words, many of them in ca-non, printed in 1607. A second part of this work was published in 1613.

The compositions of Le Jeune best known to the public are his *psalms*, adapted to the words of the version by Theodore Beza and Clement Marot : of these there are two collections extant, both of which appear to have been posthumous publica-tions. One of them contains the whole hun-dred and fifty, with the music in four and five parts, and was beautifully printed, in separate books of a small oblong form, at Paris, in 1613, by his sister Cecile le Jeune. The other was pub-

---

* Bayle, art. Goudimel.

lished at Paris in 1606, and entitled, *" Pseaumes*
" en Vers mezurez, mis in Musique, à 2, 3, 4,
" 5, 6, 7, et 8 Parties, par Claude le Jeune."
The latter are select psalms paraphrased by an unknown author, and the music abounds with all
the ornaments of fugue, point, and varied motion ;
so that thus set they may not improperly be styled
motets.

Dr. Burney has given us the following character of the productions of Le Jeune: " I have
scored several of them, but have generally been
disappointed in my expectations of excellence.
In comparing them with the works of the best
contemporary composers of Italy and the Netherlands, their author appears to have been more a
man of study and labour than of genius and facility."

Le Jeune was also the writer of a composition
entitled " *Dodecachorde*," being an exercise on
the twelve modes of Glareanus.

FRANÇOIS EUSTACHE DU CAURROY, successively
chapel-master to Charles the Ninth, Henry the
Third, and Henry the Fourth of France, and also
canon of the Holy Chapel in Paris, and prior of
St. Aioul, was born in the year 1549. Although
considered as one of the greatest musicians of his
day, he does not appear to have been much known
out of his own country. There is extant of his
composition, "*A Mass for the Dead*," which was

formerly sung once every year in the Cathedral
Church of Nôtre Dame at Paris ; and a posthumous work, published in 1610, entitled " *Mélanges*
" *de la Musique de Eustache de Caurroy.*"

He died in the year preceding the date of the
last named publication, and was interred in the
Church des Grands Augustins at Paris, where
he is celebrated by a pompous epitaph written by
his friend and patron the Cardinal du Perron.

ANTHONY FEUM or FEVIN, a native of Orleans,
is mentioned by Glareanus, with great enco-
miums, as a successful emulator of Jusquin de
Prez, and a youth whose modesty and diffidence
were equal to his genius.

There are three of his *masses* in the collection
of masses and motets deposited in the British
Museum, all of which are said to be excellent,
but particulary one entitled, " *Sancta Trini-*
" *tatis.*"

JEAN MOUTON, the master and conductor of
the choir in the Chapel of Francis the First, King·
of France, was a pupil of Jusquin de Prez, and
flourished about, or perhaps somewhat previous
to this time. If we were allowed to credit the
testimony of his contemporaries, he was one of
the most celebrated musicians of the age in which
he lived. But notwithstanding the rapture, says
Dr. Burney, with which his *masses* have been

spoken of, they appear greatly inferior in melody, rhythm, and design to those of Jusquin,
De la Rue, and Fevin. His *motets,* however, if
not more nervous and elaborate than those of his
contemporaries, are more smooth and polished.

GUILLAUME FRANC. The name of this person
is scarcely known among the musicians of the present day, except as being one of the original composers of the tunes to the French version of
psalms by Marot. These were fifty in number,
and were first printed at Strasburg in the year
1545 ; they were afterwards, with several others,
set in parts by Bourgeois and Goudimel.

CLAUDE GOUDIMEL is supposed to have been a
native of Franche-Comté. He was a member
of the reformed religion, and is said by D'Au-
bigné to have been murdered in the dreadful and
never to be forgotten massacre at Paris on St.
Bartholomew's day, 1572. This writer states, that
at the same time with M. Perot, a civilian, he
was thrown headlong out of a high window into
the street, dragged by the legs over the stones,
and finally cast into the river. According to the
assertion of Thuanus, it was at the massacre at
Lyons that he suffered.

Goudimel's music to the metrical translation of
the French psalms obtained so much repute as
to pass through several editions. He " has been

much celebrated by the Calvinists in France," says Dr. Burney, " for this music, which was never used in the church of Geneva, and by the catholics in Italy for instructing Pales'rina in the art of composition, though it is doubtful whether this great harmonist and Goudimel had ever the least acquaintance or intercourse with each other.   He set the ' Chansons Spirituelles' of De Muret, in four parts, which were printed at Paris, 1555. We may suppose Goudimel at this time to have been a catholic, as Muret is never ranked among heretics by French biographers.   Ten years after, when he set the psalms of Clement Marot, this version was still regarded with less horror by the catholics than in later times; for the music which Goudimel had set to it was printed at Paris by Adrian Le Roy and Robert Ballard with a privilege, 1565.   It was reprinted in Holland, in 1607, for the use of the Calvinists, but it seems to have been too difficult ; for we are told by the editor of the psalms of Claude le Jeune, which were printed at Leyden, 1633, and dedicated to the States-General, that, ' in publishing the psalms in parts, he had preferred the music of Claude le Jeune to that of Goudimel ; for, as the counterpoint was simply note for note, the most ignorant in music, if possessed of a voice, and acquainted with the psalm-tune, might join in the performance of any one of them ; which is impracticable in the compositions of Goudimel, many of whose psalms being composed in fugue, can only be performed by person's well skilled in music."

The works of Goudimel, who was certainly the greatest musician in France during the reign of Charles the Ninth, are become so scarce, that his name and reputation are preserved by protestant historians more in pity of his misfortunes than by any knowledge of their excellence. " His motets in four parts," continues Dr. Burney " resemble, in gravity of style, simplicity of the subjects of fugue, and purity of harmony, the ecclesiastical compositions of our countryman Bird."

VERDELOT is mentioned by Rabelais among the musicians of his acquaintance in France, and his name frequently occurs in the Italian catalogues. He lived in the middle of the sixteenth century.

Though he has been ranked among the best composers of his time, his works contain no characteristic excellence that can entitle him to that place.

HENRY DUMONT, chapel-master to Louis the Fourteenth, is celebrated by the French writers as having been a masterly performer on the organ. He was born in the diocese of Liege in 1610, and was the first French musician that introduced thorough-bass into his compositions. He died at Paris in the year 1684.

There are extant some of his *motets*, which are

held in great estimation; and five *grand masses,*
called royal m.sses.

SEBASTIAN DE BROSSARD, an eminent French
musician, was born in the year 1660. In the
former part of his life he was a prebendary and
the chapel-master of Saltzburg; but he afterwards
became grand chaplain and also maître de cha-
pelle in the Cathedral of Meaux.

There are extant by this composer, " *Prodro-*
" *mus musicalis, ou Elévations et Motets à Voix*
" *seule, avec une Basse-continue,*" the second edition of which was printed in the year 1702 ; and
" *Elévations et Motets à 2 et 3 Voix, et à Voix*
" *seule, deux dessus de Violin, ou deux Flûtes,*
" *avec la Basse-continue,*" being a second part of
the same work, published in 1698.

De Brossard was also the author of a very useful book' entitled, " *Dictionaire de Musique,*
" *contenant une Explanation des Termes Grecs,*
" *Latins, Italiens, et François, les plus usitez*
" *dans la Musique,*" printed at Amsterdam in
1703. At the end of this book, which appears to
have been the earliest musical dictionary of any
excellence that has been published, there is a
catalogue of nine hundred musical authors, ancient
and modern ; and it also contains many curious
observations relative to the history of music. This
writer died in the year 1730.

Jean Baptiste Moreau, a musician who resided at Angers, was led by the consciousness of his musical talents to try his fortune at Paris. Having succeeded in a bold attempt to get unperceived into the closet of Madame the Dauphiness Victoire de Baviere, who was fond of music, he had the assurance to pull her by the sleeve, and ask permission to sing to her a little air of his own composing. The Dauphiness, laughing at the singularity of the incident, allowed him to do so. He sang without being disconcerted, and the princess was pleased. The story came to the ears of the king, and he desired to see him. Moreau was introduced to his Majesty in the apartment of Madame Maintenon, and sung several airs, with which the king was so much delighted, that he ordered him to compose a musical entertainment, which was performed at Marli two months afterwards, and applauded by the whole court. He was also engaged to compose the *interludes* for the tragedies of Esther, Athalie, Jonathas, and several other pieces for the house of St. Cyr.

His chief excellence consisted in giving the full force of expression to all kinds of words and all kinds of subjects. The poet Lainez, with whom he was intimate, furnished him with several *songs* and little *cantatas*, which he set to music, but none of them have been published.

Michel Lambert was born, in 1610, at Vivonne, a small village of Poictou. He was an exquisite performer on the lute, and sang to it with peculiar grace and elegance. His merit alone procured him the office of master of the king's chamber music. After receiving this appointment, he became so eminent, that persons of the highest rank were proud of being considered his pupils, and resorted in great numbers to his house, in which he held a kind of musical academy. Lambert is esteemed the first who gave to his countrymen a just notion of the graces of vocal music.

His compositions, however, contain in them nothing remarkable. They consist of *motets*, of music for the " *Leçons de Ténébres*," and a collection containing several *airs* in one, two, three, and four parts, with a thorough-bass.

Lambert died at Paris in the year 1690.

———— Gauthier, generally denominated *the Elder*, was an admired French lutenist. In conjunction with his relation, Pierre Gauthier, he published a collection entitled, " *Livre de Ta-* " *bleau des Pièces de Luth sur différens Modes ;*" the preface to which contains a set of rules for playing on the lute.

The principal compositions of the Elder Gauthier are his lessons, entitled, " *L' Immortelle,* " *la Nonpareille, le Tombeau de Mezangeau.*"

PIERRE GAUTHIER was a musician of Ciotat, in Provence, and the director of an opera company which played alternately at Marsellies, Montpelier, and Lyons. He perished by shipwreck, in 1679, in a vessel in which he had embarked from the Port de Cette. At the time of his death he had just attained the age of fifty-five.

The chief of his compositions are, *A Collection of Duos and Trios,* which have been much admired.

MARC-ANTOINE CHARPENTIER was superintendant of the music of the Duke of Orleans, and his instructor in musical composition. He died at Paris in the year 1704.

One of his operas, entitled *Medée,* obtained great celebrity.

PASCAL COLASSE, chapel-master to Louis the Fourteenth, was born at Paris in 1636. He was a pupil of Lully, whom he imitated in all his compositions. Colasse destroyed both his fortune and health in an infatuated pursuit of the philosopher's stone.

There are extant of his composition several *motets* and *songs.* His opera of *Thetis and Pelcus* is esteemed an excellent production.

GUILLAUME MINORET was one of the four masters of, or composers to, the Chapel of Louis the Fourteenth. He composed many *motets,* which, though greatly admired, have never yet been printed. He died about the year 1717, at a very advanced age.

ANDRÉ CAMPRA, born at Aix, in Provence, in 1660, was at first a chorister in the cathedral of that city ; but soon after his leaving the choir, he became distinguished by his *motets,* which were performed in numerous churches and private concerts. So well were these received, that they procured him the rank of the director of music in the Jesuit's Church at Paris, and some other preferment in that metropolis. His genius having been too much confined while restrained to the narrow limits of a motet, Campra set himself to compose for the stage, and wrote the music to several operas. His progress in this new course of study was answerable to his industry ; and by following the style of Lully, he acquired a degree of excellence but little inferior.

His *Europe Galante, Carnaval de Venise,* and *Fêtes Venitiennes ;* his *Ages,* his *Fragmen de Lulli,* which are *ballets ;* and his operas of *Hesione, Alcide, Telephé, Camille,* and *Tancrede,* were greatly applauded, and are still admired. The grace and vivacity of his airs, the sweetness of his melody, and, above all, his strict attention to the sense of the words, render the compositions of this master truly estimable.

Towards the close of his life, the king of France appointed Campra music-master of the Royal Chapel, and gave him a pension. He died at Versailles, in the year 1744, at the great age of eighty-four.

JEAN GILLES, a native of Tarascon, in Provence, was originally a singer in the Cathedral Church of Aix, and afterwards chapel-master of the Church of St. Stephen in Thoulouse.

There are extant of his composition many fine *motets*. His most capital work, however, is a *Masse des Morts*.

MICHEL RICHARD DE LALANDE was born at Paris in the year 1657. Having had during his childhood a fine voice and a strong propensity for music, he was admitted into the choir of the Church of St. Germain Auxerrois. In this situation he applied with great diligence to the study of his profession, frequently spending whole nights in practice on various instruments, but more particularly on his favourite instrument the violin. Conscious of his superior talents, he applied to Lully, requesting to be taken into the opera band ; and on being rejected, he broke his violin, and renounced the use of it for ever.

Not long after this incident he was requested by the Duke de Noailles to undertake the instruction of one of his daughters. The Duke was so well pleased with him that he recommended him to the notice of Louis the Fourteenth, in consequence of which he was appointed musical preceptor to the French Princesses. He frequently composed little pieces of music, at the express desire of the king, who conferred on him numerous favours.

Lalande enjoyed, in succession, the two offices of music-master of the king's chamber, the two of composer, that of superintendant of the music, and the four offices of the Royal Chapel.

His *motets* have been collected and published in two folio volumes.

He died at Versailles in the year 1726.

JEAN FRANÇOIS LALOUETTE was a pupil of Lully. He successively conducted the music in the churches of St. Germain l'Auxerrois and Nôtre Dame, and died at Paris in the year 1728, at the age of seventy-five.

Several of his *motets* for a full choir have been much admired. A few only of those for the principal anniversary festivals have been published.

MARIN MARAIS, born at Paris in the year 1656, is said to have made so rapid a progress in playing on the viol, that his master, at the end of six months, would give him no further instruction. He carried the art of playing on this instrument to the highest perfection. Marais was the first who thought of adding to the viol three strings of brass wire in order to deepen the tone.

He was a member of the chamber-music to the king of France, and the composer of several operas, namely, *Alcide, Ariane, Bacchus, Alcione,* and *Semele ;* and of three collections of pieces for the bass-viol. His works are said to bear the marks of a fertile genius united to great taste and judgment.

Marin died, in the year 1728, in the Fauxbourg S. Marceau, and was interred in the Church of S. Hippolite.

ELIZABETH CLAUDE JACQUETTE DE LA GUERRE, a female musician, was the daughter of Marin de la Guerre, organist of the Chapel of Gervais in Paris. She was born in the year 1669, and received instruction in the practice of the harpsichord, and the art of composition, from her father. To so great a degree of excellence did she attain both in the science and practice of music, that very few of her sex have equalled her. She died in 1729, and was buried in the Church of St Eustace at Paris.

An opera of her composition, entitled " *Cephale* " *and Procris*" was represented at the Royal Academy of Paris in the year 1694, and was afterwards published.

SALOMON, a native of Provence, was a player on
the bass-viol in the Royal Chapel, and the composer of an opera entitled " *Medée et Jason.*"
This was performed at the Royal Academy, in
1713, with great applause, and is now extant in
print.

He died at Versailles in the year 1731, at the
age of seventy.

JEAN LOUIS MARCHAND was born at Lyons in
the year 1669, and, in the early part of his life,
was organist in some church of that city.   Whilst
he was very young he went to Paris ; and one day
strolling, as if by accident, into the chapel of the
College of St. Louis le Grand, he obtained permission to play the organ for a little while before
the service began.   The Jesuits were so greatly
delighted with his performance, that they earnestly
requested him to remain with them.   Marchand
assented, and they afforded him every means of becoming perfect in his art.   His situation in this
college was so agreeable to his wishes, that, although many advantageous offers were made to
him, nothing could tempt him to relinquish it.

He died at Paris in 1732, and left of his composition two books of *Lessons for the Harpsichord,* which have been greatly admired.

LOUIS COUPERIN.   The family of Couperin has
produced a succession of persons eminent in music.

Of these, Louis and François were brothers, and natives of Chaume, a little town in Brie. The former,
who was the oldest, was a celebrated performer on the
organ, and, in consequence, obtained the place of
organist in the King's Chapel ; and, as a further
reward for his merit, a post was created for him
called *Dessus de Viole.*

He died about the year 1665, aged thirty-five
years ; and has left of his composition three suits
of *Lessons for the Harpsichord.* These, however are still in manuscript, and only to be found
in the collections of the curious.

FRANÇOIS COUPERIN, the most celebrated of this
musical family, was the son of Charles Couperin,
and the nephew of the above-mentioned Louis.
He is considered by many persons to have been the
finest composer for the organ and harpsichord that
the French nation can boast. He was organist of
the Chapel of Louis the Fourteenth, and a member
of his chamber music.

His *Lessons for the Harpsichord* were published by himself, the first of them in 1713, and
occupy, in the whole, six volumes in folio. They
were so difficult of execution, that, four years
afterwards, he found it necessary to publish a work
on the art of playing the harpsichord, under the
title of *L' art de toucher le Clavecin,* which contains much good and useful instruction.

François Couperin died in the year 1733, aged

sixty-five, leaving two daughters equally celebrated for their performance on the harpsichord, which appears to have been the favourite instrument of the family. One of these daughters was a nun in the abbey of Maubuisson; and the other succeeded her father in the charge of the harpsichord in the king's chamber, an employment which, except in this instance, was never conferred on a woman.

FRENCH MUSICAL WRITERS,

Who flourished from the Middle of the Sixteenth to the Conclusion of the Seventeenth Century.

MARIN MERSENNE, or, as his name is written in Latin, MARINUS MERSENNUS, was born on the 8th of October, 1588, at Oyse, in the province of Maine. His first instructions were received in the College of Flêche. On quitting that seminary, he studied divinity for some years in the College of Sorbonne. He afterwards entered himself amongst, and in 1611 received his habit of, the Minims. He applied himself diligently to the study of the Hebrew language, and was appointed a teacher of philosophy and theology in the Convent of Nivers. This station he held till the year 1619, when, in order to prosecute his studies, and enjoy the conversation of the learned, he returned to Paris. During his abode at La Flèche, he contracted a friendship with Des Cartes. The residence of Mersennus at Paris did not prevent his making several journeys into foreign countries. He visited Holland, and went four different times into Italy. During the hot weather of July, 1648, having been upon a visit to Des Cartes, he returned to his convent excessively heated ; and, in order to allay his thirst, drank some cold water. The consequence of this was his being seized with an illness, which produced an abscess in his right side. The physicians, supposing his disorder a pleurisy, bled him several times to no purpose. At length they determined to open his side. The operation was begun, but he expired under it, in the month of September, 1648. He had directed that, if the operation should not succeed, they should open his body. This they did, and found that they had made the incision two inches below the abscess.

Mersennus was a man of great learning and deep research. He had also a correct and judicious ear, and was a passionate admirer of music. These gave a direction to his pursuits, and were productive of numerous experiments and calculations tending to demonstrate the principles of harmony, and to prove that they had their foundation in nature, and in the original constitution of the universe.

In the year 1636, Mersennus published at Paris, in a large folio volume, a work entitled " *Har-* " *monie Universelle,*" in which he treats of the nature and properties of sound, of instruments of various kinds, of consonances and dissonances, of composition, of the human voice, of the practice of singing, and a variety of other particulars on the subject of music.

This book consists of several separate and distinct treatises, with such signatures for the sheets, and such numbers for the pages, as render them independent of each other. The consequence is, that there are scarcely any two copies to be met with which contain precisely the same number of tracts, or in which these follow in the same order.

The substance of the several treatises in this work is also contained in a Latin work of Mersennus, entitled, " *Harmonicorum Libri XII. in* " *quibus agitur de Sonorum Natura, Causis, et* " *Effectibus; de Consonantiis, Dissonantiis, Ra-* " *tionibus, Generibus, Modis, Cantibus, Com-* " *positione, Orbisque totius harmonicis Instru-* " *mentis.*" This book is a translation of the other work, but with considerable additions and improvements. Its most material contents are dissertations on the nature and properties of sound ; on the causes of sound ; on strings ; on consonances and dissonances ; on ratios, proportion, and the division of consonances ; on the modes and genera of the ancients; on singing and the human voice; on composition; and on musical instruments.

The doctrines delivered by Mersennus are founded on a variety of well-tried experiments, and his reasoning upon these is generally very close and satisfactory.

René des Cartes, the famous French philosopher, who was born at La Haye, in Touraine, on the 31st of March, 1596, and the particulars of whose life and character are well known to the public, was the author of a treatise entitled " *Mu-* " *sicæ Compendium.*" This was written in the year 1617, whilst he was very young; and, what may appear somewhat extraordinary, whilst he was engaged in the profession of a soldier, in the garrison at Breda. It is comprehended in fifty-eight quarto pages, and contains many curious particulars relative to the science of music, in observations on the different measures, on consonances and dissonances, the division of the octave and the proportions, and on the modes.

An English translation of this book was published, in 1653, by William Lord Brouncker, president of the Royal Society, with some animadversions, which prove the translator to have been deeply skilled in the theory of the science.

Des Cartes died at Stockholm in the year 1650.

Claude François Menestrier, a French Jesuit, wrote, in 1681, a treatise " *Des Representations en* " *Musique anciennes et modernes.*" In this book, among a great variety of curious particulars, is contained a brief inquiry into the music of the Hebrews. The author states that dramatic music was first introduced into France by the pilgrims, who, returning from the Holy Land at the time of the crusades, formed themselves into parties, and exhibited spectacles of devotion accompanied with music and songs. There are likewise many curious accounts of public amusements, and of dramatic and musical representations, in several of the courts of Europe.

In the year 1682, Menestrier published, " *Des* " *Ballets anciennes et modernes, selon les Règles* " *du Théâtre.*"

He died in the month of January, 1705.

Gabriel Nivers was one of the four organists of the Chapel of Louis the Fourteenth, and also organist of the Church of St. Sulpice at Paris.

He published, in 1683, a tract entitled, "*Disser-* " *tation sur le Chant Gregorien,*" written for the purpose of restoring the cantus Gregorianus to its primitive purity. This work had so much influence, that the antiphonary of the French church was republished according to his corrections, at the express command of the king.

At the end of the dissertation are contained the

forms of the offices, with the musical notes adjusted to rules laid down by the author. These are followed by a short treatise on the mode of singing according to the eight tones of the cantus Gregorianus ; and the book is concluded with some select church services.

The author appears to have been well skilled in ecclesiastical history, and the present work contains one of the best histories of church music that is extant.

In the year 1697, Nivers published at Amsterdam " *Traité de la Composition de Musique ;*" and the two following works have been ascribed to him, " *Le premier Livre des Motets,*" and " *Le* " *premier Livre des Pièces d' Orgue.*"

LOULIE, a musician of considerable eminence, was the author of an ingenious and useful book published in 1698, at Amsterdam, entitled, " *Elé-* " *ments, ou Principes de Musique, mis dans un* " *nouvel Ordre ;*" in which, after teaching the method of solmization, he explains the nature of transposition, and suggests the method of reducing music, in any of the keys denoted by either flat or sharp signatures, into their original or radical keys. In the course of his work, the author lays down a rule for dividing the monochord, and assigns the proportions of the natural sounds in the octave, distinguishing between the greater and lesser tones. Towards the end of the book, he describes an instrument which he calls a chronometer, contrived for the measuring of time by means of a pendulum.

PIERRE JEAN BURETTE was a French physician, and born at Paris in the year 1665. During his infancy he was so feeble and sickly, that he was chiefly allowed to amuse himself by playing on the spinet, which he had been taught to do by his mother ; and so early was he a proficient in music, that at the age of eight years he was invited to play in concert before the king, who expressed himself well satisfied with his performance.

Not long after this period he assisted his father, who was at that time a teacher of music, in instructing his pupils ; but, having a turn for literature, as well as for music, he determined, when at the age of eighteen, to adopt one of the learned professions. He consequently became a student in the College of Harcourt, and, in 1690, was admitted to the degree of Doctor of Physic.

Besides the Latin and Greek languages, which he had previously acquired, he attained, whilst at Harcourt and afterwards, a knowledge of Hebrew, Syriac, Arabic, Italian, Spanish, German, and English. He afterwards became eminent as a physician, read a course of lectures on the materia medica, and, in 1710, was nominated professor of medicine in the Royal College at Paris.

His literary attainments were such, that he had

a considerable share, for more than thirty years, in the publication of the " Journal des Sçavans ;" and, in 1718, had an appointment in the Bibliotheque du Roi.

Amongst his other productions there is, in the Memoirs of the French Academy, " A Transla-" tion of Plutarch's Treatise on Music," accompanied by notes and remarks. In this work, to which almost all late writers on the subject have been under great obligations, he has exhibited much diligence and learning; " but," observes Dr. Burney, " he does not seem always to have been possessed of an equal share of sagacity, or of courage sufficient to confess himself unable to explain inexplicable passages in his author. He never sees a difficulty—he explains all. Hence, amidst great erudition and knowledge of antiquity, there are a thousand unintelligible explanations in his notes."

He died in the year 1742, at the great age of eighty-two.

CHAP. X.

ENGLISH
MUSICAL COMPOSERS AND WRITERS,
WHO FLOURISHED
From about the Year
1700 to 1725.

CLAYTON. — CLARK.—WELDON—JOHN AND HENRY ECCLES.—BRITTON.—DR. TUDWAY.—DR. CROFT.— DR. CREIGHTON.—DR. TURNER.—GOLDWIN.—KING. —ISHAM.—HENSTRIDGE.—HESELTINE.— KELLER. — CORBETT. — LOEILLET. — BANISTER, JUN.— ROSEINGRAVE.— BARRETT.— RAMONDEN.—HART.— MONRO.—HAYDEN.—BABELL.—SHEELES.— SHUTTLEWORTH.—SYMONDS.—WHICHELLO.—MALCOLM.

We are now arrived at an highly important era in the musical history of this country. The Italian Opera, which, on the Continent, had for many years been gradually advancing towards perfection, was at length introduced into England a short time after the commencement of the eighteenth century. The first opera performed in London was that of *Arsinoë*, in the year 1707.

The music of this opera was selected and in part composed by Clayton. In the preceding year a new theatre had been erected in the Haymarket, which was opened with a pastoral entertainment called the " *Loves of Ergasto*," set to music, after the manner of the Italian opera, in recitatives, with airs intermixed, by Greber, a German musician, who had studied in Italy. It was not favourably received, and was succeeded by another of the same kind, " *The Temple of Love*," composed by Saggioni, a Venetian, which likewise failed.

The bad success of these performances at the Haymarket induced the managers of Drury-Lane Theatre to attempt the exhibition of an Italian opera ; and they fixed upon that of *Camilla*, composed by Bononcini, then resident in the court of the Emperor of Germany. In order to accommodate the singers of our own country, many of the recitatives were translated into the English language ; and, notwithstanding the glaring absurdity of so motley a performance, it is said that Camilla did not meet with so favourable a reception in any of the countries of the Continent as it did in England.

The first genuine Italian opera performed in London was that of *Rinaldo*, represented at the theatre in the Haymarket in the year 1710. The music was composed by Mr. Handel. Its success was so great as to prove irretrievably injurious to the interests· of those persons whose employment it had been to furnish operas by selection from various masters. From this time the opera was conducted in a manner much less liable to exception than at first ; and to this reformation it is probable that the ridicule of Addison, in several of the Spectators, and the censures of critics less humorously disposed than himself, might not a little contribute.

In the year 1710, a plan was formed by many persons of distinction, aided by some of the most eminent musicians of the time, of an academy for the study and practice of vocal and instrumental harmony, to be holden at the Crown and Anchor Tavern, opposite St. Clement's Church in the Strand. They began by forming a library, consisting of the most celebrated compositions, as well in manuscript as in print, that could be procured either at home or abroad. With the assistance of the gentlemen of the Chapel Royal and the choir of St. Paul's, and the boys belonging to each, the academy commenced its performances. This institution was the origin of the *Academy of Ancient Music*.

In the early part of the eighteenth century there were not only several private, but some *subscription concerts* held in different parts of London. The latter were, in a great measure, discontinued about the year 1724, upon the establishment of the concerts at the Castle Tavern, in Paternoster Row, thence called the *Castle Concerts.* To these both auditors and performers were admitted subscribers ; and the fund was sufficiently great to allow of several second-rate singers from the Opera and other persons being hired to assist in them. About the year 1744, the subscription was raised, from its former sum of two, to five guineas, for the purpose of enabling the society to introduce the performance of *oratorios.* These concerts were afterwards removed to Haberdasher's Hall, where they continued for fifteen or sixteen years ; and from whence they were subsequently removed to the King's Arms, in Cornhill.

The account of *Britton's concerts,* the most celebrated of any that were held about this time in private houses, will be found in a subsequent part of the present chapter.

THOMAS CLAYTON was a member of the royal band of music in the reign of William and Mary. Although a man of very inferior talents in his profession, he was induced, in the early part of his life, to travel into Italy for the purpose of improvement. At his return to England, he so far imposed on the good sense of the public as to obtain the reputation of an eminent musician. Several persons of distinction were persuaded into a belief, that by means of Mr. Clayton's assistance, rusticity would be no longer the characteristic of English music ; and that, if due encouragement were given to him, our music would, in a very short time, emulate that of Italy. This is a kind of artifice that has more than once been practised on the English people, but never with the success of the present instance.

He had brought along with him a collection of Italian airs, which he set a high value on. Some of these he mangled and adulterated, and then, adapting them to the words of the drama of *Arsinoë*, had it performed in the theatre in Drury Lane as an opera composed by himself. He afterwards, in the same manner, adapted music to Mr. Addison's opera of *Rosamond*. The former, from the public prejudice in his favour, met with some success ; although it is in reality one of the most execrable performances that ever disgraced the stage. The latter, if possible, still worse, was condemned on the third night it was acted, and could not afterwards be revived.

JEREMIAH CLARK was educated in the Royal Chapel under Dr. Blow, who entertained so great a friendship for him as at length to resign in his favour the places of almoner and master of the children of St. Paul's. Clark received these appointments in the year 1693, and shortly afterwards became the organist of that cathedral. In July, 1700, he was appointed a gentleman-extraordinary of the Chapel Royal; and at the expiration of about four years, was also made organist.

The compositions of Clark are not numerous, as an untimely and melancholy end was put to his existence before his genius had had time to expand.

Early in life he was so unfortunate as to conceive a violent and hopeless passion for a very beautiful lady, of a rank far superior to his own; and his sufferings under these circumstances became at length so intolerable that he resolved to terminate them by suicide. Being at the house of a friend in the country, he found himself so miserable that he suddenly determined to return to London. His friend observing in his behaviour great marks of dejection, furnished him with a horse, and a servant to attend him. In his way to town a fit of melancholy and despair having seized him, he alighted, and giving his horse to the servant, went into a field, in the corner of which was a pond surrounded with trees. This pointed out to his choice two ways of getting rid of life; but not being more inclined to the one than the other, he left it to the determination of chance. He took out of his pocket a piece of money, and tossing it in the air, determined to abide by its decision. The money fell on its edge in the clay, and thus seemed to prohibit both these means of destruction. His mind however was too much disordered to receive comfort from, or take advantage of, this delay. He therefore mounted his horse and rode to London, determined to find some other means of ridding himself of life ; and in July, 1707, not many weeks after his return, he shot himself in his own house in St. Paul's Church-yard.

His *anthems* are remarkably pathetic, at the same time that they preserve all the majesty and dignity of the true church style. The most celebrated of them are, " I will love thee," printed in the second book of Harmonia Sacra ; " Bow down " thine ear ;" and " Praise the Lord, O Jerusa-" lem :" these, with some others, are also still in print as single anthems.

He published some *Lessons for the Harpsi-chord;* and several of his *songs* are to be found in the collections of the day, particularly in the Pills to Purge Melancholy ; but they are there printed without the basses. He also composed for D'Urfey's comedy of the Fond Husband, or the Plotting Sisters, that sweet ballad air, " The bonny " grey-eyed man," which is introduced into the Beggar's Opera, and sung to the words, " 'Tis " woman that seduces all mankind."

JOHN WELDON, a native of Chichester, was originally a pupil of Walter, the organist of Eton, and afterwards of Henry Purcell. His first important engagement in his profession was as orga-nist of New College, Oxford. In 1701, he was

appointed a gentleman-extraordinary of the Royal
Chapel ; and seven years afterwards, he succeeded
Dr. Blow as organist there.   In 1715, upon
the establishment of a second composer's place
(mentioned in the preceding account of Blow),
Weldon was admitted to it.   He had been in this
station but a short time before he gave a specimen
of his abilities in the composition of the *Communion Service* and several *anthems*, agreeably to
the terms of his appointment.

At the same time that Weldon was organist of
the Chapel Royal, he was organist also of the
Church of St. Bride, London ; and King George
the First having given an organ to the parish
of St. Martin in the Fields, he was likewise chosen
organist there.

The studies of Weldon were chiefly confined to
church music ; yet he set to music Mr. Congreve's masque, the " *Judgment of Paris*," and
obtained by it the first of four prizes paid out of a
sum of two hundred pounds subscribed by several
persons of quality for the best compositions on this
subject.

Some of Weldon's *songs* are to be found in a
book entitled " *Mercurius Musicus*," and in
other collections of the time.

When he first became a member of the Chapel,
Mr. Elford was a singer there, and was celebrated
for a very fine counter-tenor voice.   Weldon composed for him several solo anthems, six of which

he published about the year 1730.   We say *about*
that period, because, in the course of the last
century, musical chronology has become a very difficult study.   The late Mr. Walsh, finding that
old music-books were like old almanacks, ceased,
very early in the eighteenth century, to ascertain
the time of their birth by dates, which have ever
since been as carefully concealed as the age of antiquated virgins.

These solos have considerable merit ; but in
point of excellence they fall far short of his full
anthems, particularly those to the words, " In
" thee, O Lord," and " Hear my crying," of which
it is difficult to say whether the melody or harmony of each be its greatest excellence.   One of
his solo anthems, " I will lift up mine eyes," is inserted in the first volume of Page's Harmonia
Sacra ; and with another, " O Lord, rebuke me
" not," is also in print as a single anthem.

Weldon died in the year 1736, and was buried
in the church-yard of St. Paul's, Covent Garden.
The successor to his place in the Royal Chapel
was Dr. Boyce.

JOHN ECCLES was the son of Solomon Eccles, a
performer on the violin, and the composer of some
grounds with divisions thereon, published in the
second part of the " Division Violin," printed in
London in 1693. He was instructed by his father in
music, and became a composer for the theatre of

act-tunes, dance-tunes, and some incidental songs, a collection of which he published.   He wrote the music to a tragedy called " *Rinaldo and Armida,*" in which there is a song for a single voice, " The " jolly breeze," that has been greatly admired. Eccles set to music an *Ode for St. Cecilia's Day,* written by Mr. Congreve, and performed in 1701 ; and also his masque, the *Judgment of Paris,* for which he obtained the second of the prizes mentioned in the preceding article.   The music to this masque is published.

In the above-mentioned collection there are many well-known songs, particularly two, each for three voices, " Inspire us, Genius of the Day," and " Wine does wonders every day."   It contains also a very spirited song for two voices, sung in the play of King Henry the Fifth, " Fill all " your glasses ;" and a solo sung in D'Urfey's play of Don Quixote, " I burn, my brain con- " sumes to ashes."   Eccles composed the tune to " A soldier and a sailor," in Mr. Congreve's comedy of Love for Love, which is also one of the songs in the Beggar's Opera, adapted to the words, " A fox may steal your hens, Sir."   There are several good songs by Eccles in the Pills to Purge Melancholy.

About the year 1698, upon the decease of Dr. Staggins, Eccles was appointed master of the Queen's band.   The latter part of his life was spent in retirement at Kingston, in Surry.

HENRY ECCLES, one of the brothers of the last-mentioned musician, was a violin-player of considerable eminence. Not finding, however, that recompence in his native country which he thought due to his abilities, he went to Paris, and was fortunate enough to obtain admission, as a performer, into the king of France's band.

He was the composer of *Twelve excellent Solos for the Violin*, published in Paris in the year 1720.

THOMAS BRITTON,* the famous musical small-coal man, was born at or near Higham-Ferrers, in Northamptonshire; from whence he went to London, and was bound apprentice to a dealer in small-coal in St. John Street. After he had served his time of seven years, his master gave him a sum of money not to oppose him in business. On this he went again into Northamptonshire; but after he had spent the money, he returned to London, and, notwithstanding his agreement, set up in the small-coal trade. He hired a stable in Aylesbury Street, Clerkenwell, which he converted into a dwelling-house. Some time after he had been settled here, he became acquainted with his neigh-

---

* Britton is not known as a composer of music; but his history is so interesting, and involves so much of the state of the art in his time, that we cannot resist the inclination to insert here some of the principal circumstances connected with it.

bour Dr. Garenciers, through whose instructions
and assistance he obtained an extensive knowledge
of chemistry.

He was likewise celebrated for a great degree of
skill both in the theoretical and practical parts of
music. He himself copied a collection of music,
so valuable, that after his death it sold for nearly
a hundred pounds. He collected also a great
number of books, which he left behind him ; and
some years previously to his death, he sold a large
collection, chiefly on the occult sciences, of which
he is said to have been a great admirer, and among
which there were many manuscripts. He had also
a collection of musical instruments that after his
death were sold for eighty pounds.

Of the origin of Britton's concert, which was
the first meeting of the kind in London, an account
has been left us by his neighbour Mr. Edward
Ward, the facetious author of the London Spy.
This club, he informs us, was first patronised by
Sir Roger L'Estrange, who was a lover of music,
and himself a performer on the violoncello. " The
attachment of this person and of other gentlemen
to Britton," he says, " arose from the profound
regard which they had in general for all manner
of literature. The prudence of Britton's deport-
ment to his superiors procured him great respect ; and men of the best wit, as well as some
of the best quality, honoured his musical society
with their company. He was even so much dis-

tinguished that, when passing the streets in his blue linen frock, and with his sack of small-coal on his back, he was frequently accosted with such expressions as, ' There goes the famous small-coal man, a lover of learning, a performer of music, and a companion for gentlemen.'   At its first institution this concert was held in Britton's own house.   On the ground-floor there was a repository for small-coal, and over that was the concert room, which was very long and narrow, and had a ceiling so low that a tall man could but just stand upright in it.   The stairs to this room were from the outside of the house, and could scarcely be ascended without crawling.   The house itself was very old and low built, and in every respect so mean as to be a fit habitation for only a very poor man."   Notwithstanding all these disagreeable circumstances, this mansion had such attraction as occasionally to draw together even the genteelest audiences.   The admission is said, for some time, to have been gratis ; and the following lines of Ward confirm this :

> " Upon Thursdays repair
> To my palace, and there
> Hobble up stair by stair ;
> But I pray ye take care,
> That you break not your shins by a stumble:
> And without e'er a souse
> Paid to me or my spouse,

Sit as still as a mouse
At the top of the house,
And there you shall hear how we fumble."

But Mr. Walpole, who, in his Anecdotes of
Painting, takes occasion to mention Britton, says
that there was a subscription of ten shillings a
year; and that the subscribers were supplied with
coffee at a penny a dish. By this it should seem
that he afterwards departed from his original institution.

The principal performers were Dr. Pepusch,
and frequently Mr. Handel, who played the harpsichord, Mr. Banister, Mr. Henry Needler of the
Excise Office, Mr. John Hughes, author of the
Siege of Damascus, Mr. Woolaston the painter,
Mr. Philip Hart, Mr. Henry Symonds, Mr.
Abiell Whichello, Mr. Obadiah Shuttleworth,
and others; of whom some constantly and others
frequently performed there. That afterwards fine
performer, Mr. Matthew Dubourg, was then but
a child; but the first solo on the violin which
he ever played in public was at Britton's concert,
standing upon a joint-stool. So terribly was the
child alarmed at the sight of such a splendid
audience, that at first he was near falling to the
ground from dismay.

Britton, in his person, was a short stout man,
with a very honest and ingenuous countenance.
There are two pictures of him extant, from both
of which mezzotinto prints have been engraved.

One of these was painted by Mr. Woolaston, and
is now deposited in the British Museum. The
occasion of its painting, which is deserving of
notice, was as follows :—Britton had been out one
morning, and having nearly emptied his sack
earlier than he expected, wished to call on his
friend Mr. Woolaston. He had, however, always
been accustomed to consider himself in two capacities, namely, as a man who subsisted by a very
mean occupation, and as a companion of persons
in a station of life much above himself; and he
could not, consistently with this distinction, drest
as he then was, make his visit. He did not, however, like to defer it, and he determined upon the
following expedient, that he would vary his usual
round, and, passing through Warwick Lane, in
which Mr. Woolaston lived, would cry small-
coal so near his door, as to stand a chance of
attracting that gentleman's notice. Accordingly
he had no sooner done this, than Mr. Woolaston,
who had never heard him there before, threw up
the sash and beckoned him to come in. After
some conversation, Mr. Woolaston intimated a
desire to take his picture. This Britton modestly
yielded to, and Mr. Woolaston then, and at a few
subsequent sittings, painted him in his blue frock,
and with his small-coal measure in his hand. From
this picture a mezzotinto print was engraved, for
which Mr. Hughes wrote the following lines :

> " Though mean thy rank, yet in thy humble cell
> Did gentle Peace and arts unpurchas'd dwell;
> Well pleas'd Apollo thither led his train,
> And Music warbled in her sweetest strain.
> Cyllenius so, as fables tell, and Jove,
> Came willing guests to poor Philemon's grove.
> Let useless pomp behold, and blush to find
> So low a station, such a liberal mind."

There is another picture of Britton, painted also by Woolaston, in which he is represented in the act of tuning a harpsichord. Under a mezzotinto from this are inserted the following lines of Prior, which (probably in order to recommend virtue to notice) contain little less than a sarcasm both on the painter and the engraver.

> " Though doom'd to small-coal, yet to arts allied,
> Rich without wealth, and famous without pride;
> Music's best patron, judge of books and men,
> Beloved and honoured by Apollo's train;
> In Greece or Rome sure never did appear
> So bright a genius in so dark a sphere;
> More of the man had artfully been sav'd
> Had Kneller painted, and had Vertue grav'd."

Britton was well skilled in the titles and prices of ancient books and manuscripts, which he was very assiduous in collecting. The method adopted by himself and others in doing this has been thus related. " About this time a passion for making these collections had seized many of the nobility; of whom the chief were Edward Earl of

Oxford, the Earls of Pembroke, Sunderland,
and Winchelsea, and the Duke of Devonshire.
These persons, on Saturdays during the winter
season, used to resort to the City, and there sepa-
rating, took several routes to the booksellers'
shops in different parts of the town to search out
old books and manuscripts. Some time before
noon they would assemble at the shop of Christopher Bateman, a bookseller at the corner of
Ave-Maria Lane, in Paternoster Row, where they
were frequently met by other persons engaged in
the same pursuits, and a conversation always
commenced on the subject of their inquiries.
As nearly as possible to the hour of twelve by
St. Paul's clock, Britton, who by that time had
finished his round, clad in his blue frock, and
pitching his sack of small-coal on the bulk of
Mr. Bateman's shop window, used to go in and
join them. After about an hour's conversation
the noblemen adjourned to the Mourning Bush
Tavern at Aldersgate, where they dined and p ent
the remainder of the day."

The singularity of his conduct, the course of
his studies, and the collections he made, induced
suspicions that Britton was not the character he
seemed to be. Some persons fancied his musical
assembly was only a cover for seditious meetings;
others for purposes of magic; and he was himself
taken, by different persons, for an atheist, a presby-
terian, and a jesuit. These however were all ill-

grounded conjectures; for Britton was a plain, simple, honest man, perfectly inoffensive, and highly esteemed by all who knew him.

The circumstances of his death are not less remarkable than those of his life. A person of the name of Honeyman, a blacksmith by trade, lived about this time in Bear Street near Leicester Square. This man was celebrated as a *ventriloquist*, and was secretly introduced by Mr. Robe, a Middlesex magistrate, who frequently played in Britton's concerts, for the sole purpose of terrifying him, and he succeeded but too seriously. Honeyman, without moving his lips or seeming to speak, announced from a distant part of the room the death of poor Britton within a few hours, unless, to avert the doom, he would fall on his knees immediately and repeat the Lord's prayer. The poor man did as he was told, but it did not answer the purpose. He was so dreadfully alarmed that he died within a few days afterwards.

This event took place in the month of September, 1714, when he was upwards of sixty years of age. He was interred in the churchyard of Clerkenwell, attended by a great concourse of people, particularly of the attendants of his musical club. His wife survived him, but he left very little property besides his books, his collection of manuscript and printed music, and his musical instruments, all of which were afterwards sold by auction.

THOMAS TUDWAY was educated in the Chapel Royal under Blow, and was a fellow-disciple of Turner and Purcell. In April, 1664, he was admitted a tenor-singer in the Chapel at Windsor. Seven years after this he went to Cambridge to take the place of organist of King's College Chapel; and in 1681, was admitted to the degree of Bachelor in Music. In the year 1705, Queen Anne paid a visit to the University of Cambridge, on which occasion Tudway wrote an *anthem*, " Thou, O God, hast heard my " vows," which he also performed as an exercise for the degree of Doctor in Music. He composed an anthem, " Is it true that God will dwell " with men upon the earth?" on the occasion of her Majesty's first going to her Royal Chapel at Windsor; and, for these compositions, and perhaps some others on similar occasions, he was permitted to style himself composer and organist-extraordinary to Queen Anne. He succeeded Dr. Staggins as professor of music in the University of Cambridge.

A few *songs* and *catches* are the whole of his works that are in print; it appears nevertheless that he was a man studious in his profession, and a composer of *anthems* to a considerable number.

Dr. Tudway had a son whom he intended for his own profession; and, for the information of this youth, he drew up, in the form of a letter, such an account of music and musicians as his memory enabled him to furnish. Many curious particulars are there related, and some facts, which, but for him, must have been for ever buried in oblivion. The sentiments expressed in it on music are somewhat singular. He manifests an uniform dislike to the practice of fuguing in vocal music, alleging as a reason, that it obscures the sense of the words; and it is perhaps owing to this singularity of opinion, that the best of his compositions do not rise above mediocrity, and that scarcely any of them are now in use.

In the latter part of his life Dr. Tudway was chiefly resident in London. Having a general acquaintance with music, and being personally intimate with nearly all the most eminent men of his profession, he was employed by Edward Earl of Oxford to make a collection of musical compositions. These were to consist chiefly of the works of Italian masters, and the most valuable and serviceable anthems of our own countrymen. Of these he scored, with his own hand, as many as filled seven thick quarto volumes, which are now deposited in the British Museum.

WILLIAM CROFT, Mus. Doc. who was born in the year 1677, at Nether Eatington, in the county of Warwick; received his musical education in the Chapel Royal under Dr. Blow; and on the erection of an organ in the parish church of St. Anne, Westminster, he was elected the organist. In 1700, he was admitted a gentleman-extraordinary

of the Chapel Royal ; and, about four years afterwards, was appointed joint-organist there with
Jeremiah Clark.   On Clark's decease, in 1708,
he was allowed to retain the whole place.   In
the following year he succeeded **Dr. Blow** as
master of the children and composer to the Chapel Royal, and also as organist of Westminster
Abbey.

In 1711, he resigned his place of organist of
St. Anne's, Westminster ; and in the succeeding
year published, but without his name, *" Divine
" Harmony, or a new Collection of select An-
" thems used at her Majesty's Chapels Royal,
" Westminster Abbey, St. Paul's, &c."* This collection, however, contains only the words of the
anthems.

Four years afterwards he was created a Doctor of
Music in the University of Oxford.   His exercise
for that degree is published under the title of
" Musicus Apparatus Academicus."

About this time an addition was made to the
old establishment of the Chapel Royal, of four
gentlemen, a second composer, a lutenist, and
a violist.   An allowance was also made to Dr.
Croft, as master of the children, of 80*l.* per
annum, for teaching them reading, writing, and
casting accounts; and for teaching them to play
on the organ and to compose music.

In the year 1724, Dr. Croft published, by subscription, a noble work, in two volumes (of his

own composition), entitled, "*Musica Sacra, or*
"*select Anthems in Score*," the first of which
contains the burial service which Purcell had
begun, but did not live to complete. In the preface the author observes of this work, that it was
the first attempt in music-printing of the kind,
being in score, engraved and stamped on plates ;
and that, for want of some such contrivance,
the music formerly printed in England had been
very incorrectly published.

The anthems contained in this collection are in
that grand and solemn style of composition which
should ever distinguish music appropriated to the
service of the church. Many of them were composed on thanksgivings for victories obtained during the reign of Queen Anne : others, equally excellent with these, are, " O Lord rebuke me not,"
—" Praise the Lord, O my soul,"—" God is gone
" up,"—and " O Lord, thou hast searched me
" out." Several of his anthems are inserted in
Page's " Harmonia Sacra," and Stevens's " Col-
" lection of Sacred Music."

Dr. Croft died in August, 1727, of an illness
occasioned by attending to his duty at the coronation of King George the Second.

The turn of his genius led him chiefly to the study
of church music. He, however, also composed
and published *Six Sets of tunes for Two Violins
and a Bass, Six Sonatas for two Flutes,* and *Six
Solos for a Flute and a Bass.* There are likewise

extant, in print, *songs* of his composition to a considerable number, and some in manuscript which have never yet been given to the public.

ROBERT CREIGHTON, D.D. was the son of Dr. Robert Creighton of Trinity College, Cambridge, who was afterwards Bishop of Bath and Wells, and who attended on King Charles the Second during his exile. In his youth he had been taught the rudiments of composition ; and after he entered into holy orders, he applied himself so sedulously to the study of church music, that he attained a proficiency which has entitled him to rank among the ablest masters of his time. In the year 1674, he was appointed a canon-residentiary, and also a chanter, in the Cathedral Church of Wells. He died at this city in 1736, having attained the great age of ninety-seven years.

Dr. Boyce has given to the world one of his anthems, " I will arise and go to my father," which no one can peruse without regretting that it should be so short. It is inserted in Page's " Harmonia Sacra ;" and, as arranged for keyed instruments, in Dr. Crotch's " Specimens of Music." Several of his compositions for the church are yet extant in manuscript in the books of the Cathedral of Wells.

WILLIAM TURNER was one of the second set of Chapel children after the Reformation, and a pupil

of Dr. Blow.   When he was grown up, his voice
broke into a fine counter-tenor ; a circumstance
that procured him an easy admittance into the
Royal Chapel, of which he was sworn a gentleman in the year 1679.   He was afterwards appointed a vicar-choral of St. Paul's, and a lay-vicar
of the Collegiate Church of St. Peter, Westminster.   In 1696, he was admitted to the degree of
Doctor of Music in the University of Cambridge.

Dr. Turner died in January, 1740, at the age of
eighty-eight, and was buried in the cloister of
Westminster Abbey, at the same time and in the
same grave with his wife Elizabeth, whose death
took place but a few days before his own.   They
had been married nearly seventy years, and afforded
to the world an illustrious example of conjugal
virtue and felicity.   They left a daughter who was
married to Mr. John Robinson, organist of Westminster Abbey, and of some parish churches in
London.

JOHN GOLDWIN, or GOLDING, was a pupil of
Dr. Child, and, in April, 1697, succeeded him as
organist of the Chapel of St. George at Windsor.
In the year 1703, he was appointed master of the
choristers there.   Both these stations he continued
to hold until the day of his death, the 7th of
November, 1719.

Of the many *anthems* of his composition that
are extant, Dr. Boyce has selected one for four

voices, "I have set God always before me," that answers precisely the character which the Doctor has given of Goldwin's music, namely, that in its modulation it is both singular and agreeable. Two of them, "O praise God in his holiness," and "I will sing unto the Lord," are inserted in Page's Harmonia Sacra.

CHARLES KING, educated in the choir of St. Paul's under Dr. Blow, was at first a supernumerary singer in that cathedral, for the small stipend of 14l. a year. In 1704, he was admitted to the degree of Bachelor of Music in the University of Oxford. On the death of Clark he was elected almoner and master of the children of St. Paul's; and he continued to sing there until October, 1730, when he was admitted a vicar-choral of that cathedral. Besides these places he was also permitted to hold that of organist of the parish church of St. Bennet Fink, London. All these stations he retained till his death, in March, 1745.

He composed some *anthems* and a great number of *services*, whence Dr. Greene, speaking of him in a jocular style, was accustomed to say that Mr. King was "a very serviceable man." As a musician, however, his writings are not held in any high degree of estimation. Four of his anthems are inserted in Page's "Harmonia Sacra," and two in Stevens's "Sacred Music."

JOHN ISHAM, though little known in the musical world, was undoubtedly a man of considerable abilities in his profession. Under what master he received his instruction is not known. It appears, however, that he was admitted to the degree of Bachelor in Music at the same time that Croft received that of Doctor. He was the deputy of Dr. Croft for many years ; and, in 1711, when the latter resigned the place of organist of St. Anne's, Westminster, Isham, through his interest, was elected in his stead.

He had no cathedral employment, nor any place in the Royal Chapel. In the year 1718, he was elected organist of the Church of St. Andrew, Holborn, with a salary of 50*l.* and he resigned his former situation at St. Anne's ; but a vacancy soon afterwards happening in the organist's place of St. Margaret's, Westminster, it was offered to and accepted by him.

He died in 1726, leaving behind him, in manuscript, many valuable *services* and *anthems* for the church. In conjunction with William Morley, a gentleman of the Chapel Royal, he published a collection of *songs*, their joint composition.

DANIEL HENSTRIDGE, organist of the Cathedral Church of Canterbury about the year 1710, was the composer of several *anthems*. The words of some of them are inserted in the collection entitled, "Divine Harmony," published by Dr. Croft,

JAMES HESLETINE, a pupil of Blow, was organist of the Cathedral Church of Durham, and afterwards of the Collegiate Church of St. Catharine, near the Tower.

He was an excellent church musician, and composed a great number of *anthems.* Some of these are to be found in the choir books of most of the cathedrals of the kingdom. Others, to a great number, he caused to be copied into the books belonging to Durham Cathedral; but having (as he conceived) been ill-treated by the Dean and Chapter, he tore them all out and destroyed them.

He died, at an advanced age, about the year 1750.

GODFREY KELLER was a celebrated performer on the harpsichord about this time. In conjunction with a person of the name of Finger, he published a set of *Sonatas in five Parts for Flutes and Hautboys,* and he was himself the composer of *Six Sonatas for Violins, Trumpets, Hautboys, and Flutes.*

At present, however, Keller is known only by a work which he had prepared for the press, but was prevented from publishing by a premature death. It was nevertheless afterwards printed with the title of, " *A complete Method of attaining to* " *a Thorough-Bass upon either Organ, Harpsi-* " *chord, or Theorbo-Lute, by the late famous* " *Mr. Godfrey Keller ; with a variety of proper*

" *Lessons and .Fugues, explaining the several*
" *Rules throughout the whole Work ; and a*
" *Scale for tuning the Harpsichord. or Spinnet,*
" *all taken from his own Copies, which he did*
" *design to print.*"

This work was subsequently reprinted as an
appendix to Dr. Holder's Treatise on the natural
Grounds and Principles of Harmony, to which
indeed it forms an awkward supplement, from the
circumstance of its being altogether practical.
Matthew Lock's " *Melothesia*" was the first
treatise on thorough-bass published in this kingdom, and this was the next. Since Keller's time
however there have been others without number.

WILLIAM CORBETT, a member of the king's
band, and a celebrated performer on the violin,
was the leader of the first Opera orchestra, in the
Haymarket, at the time when Arsinoë was performed there. In 1710 he went to Rome, where
he resided many years, and where he made a valuable collection of music and musical instruments.
Some persons, acquainted with his circumstances,
were at a loss how to account for his expending such
large sums of money as he was known to do on
these, otherwise than by supposing that he had an
allowance from Government, and that his business
at Rome was to watch the motions of the Pre-
tender.

In his younger days, before he left England,

he published two or three sets of *Sonatas for Violins and Flutes, twelve Concertos for all Instruments,* and several sets of *Tunes for the Plays.* On his return from Italy, about the year 1740, he brought over with him a great quantity of music which he had composed during his residence abroad, and from the publication of which in this kingdom he hoped to derive considerable profit. Accordingly he issued proposals for publishing by subscription a work entitled, " Con" certos, or Universal Bizzarries, composed on " all the new Gustos during many Years' Resi" dence in Italy," in three books, containing thirty-five concertos of seven parts ; in which he professes to have imitated the styles of the various kingdoms in Europe, and of several cities and provinces in Italy. However ridiculous such a proposal may seem to have been, the author determined to try the experiment, and, with little or no encouragement, published his work, of which very few copies were sold.

Corbett died, at an advanced age, in the year 1748. By his will he bequeathed the best of his instruments to Gresham College, with a salary of ten pounds a year to a female servant who was to shew them. Some other singular bequests are contained in his will, but how far they were complied with we know not. A short time after his decease, there was a sale by auction of his

instruments at Mercer's Hall, and his music-books
and manuscripts were also sold by auction at his
house in Silver Street, Golden Square.

JOHN LOEILLET, a relation, as is supposed, of
John Baptist Loeillet of Ghent, was a celebrated performer on the flute, and the composer
of four operas of *solos* for that instrument. He
was also celebrated as a harpsichord-performer,
and assisted in the Opera band at the same time
with Corbett. He resided in Hart Street, Covent
Garden, and in his house held a weekly concert,
which was chiefly frequented by unprofessional
performers, who gratified him very handsomely
for conducting it.

Loeillet published some *Lessons for the Harpsichord.* In one of these there is a minuet in the
minor key of A, which has been erroneously ascribed to Jean Baptiste Lully, and which was a
great favourite with the ladies of the last age.
He died about the year 1728, having, by his application and industry, acquired a fortune of about
sixteen thousand pounds.

The works published by him are, *Six Suits of
Lessons for the Harpsichord; Six Sonatas for
Flutes, Hautboys, German Flutes, and Violins;
Twelve Sonatas for Violins, German Flutes, and
common Flutes;* and *Twelve Solos for a German
Flute, common Flute, and Violin.*

JOHN BANISTER was the son of the person of the same name, already mentioned as a famous performer on the violin in the reign of Charles the Second. He was educated under his father, and afterwards played the first violin at the Drury-Lane Theatre, both in the operas and on ordinary occasions. In this station he continued till about 1720, when he was succeeded by Carbonelli. He died in the year 1725.

Banister was the composer of several grounds with divisions, inserted in the " Division Violin." A collection of music, the joint production of himself and Godfrey Finger, was published by him, and sold at his house in Brownlow Street, Drury Lane.

THOMAS ROSEINGRAVE was the son of one of the vicars-choral of St Patrick's Church, Dublin, under whom he received the first rudiments of his musical education. As he exhibited early indications of musical genius, the Chapter of St. Patrick's allowed him a pension to enable him to travel into other countries for improvement. He accordingly went to Rome in the year 1710. How long he continued abroad is not exactly known; but in 1720, he appears to have had some concern in the management of the Opera at the Haymarket; for in that year he brought upon the stage, with some additional songs of his own, the opera of *Narcissus*, written by Rolli, and set to music by Dominico Scarlatti.

Roseingrave afterwards became a teacher of music, in the principles of which he was supposed to be deeply skilled.   His style, however, both of playing and composing, was harsh and disgusting, shewing much learning, but very little either of elegance or variety.   About the year 1725, an organ having been erected in the New Church of St. George, Hanover Square, he was appointed the organist.

A few years after he had obtained this situation, he fixed his affections on a female, by whom he was rejected at a time when he thought himself most secure of her affections.   This disappointment was so severely felt by the unfortunate lover as to occasion a temporary and very strange kind of insanity.   He used to say that the lady's cruelty had so literally and completely broken his heart, that he heard the strings of it *crack* at the time he received his sentence; and on that account he ever afterwards called the disorder of his intellects his *crepation*, from the Italian verb *crepare*, to crack.   After this misfortune he was never able to hear any noise without great emotion. If, during his performance on the organ, any one near him coughed, sneezed, or blew his nose with violence, he would instantly quit the instrument, and run out of church, seemingly in the greatest pain and terror, crying out that it was *Old Scratch* who tormented him and played on his *crepation*.

About the year 1737, on account of his occasional insanity, he was superseded at St. George's Church by Mr. Keeble, who during his life divided with him the salary. He died in the year 1750.

Roseingrave was an enthusiastic admirer of Palestrina, and the ornaments of his bed-chamber were scraps of paper containing select passages from the works of that composer.

Some time previously to his death he published a collection of *Lessons for the Harpsichord* of his friend Domenico Scarlatti, in which are contained also two or three of his own. His other works that are to be met with in print are, *Additional Songs to the Opera of Narcissus*; *Voluntaries and Fugues* for the organ and harpsichord; and *Twelve Solos for a German Flute*, with a thorough-bass for the harpsichord.

JOHN BARRETT, a pupil of Dr. Blow, was music-master to the boys of Christ's Hospital, London, and organist of the Church of St. Mary-at-Hill.

He was a good musician, and wrote tunes to *songs* in several of the plays performed in his time. In the " Pills to purge Melancholy," there are many of his songs. He composed that sweet air, " Ianthe the lovely," adapted, in the Beggar's Opera, to the words, " When he holds up his "hand arraigned for his life."

LEWIS RAMONDEN appeared as a singer in several of the English Italian operas.

He composed some of the songs in a collection published in 1716, entitled, " the Merry Musi-" cian, or a Cure for the Spleen ;" among which there is a favourite hymn upon the execution of two criminals, beginning, " All you that must " take a leap in the dark." This is one of the tunes in the Beggar's Opera, adapted to the words, " Would I might be hang'd."

PHILIP HART was organist of the Churches of St. Andrew Undershaft, and St Michael's, Cornhill. The latter of these situations he quitted, upon some diagreement with the church-wardens, and was elected organist of St. Dionis Backchurch. He was esteemed a sound musician ; but he entertained little relish for those refinements in the science which followed the introducion of the Italian opera into this country.

His name frequently occurs in the " Treasury " of Music," and in other collections of his time ; and there are extant of his composition, a coltion of *Fugues for the Organ*, and the *Morning Hymn*, from the fifth book of Paradise Lost. This is generally supposed to have been written in opposition to Mr. Galliard's composition to the same words ; but the attempt, if it was such, seems to have failed ; for the latter is a fine and elegant composition, admired at this day, whilst

that of Hart is entirely forgotten.   He died about
the year 1750 at a very advanced age.

GEORGE MONRO was a competitor with Roseingrave for the place of organist of St. George's,
Hanover Square ; but, failing in his application,
he became organist of the Church of St. Peter,
Cornhill.   He played the harpsichord in the
Goodman's Fields theatre from its first opening,
in 1729, till his death, which happened a year or
two afterwards.

Many of his *songs and ballad airs* have been
much admired.   Several of them are printed in
the " Musical Miscellany," a collection of songs
in six volumes, published in the year 1731.

GEORGE HAYDEN was organist of the Church
of St. Mary Magdalen, Bermondsey.   He composed and published (about the year 1723) three
cantatas, the first of which was much admired :
he also composed a song called New Mad Tom,
beginning, " In my triumphant chariot hurled ;"
and a pleasing song in two parts, " As I saw fair
" Chlora walk alone."

WILLIAM BABELL, organist of the Church of
All-Hallows, Bread Street, and a member of the
private music of King George the First, was the
son of a person who played the bassoon at the
theatre in Drury Lane.   He was instructed by his

father in the rudiments of music, and became an excellent performer on the harpsichord. He is stated to have been the earliest of those persons who simplified the music for keyed instruments, and divested it of the crowded and complicated harmony with which, before his time, it had been embarrassed.

His first essay in composition was to turn the favourite airs in Pyrrhus and Demetrius, Hydaspes, and some other operas, into *Lessons for the Harpsichord;* and, from the opera of Rinaldo, he composed a set of shewy and brilliant lessons, which few could play except himself. There are extant also of his composition, *Twelve Solos for a Violin or Hautboy; Twelve solos for a German Flute or Hautboy; Six Concertos for small Flutes and Violins;* and some other works.

He died, a young man, about the year 1722, having considerably shortened his days by intemperance.

JOHN SHEELES was a teacher of the harpsichord in London, and the composer of *Two sets of Lessons for that Instrument.* He was one of the chief contributors to the collection of songs called the " Musical Miscellany."

OBADIAH SHUTTLEWOTH was organist of St. Michael's, and, a few years afterwards, of the Temple Church. He was the son of a person who lived in Spitalfields, and who had acquired a small fortune, partly by teaching the harpsichord, and partly by copying Corelli's music for sale before it was printed in England.

Shuttleworth played the violin so well as to be ranked among the first performers of his day. He was the leader of the concert at the Swan Tavern, Cornhill, from the time of its institution till his death, in the year 1735.

He was likewise a respectable composer, having written *twelve concertos* and several *sonatas for violins*. None of his compositions, however, are extant in print, except *two concertos* formed from the first and eleventh solos of Corelli.

HENRY SYMONDS was a member of the king's band, and organist of the Church of St. Martin, Ludgate, and of St. John's Chapel, at the end of James Street, near Bedford Row.

He published *Six Suits of Lessons for the Harpsichord*, and died about the year 1730.

ABIELL WHICHELLO was, for some years, deputy to Mr. Hart, as organist of the Churches of St. Andrew Undershaft, and St. Michael's, Cornhill. He was afterwards elected organist of the Church of St Edmund the King, and taught the harpsichord to some of the first families in the City.

He composed many *songs*, which have been separately printed, and a collection of *Lessons for the Harpsichord*, or spinnet, containing Alamands, Courants, Sarabands, Airs, Minuets, and Jigs. The time of his death is supposed to have been about the year 1745.

———

ALEXANDER MALCOLM published at Edinburgh, in the year 1721, " *A Treatise of Music, Speculative, Practical, and Historical.*" This work is divided into fourteen chapters.

The first chapter contains an account of the object and end of music, and of the nature of the science. The author begins by explaining the nature of sound. He then inquires into the various affections of sound, so far as they relate to music, of which he makes two divisions : 1st, The knowledge of the materia medica ; 2d, The art of composition.

The second chapter treats of tune, or the relation of acuteness and gravity in sounds.

The third chapter contains an inquiry into the nature of concord and discord, and is concluded with a relation of some remarkable phenomena respecting them.

The fourth chapter is on the subject of harmonical arithmetic, and contains an explanation of the nature of arithmetical, geometrical, and harmonical proportions, with rules for the addition, subtraction, multiplication, and division of ratios and intervals.

The fifth chapter contains the uses and application of the preceding theory, explaining the nature of the original concords, and also of the compound ones.

The sixth chapter explains the geometrical part of music, and the method of dividing right lines, so as their sections or parts, one with another, or with the whole, shall contain any given interval of sounds.

The seventh chapter treats of harmony, and explains the nature and variety of it, as it depends upon the various combinations of concording sounds.

The eighth chapter treats of concinnous intervals and the scale of music ; and in this are shewn the necessity and use of discords, and their original dependence on the concords. It explains farther the use of degrees in the construction of the scale of music.

The ninth chapter is on the mode or key in music, and of the office of the scale of music.

The tenth chapter treats of the defects of instruments, and the remedy for these in general, by means of sharps and flats. This chapter is concluded by a general approbation of the semitonic division, and of the present practice of tuning the organ or harpsichord, corresponding as nearly to that as the judgment of the ear will allow. As to the pretences of nicer kinds of musicians, he demonstrates that they tend to introduce more errors than those under which the present system labours.

The eleventh chapter describes the method and art of writing music, and shews how the differences in tune are represented. Under this head the author explains the nature and use of the cliffs, and the nature of transposition. He explains also the practice of solmization. Lastly, he enters into an examination of Salmon's proposal for reducing all music to one cliff, as delivered in his " Essay " to the Advancement of Music," of which he approves.

The twelfth chapter is on the time or duration of sounds in music.

The thirteenth chapter contains the general rules and principles of harmonic composition. These are such as are to be found in almost every book on the subject of musical composition.

The account given, in the fourteenth chapter, of the ancient music, is, considering its brevity, very entertaining and satisfactory.

In a short history of the improvements in music, which makes part of this last chapter, the author particularly notices the reformation of the ancient scale by Guido, and adopts respecting it the sentiment of a very ingenious man, who says that it is " *crux tenellorum ingeniorum.*"

In the comparison between ancient and modern music the author gives a decided preference to the latter ; and on the controverted question, whether

the ancients were acquainted with music in consonance or not ? he cites a variety of passages from
Aristotle, Seneca, and Cassiodorus, to determine
the negative.

This work is replete with musical erudition ;
and, extensive as the subject is, the author has
contrived to bring under consideration all the essential parts of the science. His knowledge of
mathematics has enabled him to discuss, with great
clearness and perspicuity, the doctrine of ratios,
and other abstract speculations, in the language
of a philosopher and a scholar. In short, it is a
work from which a student may derive great advantage, and it may be justly deemed one of the
most valuable treatises on the subject of theoretical
and practical music that is to be found in any of
the modern languages.

END OF THE FIRST VOLUME.

J. Brettell, Printer, Rupert Street,
Haymarket, London.